NO SINGLE SPARROW MAKES A SUMMER

NO SINGLE SPARROW MAKES A SUMMER

NARJIS ALSAADI

YENNIFER COCA IZQUIERDO

HAFSA JAMA

ATALYA LAWLER

A'LEA MARIE SMITH

KATHERIN E. SOCIAS BÁEZ

AUTUMN WILSON

MARIA ZAMINKHAN

MEHWISH ZAMINKHAN

LOUISVILLE STORY PROGRAM

Louisville Story Program
851 South 4th Street
Louisville, KY 40203
www.louisvillestoryprogram.org

ISBN 978-0-9914765-4-1
Library of Congress Control Number: 2018952035

Edited by Joe Manning and Darcy Thompson
Book design by Shellee Marie Jones
Cover art by Kathleen Lolley
Back cover photo by Kyle Gordon

Contents

Introduction

Iroquois High School is the most diverse school in the state of Kentucky, with large populations of both foreign-born and American-born students and over forty languages spoken in its hallways. In 2017, nine Iroquois students began working with the Louisville Story Program on an ambitious project to document their lives and communities. Six of them had moved to the United States only two to four years earlier. All nine had important things to write about and a desire to tell their stories.

They began by developing interviewing skills in oral history workshops during the summer of 2017, then applied those skills to conduct interviews with relatives, neighbors, and other community members. When the school year began, they participated in daily college-level writing workshops with us and with incredible Iroquois High School teacher Kim Courtney. In these workshops, they learned about elements of craft and honed their writing skills through frequent practice and feedback. They read their work aloud and responded enthusiastically to one another's writing. They made each other laugh. They moved each other to tears. They developed an appreciation for their different life experiences, and an understanding of their fundamental commonalities. They formed a community.

The title of this book, *No Single Sparrow Makes a Summer*, is a translation of an idiom one of the authors heard frequently growing up, a sort of refrain in her family, which was comprised of some very strong women. It speaks to the power of collective effort and mutual support, to how much more we can accomplish together than we can accomplish on our own. This unity and collaboration is at the heart of the groundbreaking project these authors undertook together for more than a year.

After many, many months of hard work, the authors have skillfully and compellingly documented communities in Louisville that have, heretofore, sometimes been ignored, unaccounted for, or otherwise written out of the narrative. In this book, they offer you rich accounts of their own lives alongside memorable stories from community members they have interviewed. The pieces in this book are honest, courageous, tender, funny, and above all, humane. In a time when we are arguably quicker to dehumanize people who are different from us, the pieces in this book are necessary, important.

They've written about the ravages of war, life before and after moving to Louisville as refugees and immigrants, the foster care system, juvenile detention, motherhood, unfair representations of their communities. Perhaps most importantly, though, their book demonstrates the power of deep listening and mindful storytelling as tools to create and sustain community.

For well over a year, we have felt honored to bear witness to the authors' stories, and we hope that you feel the same way as you read this book written by and about some of your neighbors.

DARCY THOMPSON & JOE MANNING
Louisville Story Program

KATHERIN E. SOCIAS BÁEZ

No Single Sparrow Makes a Summer

Journey to La Yuma

Warm Cuban Hugs Are a Fine Thing

No Single Sparrow Makes a Summer

KATHERIN E. SOCIAS BÁEZ

When I was twelve years old, I flew to La Yuma—what the people in my life had always called the United States—to come live with my father. It was my first time on an airplane and I was traveling without a chaperone. I had no clue what La Yuma would look like, but I imagined a paradise with lots of food and angels, where everyone was rich. I worried that the humble Katherin wouldn't have a place in this luxurious world. I thought that I had to be a new person, so I decided to leave the old me behind.

I didn't want a suitcase full of memories and things that would make me reconsider the trip. Instead I packed only a small silver handbag with an image of a single flower on it. It was full of notes, letters from loved ones, and two notebooks. One of the notebooks was from my English class where I'd written words and their meanings and barely understandable pronunciations. I had photographs hidden in the cover of the notebook so my mom wouldn't find out that I had taken some of our family pictures. The other notebook held notes from my friends saying how much they loved me and would miss me. In one of the small, almost hidden pockets of the handbag I found five multicolored plastic letters. I took them out and placed them on the little table in front of my seat on the plane. I tried to make a word

out of them and spelled "*Te amo*"—"I love you." I beamed softly and felt somewhat better, yet I was still by myself, nothing to hold on to, just a handbag. Everyday things like my mom brushing my hair were going to become long-lost memories. I was excited to see what my new life would be like, but I was also terrified.

Living in a underdeveloped communist country wasn't always the best thing in the world, yet my family and I managed to survive. I was born in La Havana, where I lived on the fifth floor of an apartment building with my grandma on my father's side, my uncle Orlando, my uncle Felipe, my caring dad, and the most precious person in the world to me, my mom. My mom was always full of life. For example, when she was about sixteen, she organized a group of teenagers who would dance to her choreographies while wearing *rumbera* costumes. But in La Havana, she was mostly in the kitchen or playing with me. Outside of that house she didn't really have a life.

My dad was a carpenter. On the back of the building we lived in, he had a garage made of patches of metal, some completely oxidized. The building was secured with a big cowbell with a padlock inside it. All four of my uncles kept a key. When I was about six I entered his man cave. Inside, curled wood shavings and sawdust covered the floor like the confetti after you break a piñata. It had tables with sharp-edged circular saws and machines for polishing wood with a piece of hard sandpaper. The smell of dead trees, metal, and glue weakened me. Dad's denim jeans didn't look like denim anymore: they were smeared with car oil and had sawdust glued all over them. His hands were covered in layers of dried white glue, his fingers smashed from the hammer, a couple of purple nails turning black. His white T-shirt had holes in it and was too small for him, yet he smiled affably when he saw me. I asked him if I could help and make beautiful objects like my daddy, and he chuckled and said, "Come here, *chichi*, I got something for you." My father had made me a tiny hammer.

One of the first objects I made was a wooden hand mirror with my name carved on the handle. The frame was misshapen and the mirror inside the frame was asymmetrical and distorted. It showed a sad face standing behind me as I observed my innocent lips beam. "What's wrong, Daddy?" I asked. "Nothing, *chichi*, don't worry about it. You'll understand one day when you grow up and have your own family." He picked me up from the ground. Even though I was young I understood: yes, I was happy and so was he, but the fact that he couldn't get me a cute pink mirror like the ones in the store showcase made him sad. Yet I had a mirror my dad made just for me, and no other little girl had such a precious thing.

I was never outside running like there was no tomorrow like other kids; instead I was home with

Katherin's father Yordan, paternal grandmother Nidia, and mother Nancy (pregnant with Katherin), Havana 2001

Men playing dominoes in Katherin's father's workshop in Havana

Aunt Cheli, Tio Felipe, grandma Nidia, Tio Orlando, Yordan, and Tio Jorgito

my lovely and funny uncles, my father's brothers. I was the younger niece and grandchild, which came with a variety of privileges, like being taken to amusement parks and having snacks all the time like chocolate ice cream that came in a white paper cup with a design of blue ocean waves or *pellis de jamón*, a delicious puffy, crunchy, potato-based snack made to look like strips of bacon cut into pieces.

Tio Jorgito is a 5'5" white man with a delightful smile and great self-esteem. He made me happy even though he had his own problems, like any adult. He has a lovely wife and they've been together since their first year of high school. She wasn't able to have

children, so he considers me one of his own. Once when I was about two, he needed to get me down to the street to Tio Orlando, but he was tired from work and didn't want to go down the old crumbling concrete stairs with a two-year-old on his arms and then go back upstairs. Instead, he took a burlap sack and tied it to a brown rope, put me inside the bag, and slowly let it descend from the balcony while I looked up at the bright sky. I was excited—it all seemed like a game to me. It always did.

Then there was Tio Orlando, who is in his fifties now. He has always been special to me. Perhaps because I used to call him *nené*, as if he was my baby doll.

He would let me make a ton of tiny ponytails on his head while he swung back and forth on his rocking chair until eventually he fell asleep. When he'd wake up I would have a plate with his food and feed him the *congris con pollo* my mom made. He would leave a sip of coffee in his mug for me when my mom wasn't looking. Since he worked at the International Airport, he would bring me western magazines about the newest cars, makeup, and celebrities I didn't even know about.

Tio Felipe lived across from my grandma's house. He was an old fashioned guy who was obsessed with technology but didn't want to admit it. He loved everything that had to do with TVs, Nintendos, radios, and video cameras. He once brought his heavy, ancient video camera to my grandma's house to record four-year-old me talking about the pink nails my mom had put on me and the red rose she had painted on them. I am pretty sure he still has the videocassette somewhere in his disorganized house. I used to hang out at his garage and play with the cars he fixed. I was always the driver.

Then there was Tio Hugo, the oldest of the five brothers. He is a tranquil man who barely talks, but when he does he gets his point across. There was this time when I wanted to go over to his house to play with my cousin/godmother, but we couldn't catch the bus going to La Güinera, so he had an idea. Since I was small and didn't weigh much, he tied a plastic beer box to the back of his antique bike and put a pillow on the bottom of it for my accommodation. As we rode the bike, people looked at us and whispered in their neighbor's ear like he was an unconcerned dad with a baby on the back of his bicycle.

Meanwhile, my parents started to have problems. My dad had cheated on my mom too many times to count and she was tired of it all. Ma decided that it was time for her to leave and make her own life, so when I was four and my mother was twenty-three we packed everything and headed to Manzanillo, her hometown. There we lived with my grandma (whom I call Abu), Tio Danilo, his wife Yudi, my cousin Anita, my cousin Brayan, and his mom Iraida. Manzanillo is such a beautiful place: palms, fruits, beaches, and pacific landscapes. It felt like home.

Abu was happy that my mom was back, but my mom wasn't. My dad was entangled with another woman and couldn't see what was going on around him. When he finally faced reality, he called and apologized to my mom. Since she loved him very much, she doubted the decision she had made a month ago, but Abu—smart woman that she was—told my mom to bite the bullet. He wasn't going to change, not now, not in a million years.

Then my mom found out she was pregnant. The first months everyone seemed to have the word "worry" written on their forehead because she was a single mom, but we made peace with the baby growing in her womb. I often lay in bed with my mom and massaged her belly and talked about names for my little brother. My friend's mom was also pregnant and another friend had a newborn baby brother, so our hobby was trying martial arts against the wall and talking about how the three of us would protect the boys. After the baby boy was born he was named Yordan after my father and he looked exactly like him.

Katherin and Yordancito with their father during one of his visits to Manzanillo

My dad visited us once in a while in the summer. He would take my brother and me to eat ice cream and we would visit the zoo. During one visit when I was seven years old, I had the feeling that this might be his last visit. He was drunk and couldn't speak the words he really wanted to say. He gave me the chain that was hanging from his neck and said that it was precious to him and it should be to me as well. The pendant was a crescent sun. I didn't know the meaning of it, but apparently it symbolizes strength, power, and rebirth. The next morning, my grandma told me he had gone back to La Havana. A

few months later I heard my dad was in the United States. He had taken a boat to Central America, and gone through Mexico, and was living in Las Vegas.

My mom remarried and I gained a stepsister and a stepbrother in the process. Life was good. On the weekends my mother would listen to telenovelas on the radio while washing our clothes with her bare hands. It was amusing to see her smile and bite her nails when a mysterious and intense song played in the background. "What are you listening to, Ma ?" I would ask.

"Maria is waiting for Roberto tell her the truth about his affair, but he doesn't know she knows. This is so good!"

I'd almost laugh at her, but opt not to. "Ma, can I go to Abu's house? I think she's making *pollo en salsa*," I would say with sweet puppy eyes.

"Of course, *niña*."

I would jog to the sink, embrace her, and kiss her on the cheek. She would smile and kept listening to the *'novela* and making expressive faces.

I would get together with my slightly-older stepsister Yami, my friend Danielis, and the rest of our neighbors at Abu's house and jump rope, string up a net from a fishing boat for a volleyball match, or play *cachola* (hopscotch), baseball, or *muerte al tres*, our favorite card game. My brother would go to our stepbrother Dayan's house, which was two houses down from ours, to play with a skateboard that left scars on their knees and elbows every time they used it. At 6:00 p.m. I would hear Ma yelling, "Katherin y Yordan!" My brother and I would come back to the house and take turns showering. Then Ma would send me to get Yami and Dayan so we could all eat supper. When I got back with them, their father Yoni would be home. We all hugged him and asked, "What did you get for us today?" He would glance at my mom like he was looking for an answer, then she would grab us and kindly push us to our chairs and say, "Come on, let's eat. The food is getting cold."

After we ate, Ma would turn the radio on. They would play something like Marc Anthony's new song "Flor Palida." She would tell me to get a paper and pencil, then make everyone hush while she copied the song lyrics on the paper. Every once in a while when a song became really popular they would play it in the radio and then dictate the lyrics. Mom often complained about the host dictating the song too fast, yet in the end we would get the lyrics. Sometimes she would call her uncle René, who sang at the Granma Radio Station, so he could dictate the song again. Now every time we heard the song she could pull up her notes and sing along.

At 9:00 p.m. it was time for the Brazilian 'novela to be broadcast on the main TV channel. Yordancito would sit at the kitchen table and draw his favorite characters from the kids channel cartoons. Yoni would rush out of the shower so he could sit in the living room with my mom, Dayan, Yami, and me. I hated this TV, but my mom seemed to love it. I never understood what it was about black and white TVs that was so special. I liked colors. My grandma had just gotten her color TV from the government since she had been doing her neighborly surveillance, but we hadn't gotten ours because we moved right after my grandpa died. When he died, all the things

Katherin's mother Nancy and stepdfather Yoni (furthest on the right) with family friends Juan Jose, Yalien, and Yunier at Manzanillo's Carnaval, ca. 2013

that he owned went to his family. This TV screen was about the size of an iPad and was rounded and popped to the front. Sometimes we had to hit it a few times in the corner so it would get the signal, and the volume button was crooked and would do whatever it wanted. Ma preferred to hear the 'novelas on the radio, because there she could imagine what the characters would look like instead of having them made for her. After we watched the 'novela, we would sit on the porch and Yami, Dayan, Yordancito, and I took turns riding the bicycle. My mom and Yoni would sit on the porch watching us and enjoying

Katherin (far left) with cousins and neighbors in Manzanillo

an inexpensive wine. We were one big happy family. I can't wait for the day we are back together, even if it's on Mars.

Yoni would walk Dayan and Yami to their houses, which were close by. My mom told us we had to brush our teeth and then go to bed, and she specifically told me not to stay up late reading *Habia una vez,* a collection of children's stories. She kissed our foreheads and tucked us into bed. Before she left to her room she said, "*Que Dios los bendiga y tengan dulces sueños y que sueñen con los angelitos. Los amo.*" We repeated the same to her: "God bless you, I hope you have sweet dreams and dream of angels." I don't know why we always said that—we aren't religious people—but my mom was a strong believer in her own way.

Sometimes Ma, Yordancito, and I would sleep together. I loved listening to her breath, I loved watching her stomach ascend and descend, I loved when she moved around and pulled the blanket half asleep so she could cover us, I loved how she woke up in the middle of the night to see if we were sleeping well, I loved how she sometimes stared at us and smiled for no reason. I love her.

Yordancito in front of school with teachers Marelis, his and Katherin's mother Nancy (who taught at the school), and his pre-school teacher Mayulis

The screams of the blender woke me up. I went to the kitchen half asleep, sat at the trembling table, drank the guava smoothie Abu made, and ate my scrambled eggs. Since we were trying not to eat our chickens' eggs so they could hatch and become adults, my brother had stolen the eggs from our neighbors' chickens. I ran to the restroom so my brother wouldn't shower first. But I went to the kitchen and realized the water was still boiling, so I had two options: either shower with the cold water in the plastic bucket or patiently wait for the water to boil so I can mix it with the water in the bucket. I knew that if I waited, there was a chance my brother would distract me and get me out of the bathroom. And since it was 90 degrees outside, showering with cold water didn't seem like a bad idea. Abu yelled at me for showering with cold water: *"Mija, te vas a enfermar!"* She started sharing all her theories that I would get sick because of the cold water. I rapidly rolled myself in a pink towel and ran to my room. Once I was dressed I told Abu that I was going to my friend's house.

Arletis was quite a sleeper, and that's exactly what she was doing when I arrived at her house. We were supposed to go to a haunted house to learn about the birds we were studying. I woke her up by giving her soft slaps on her pale cheeks. After a half hour she was ready. We wouldn't just come out to our parents and say, "Hey Mom, we're going to Juan's house because it seems mysterious and now that he is at work we can get in by the broken window and see what he's hiding inside and also check out the ravens that are always surrounding his house." We just lied and took off.

Arletis carried a small notebook that contained all the witch's spells and diabolic games we liked to play. On our way to his house we noticed a one-of-a-kind mango tree. This tree was tall but its fruits were small and sweet, unusual since all the mangoes on trees in my neighborhood were big and not matured yet. We sat on the crispy grass and with a long heavy stick pulled the mangoes from the tree. We asked our neighbor Mamita for some salt and she didn't question us because she was on her way to her job. Once we were full we kept going to our destination.

The lights of Juan's house were turned off and there was no one around to witness the breaking and entering, though we didn't break anything. Arletis got in first, then me. By the vandalized window there were million-year-old flowers in a vase that looked like it was made of bone. I wondered if what we were doing was right, but I was also curious about what he had inside the house. The living room didn't have many accessories, just an old couch. On our way to the kitchen we saw a dining table covered in dust and spider webs. The kitchen itself consisted of a non-functioning metal fridge and the cooking pots the government had given everyone when the revolution first triumphed. We made our way to the bedrooms. One was full of old abandoned stuff and another with metal pieces and clothes. When we went to his room we saw a dorm bed with plain white sheets, though it didn't seem like a bed someone would want to sleep on. It looked like he was borrowing the place. Nothing seemed to belong to him. We made our way to the patio so we could check out the ravens, but once we got there the birds flew away and we were left with the green forest and tall grass. Most houses in Cuba have huge backyards and they're mostly used for personal crops and fruit trees. This was no different, except he had no crops and didn't take care of the enriched land. We walked around the patio to see what we could find. But there was nothing, just tall grass.

As we were finishing exploring Juan's house, we wanted to go on more adventures. I suggested that instead of going home so early we should go to the school's basketball courts, where our classmates hung out all the time. Just as I expected, they were all there running and playing tag. One of them, Sadiel, said that he was going to his uncle's estate (small farm). We all wanted to tag along so we could get some tamarinds and guava. I didn't ask for permission, I just went with them. When we got there it turned out that Sadiel's uncle had left and closed the fences. Sadiel suggested that we go through the neighbor's estate and cross the small fence dividing it from his uncle's. I thought that we were going to ask the guy if we could go onto his estate and cross the fence, but Sadiel said it would be too troublesome. So we trespassed and tried to make it to his uncle's. It was a long walk and it was full of goats. We walked cautiously, but the farm owner's dog started barking at us. We had to run to get out of there. Some of us struggled to catch our breath and get out of there alive. Once we got to the street, I asked Sadiel why we had to run to the street instead of going to his uncle's. He gave me that look people give when they have just been caught lying, so we knew it wasn't his uncle's estate. We had become fruit delinquents.

Ma woke up at 6:00 a.m., made breakfast, woke us up, bathed us, clothed us, and fed us, then got herself ready and walked with us to our school where she was a teacher, shielding us from the sun with a white and black umbrella. We walked for about 30 minutes and around 7:30 a.m. we got to school. We made our way to the big room located right next to the half-staff flag. It was the death anniversary of Camilo Cienfuegos, one of the martyrs of the Cuban Revolution. On October 28, 1959, his small plane disappeared into the sea. So every October 28 we picked flowers and let them float on the ocean in remembrance of the hero our nation had lost.

José Martí, a famous Cuban poet and revolutionary young man who died in a battle to obtain Cuba's independence from Spain, always gets flowers, no matter what day it is. His white marble bust is always garnished with some colorful flowers, especially *la flor mariposa*. This perfumed flower plays an important role in Cubans' lives, since during the independence struggles women would hide messages in its butterfly-shaped petals and send them to insurgent forces. This flower is now a symbol of purity,

peace, and love towards the Cuban people. Ma was like this aromatic flower to me.

Since I am a huge fan of his writing, I placed a flower on the bust of José Martí and made my way to my assigned file of students from fifth grade. We were facing each other's heads, not an centimeter behind or to the side, both hands at our side, standing firmly until told otherwise. A student leader announced, "1, 2, and 3!" Everyone started singing the national anthem, like soldiers would: loud, raising our right hands to salute the flag. After we were done we all repeated a phrase, "Pioneers for Communism, we will be like Che!" Shortly after, some students read a poem about Camilo Cienfuegos and how heroic he was, and others did a play. We all went to our classrooms holding our bouquets of flowers that we had stolen from our neighbors' yards.

Not long after, we marched to the nearest seashore to throw our flowers in the ocean. Smaller kids went first and older kids followed. When it was my turn, I glanced at the water enriched by flowers and leaves and for a second wondered what really happened to Camilo, though I couldn't touch that rose unless I wanted to be pricked by its thorns. I might end up in juvie if I even tried to talk about it with my closest friends.

I grew up hearing theories Abu had about Camilo's death, and how the Castro brothers could've been the cause of it and sent someone to assassinate him and all the people who knew about it. I wanted to ask my history teacher, but I knew I would get in trouble since school in Cuba is based on what they tell you: you believe it and in a test you say exactly what they want you to.

Abu as a young woman

Abu today

My grandma was an activist. She organized patriotic marches in July, October, and all those months that meant a lot to our nation. As the head of the CDR (Committee for the Defense of the Revolution) she would march on the large streets of our neighborhood, proudly holding a bright Cuban flag and yelling, "*¡Viva Cuba libre! ¡Viva Fidel!*" and I would follow her along with the huge crowd of students repeating after her. I loved helping Abu organize all these patriotic acts. I felt the adrenaline running through my veins every time we raised our fists and yelled something. I felt like I could do anything just by speaking up, which is ironic since I was demonstrating my "loyalty" to the Cuban government, not fighting against it. I was there not because I truly believed in what the Castro brothers were making out of Cuba, but because I wanted to feel some kind of power by screaming for the whole country to hear. Abu liked when I was this fierce about helping her because then we wouldn't be seen as traitors, but as honorable citizens of the Cuban nation.

In Cuba most people are involved in the government, even if you want out. Your job, friends, school, cartoons—your whole life experience—is because of the Cuban Revolution. Most Cubans can recite the entire Cuban history along with the biographies of all the martyrs. For me, it was normal to know all these things and have debates over wars and how things could've been different if they hadn't taken the risky measures they did.

At home it was different. Most days we would watch the news, and if Abu didn't agree with something heroic they said about Fidel, she would comment, "There they go again, making him some kind of hero. They're giving us cat instead of hare— we all know Fidel killed Camilo Cienfuegos, a martyr for Cubans." She said that the government was constantly lying to us about what had really happened. Abu always told us that we had to look communist and pretend we buy what they're selling us. It was easy to do because all we had to do was do the most and be proud of our nation. She said that we had to believe those ideals and apply them outside of the house, but that under her wing we could roast the government all we wanted. She explained to us that we had to live like that in order to be safe. Because Abu was the president of the CDR, our family wasn't targeted; to the public we looked like true revolutionaries. Her way of protecting us was showing people how outgoing and supportive of our dysfunctional government our family was. Most of our lives were based on protests demanding freedom from the United States.

At school I was an outstanding student because I would give good arguments on why we are the best nation and why we always make the right decisions, but I questioned myself and couldn't understand whether I believed what was coming out of my mouth or I was *más rollo que película:* falsely portraying myself.

As I got older it was hard for me to agree with those who really thought the government was doing the right thing, hard to not say what I really thought, so I chewed up my internal thoughts and spit what they wanted me to say.

Abu's disillusionment with the government started when my uncle Danilo was fourteen years old. He was the smartest kid in his class, read books a lot, and had his future already figured out. Even if he was as mature as everyone thought he was, he was still a kid, and kids make mistakes. There was a time he and a couple of friends heard about a stash of guns belonging to the government and went to find it. Without even giving his brain time to process the information, he went on an adventure to get those guns. He was curious to see what they were like since guns aren't part of our culture. And he did, but he was caught. The Cuban government has little mercy for sinners and he had just committed a big crime, so they said he should be punished. Uncle Danilo was sent to a correctional institution where the worst of the worst kids were prisoners. Abu suffered a lot because her first born child, who was a great kid, made a mistake. My mom tells me that Abu resented the government, yet knew there was nothing she could do but prove that she was loyal. Eventually he got out at the age of eighteen, but after being locked up for four years he wasn't the same. He couldn't get a stable job and alcohol was his best friend. It saddens me that light was stolen from such a bright person. To this day, he is the most crafty person I know. He would go near the slaughterhouse and get bulls' heads, then use the horns to make earrings, necklaces, rings, keychains, and *espuelas de gallo*, which were glued to roosters' natural spurs during cockfights. Tio Danilo also fixed shoes with a huge needle and thread which he strengthened by using resin from the Indian-almond tree in our back yard or wax from chewed honeycomb. Although Abu loves Danilo, what happened to him left a scar on her. She never forgot.

Katherin's grandfather Valerio, uncle Danilo, uncle Amaury, Abu, and aunt Berenis

Strong women guard my family, and I am who I am because of them. My grandma, mother, and aunt are as strong as concrete on a paved road. Abu raised her children plus some of the children my grandpa had after their divorce. My aunt was a single mother until she married her current husband and raised his two kids. My mom raised me and my brother by herself while going to teaching school and becoming a teacher.

Since there were no influential males in my family, women governed the household, and we were taught to be fierce and that we are not less than men. When I went to visit my family in La Havana, however, it was the other way around. I was corrected by men and put last because apparently I wasn't smart enough to talk about politics, but I was smart enough to learn millions of recipes, and to learn how much salt, oil, and lemon to put in salads so my uncles wouldn't complain. My mom didn't like the way they tried to "shape" me. She taught me to be independent. She always said that when I got older I should be in a trusting relationship where equality overflows. She didn't want me to live my life with no voice, thinking it was okay to be put down. She said that since it was just Abu, my aunt, her, and me, we had to trust each other unconditionally because if we stuck together we could be stronger. "*Un solo gorrión no compone verano*—a single sparrow doesn't make a summer. There's got to be more sparrows in order to make it together," she said.

My mom always kept a notebook in the bottom of her right side drawer. It contained poems and idioms that she either came up with or copied out of a book. She was really careful about letting my brother get to it—she protected that little notebook like it was a treasure found at the bottom of her sea. Ma let me borrow it on occasion since I liked to show it to my friends and we would talk about its meaning. I can't help but wonder where that notebook is now. Did it sink back to the bottom of her sea? Or is it at the surface of her soul?

Abu had a cookie box that no one could touch where she kept all her sewing needles and embellishments for clothes. She said that the most important things for a woman were those little memories that they can hold on to when times are hard. I didn't quite understood the meaning behind it, but being in a foreign country where patriarchy rules the nation has made me figure out the riddle of life. Now I know what she meant: women do suffer and face inequality, but that's when we need to remain stronger than ever.

When I was around ten years old my mom talked to me about coming to the United States to live with my father. She encouraged me to think of the trip as a way of expanding my mind and someday becoming someone important. It's what she had always dreamt of for me. She said I could think about it and tell her later. I was happy that this meant I could see my father. And the U.S. seemed like a paradise everyone would want to live in. I was hesitant because I knew this was going to change my life drastically, and I didn't want to be away from the most beloved people in my life. I wanted to stay in Cuba, but everybody had always said that I would never succeed in a communist country. I wanted more, and I knew that in order to *be* more I had to come to the United States, even if that meant leaving my whole world behind.

My mom always told me that no matter where I was, she would always be thinking of me and would love me forever. I didn't want to be a thousand miles away from her; I wanted her as close as my fingernails are to my fingers. I understood why she suggested that I think about it, though—it would shape my future. Ma explained that this was a long process and that it would take time before I get to live with my dad. I made a decision right there. I said, "Yes, I would like to move to the United States." We then left this conversation aside and lived our normal lives because this day was too far away to feel real.

I still remember the first time we got telephones in the houses of everyone who had been a good neighbor in the eyes of the government. Some guys from ETECSA, the only telephone company in Cuba, came to each house and did the installations and gave each house a white telephone. There were six numbers to each landline and the only thing that changed was the last two digits, so basically we knew everybody's phone number. When the installations were done they gave us a huge book with colorful pages full of phone numbers and area codes. I sent my friends to their houses so I could call them and giggle over the line. Everyone in my house wanted to play with the phone. My cousins and I were always arguing and competing to get the phone every time it made a sound. Changing the ringtone became our favorite game—we were so amazed by the sounds it could project that we kept changing it. We also prank called people. We would call and ask for the older member of the family, usually a grandma, and we would say to her, "It's the funeral home. We got a call about some old lady who died. We are calling to ask what time we should go pick up the body." It was funny because she would think that one of her sons was trying to bury her alive, or that someone wanted her dead. One time *la señora* yelled at me, "I am not dead, you fool!" I know this was very obnoxious of me, but that was our new way of having fun.

Before we got telephones it was so different. My friends and I were always doing *mandaos*, running errands. Our parents would send us to go get someone and deliver messages. Most times I was sent to my aunt's house, I would repeat the message the whole way, but by the time I got to my destination I would forget. So I had to go back home, ask again, and write it down on a little piece paper so I wouldn't have to walk back again.

Before my grandfather was hospitalized with esophageal cancer, I had never spoken with him over the phone. On April 30, 2012, I pressed the bleached buttons of my phone to call the hospital in hopes of reaching to him. Classical music played as I impatiently waited to get through to the front desk. I remembered that time when I asked him for a peso to buy a snack from a woman selling *chicharrones de viento*. It turned chaotic when all my cousins and my brother came asking for a peso too. He looked through his wallet, and soon after met our eyes with disappointment. He didn't have enough. Instead of just saying, "I don't have money," he elaborated a story about a plant that instead of flowers had money blooming like fruits, saying it died because for it to produce money you have to give it half of what you take. His eyes told me what I needed to know. Now I was starting at the only symbol of closure I had, the telephone, impatiently waiting for the front desk to please speak to me so I can talk to my *abuelito*.

The classical music stopped, and a kind yet rushed voice said, "Hello, you are on the line with the Hospital Celia Sánchez Manduley. How can I help you?" I replied desperately, but managing to sound as professional as possible, "Oh, hi. I want to speak to my grandfather. He's been admitted to the recuperation area in Room #115." This time she sounded more comfortable. "Yes ma'am. I am going to put you through the line, so please hold." And then the sad song was playing again. When he answered, Abuelito surprisingly sounded pretty hyped up about *El Primero de Mayo*.

The first of May is a festive holiday when we celebrate laborers and the working class. Everyone has the day off and gathers in La Plaza, the biggest street in Manzanillo, wearing the colors of the flag: blue, red, and white. We carry posters with revolutionary quotes and pictures of our martyrs. There's loud *salsa*, *casino*, and reggaeton music everywhere, you can feel it pounding on your feet and everything you touch. There is food on almost every corner, though those people shouldn't be working. My family never missed one of those marches, and like any other year Abuelito wanted to go.

My mom later called me and said she was going to take him to the festivities if he looked all right the next morning. I went to bed like I normally do, but woke up to despondent news. Life could be evil sometimes, and I couldn't handle the injustice God had committed. At 2:20 a.m. of May 1, 2012, God decided that Abuelito didn't belong to this world anymore. God was the jury and in his court it was the right thing to take him away from us. Who do I blame? God for taking him? Cancer for making his last days miserable? I refused to acknowledge his death.

My family had left for the hospital, and I was left with my great-aunt. I got up, walked to my closet picked a black spaghetti strap shirt and a skirt, went to the restroom, took a shower and walked out the door. I could feel my aunt staring at my back as I walked down the street. She didn't speak, and neither did I. I went to the beer brewing place where my friends and I used to hang out. There was music playing in the background, people talking, smiling, and having a great time celebrating *El Primero de Mayo*. I couldn't hear anything. I was trapped in my own universe, watching everything going on around me in slow motion with distorted sounds, unable to speak or move. I knew that if I freaked out it would just bring questions that I didn't have answers to. I blended into the conversation my friends were having and tried to believe that it was just a bad dream. As I tried to be myself again with my friends, I told them, "Hey can you guys believe my grandpa just died? Haha, crazy I know." I realized I had messed up. I immediately responded, "I'm just kidding. Abuelito is still in the hospital, but he is getting better. Who knows? Maybe he will be released today." Their faces were confused,

unsure whether to cool down or get warmer. At the moment I believed what I said: my *abuelito* wasn't dead—at least not to me. I don't believe something until I see it.

At about 2:30 p.m. I walked towards Abuelito's house. I kept thinking maybe he would be at home. When I arrived, I saw an enormous crowd of family and friends hanging out on the block. I entered the front door to find my mother sobbing, short of breath, red eyes, tears running down her peach cheeks, hugging a long brown wooden box with colorful flowers made into a circle. I slowly approached the coffin and saw Abuelito laying there, his skin like royal silk, his eyes closed like when he was in a deep sleep, his gray mustache not moving like it used to when he breathed. Every tear my family shed for him was demanding him to come back. But wasn't it unfair for them to want him to come back when all he did when alive was feel pain and wish it all went away? We knew the cancer had been eating his soul. He couldn't talk much, and he was fed by a rubber tube connected to his lower abdomen. Tears sprinted down my cheeks, meeting my lips. I was hoping one of those tears would wake him up from the eternal sleep. I was crying an ocean and it wasn't enough.

We spent a long time coping with his death. We came to see it as Abuelito getting the peace he deserved. One way for our family to stay together through this hard time was celebrating the most important Cuban holidays, like New Year's. My family spends the entire year working so they can celebrate this

Roasting a pig for New Year's

don't like about the holiday. Since we have had the pig for a long time, I have grown affection for it and I really don't want to hear those lamentable screams while it is being stabbed in the heart. Once the pig is dead but still warm, we let the blood fill up a big bowl which later will be used to make *morcilla,* or blood sausage. As I observe this sad but festive thing happening, Abu comes from the kitchen with a huge metal bowl of boiled water, her hands grasping it by the sides with two old towels protecting her hands from the heat. Then my uncle Andrés takes his fishing knife with his right hand, his left hand holding a cup to pour the hot water into the pig's body, and shaves off its hair. When the pig is nice and clean my uncle cuts it open as if doing an autopsy and pulls out the guts and places them in another bowl. The liver, the tongue, the heart, and most importantly the intestines are saved. The women clean the intestines thoroughly multiple times with water by hand so the blood can be poured inside and later boiled to make *morcilla.* The liver and heart are made into *gandingas* after they are cut in pieces and cooked in sauce. Abu is the only one who knows how to make *gandingas* properly. The tongue is roasted with the rest of the pig. Once the pig is empty and all that's left is the flesh, we season it with garlic cloves, onions, cumin, oregano, and some other seasonings. Then one member of the family sews up the pig from its belly button to its chest with hard silver wire while it is laying on the cold table. Then it is ready to be placed on the spit. My uncles and cousins measure and dig a rectangular hole in the ground, as long as the pig is, not deeper than one foot. Then they put some homemade charcoal in it. On the ends of the

expensive holiday. We have everything arranged a month in advance. My family collects their money and buys a pig. The pig must be fed with everyone's leftovers—kind of gross, but we need the pig to be as fat and big as possible. Once we have the pig ready, we worry about the new clothing we are going to wear that day: new year, new me. Everyone has to wear new clothes even if most people don't have money. We help each other or we ask the seller to let us buy clothes on credit until we can pay. My brother and I get really excited about these new clothes; we want to wear them the same day they're bought.

Finally the day arrives. My entire family wakes up early in the morning. We play music from a CD while we prepare the pig, which is the only part I

hole we place two Y shaped sticks which are taken from a mango tree we have on the left side of my aunt's house. These sticks have to be strong so they can hold the pig for more than five hours. After we have those placed, my uncle Andrés puts the pig on the stick with the help of my cousins. He places the stick inside the pig and ties its legs to the stick so it doesn't move. Then the men take turns roasting the pig because they have to go in circles in a slowish pace so it cooks just right.

The women are concentrated in the kitchen making *congris*—dark rice with beans—and a salad of cucumbers, lettuce, white cabbage, red tomatoes, and avocado mixed in a huge bowl along with vegetable oil, vinegar, salt, and lemons from our tree. Most of the cooking essentials we use come from either the *organopónico* on the corner of the street, where I once volunteered, or from our own patio. *Organopónicos* are urban organic gardens that are located everywhere in Cuba. In the kitchen they are also making the *morcilla*. Once the intestines are sterilized, we place blood inside them, seasoned it with garlic, onions, red and green peppers, salt, and a *pastillita*, a bacon bouillon that makes everything taste delicious. We carefully coil this really long intestine full of blood in a big pot of boiling water and cook it until it becomes solid, then we cut it into smaller pieces.

Then Abu makes the yuca by taking the long roots, peeling them, and cutting them into three parts if they're long or two parts if they're not. These are also placed in boiling water until they get soft. While all this is happening Ma is making the *mojito*, a sauce of vinegar, salt, limes, onions, garlic, red and green peppers, and oil mixed together. This is used as a topping on the yucas so they have a nice taste. My cousin Anita is in charge of buying lots of grapes, which will be important that night. My uncle Danilo is in charge of buying the rum, wine, and beer. Ma makes the *crema de vie,* or eggnog.

Around 7:00 p.m., everyone is drinking and dancing, wearing their new clothes. My cousins Rafael and Rafael—Rafe and Kiki for short—are in their twenties and look a lot alike. They're wearing polo shirts, jeans, old-fashioned Nikes, sunglasses, and too much hair gel. Their father left for the United States when they were just a few years old, so they don't know much about him—they just know that they have an American sister whom they've seen once and whose Spanish is not that good. Rafe and Kiki always have a microphone in their hands, they're like the hosts of the party. They are making people sing Ricardo Arjona's song "*La mujer que no soñe*" along with them. It's not an exciting song, more like a calm and melancholic one. This song came out in 1991, way before I was born, but we all still sing along to these songs. When they played "*Mi historia entre tus dedos*" I screamed, that's one of my favorite songs, and is my uncle Andrés's and my song. Everyone knows that when that song comes up we will get the first object that resembles a microphone and start singing with emotion, like the song belongs to us. It has nothing to do with what the song says; it is more of the feeling the singer puts into the song that gets our attention.

When the *puerco* is ready everyone goes crazy because they all want to eat *el cuerito,* the pig's crispy skin. Others fight over the tail, tongue, and ears, which aren't my favorites. Each plate has *congris*, big chunks of meat, *cuerito*, and salad. Even after everyone is full we keep partying. Everyone dances *casino*, *salsa*, and our traditional dances. We can't be sitting in a chair waiting for the clock to hit 12:00; we've got to have fun while we wait.

When there's ten seconds left until the New Year everyone starts the countdown:

9. Everyone gets twelve grapes.

8. They get their suitcases ready.

7. I can assure you that more than half of these people are wearing red underwear, which protect you and keep bad things away so you have a peaceful year.

6. Tio Danilo has the champagne in his hand waiting to open it. It will end up in our hair and on our clothes.

5. Everyone has empty cups.

4. We are up and reunited. We get in a circle and hug each other. I like to stare at their smiles; that's what makes this day worth celebrating. There are no worries, just joy.

3. If you have fireworks, now is the time to light them.

2. A quick moment to remember those who were there in past years but lamentably aren't now, like Abuelito. We feel somewhat empty, since parts of our heart have gone along with those who we once loved and cherished.

1. All of this happens at the same time. It's nice to step out and see all this going on so fast, like watching the metro fly with blurry faces but better.

Everyone screams, laughs, cries, hugs, and greets each other because they've just been granted another year. Once everyone eats the twelve grapes for good luck on the twelve months of the year, they walk with a full suitcase around the block. Our neighbors are out with their suitcases, too. My family always does it proudly, since we honestly want to have journeys throughout the year.

In the first moments of 2014, when I walked around with my suitcase, I was thinking about moving to La Yuma. My interview with the American Embassy was just six days away. I had to travel to La Havana for the interview. My mom, cousin, and I went to the huge building surrounded by American flags and entered by the fancy silver doors. A tall foreign man was guarding the door. There was a huge line of people, and then there was an enormous line of elders who were constantly yelled at. Soon after we signed in, we sat next to one another and held hands for a while. The cold in that place was similar to winter in Manzanillo. My mom was as nervous as I was. We silently sat there moving our legs side to side until my name was called out. While we were waiting we observed the people waiting, with us, some holding photo albums to prove themselves, and others so nervous that they would go to the restroom due to emergencies.

As one young woman went into one of the embassy's offices, she fixed her hair, tightened the bottom of her shirt, and cleared her throat a few times, then she quickly crawled into her shell, like she was trying too hard and couldn't handle the situation. A few minutes later she walked out of there in tears. I could see how important this was to some people. Everyone prepares for a pamphlet full of questions. Most people that got out of there mentioned the fact that they ask many questions and how terrifying it is.

We proceeded to the office we were assigned, and inside was a pale lady in a suit with red lips and long golden hair. Somehow she was kind, yet intimidating. She began speaking with a strong gringo accent. "Please tell me your name and date of birth." My mom and I looked at each other and I responded to the question. Then she asked my mom how old I was and my mom said, "Eleven." The woman signed a paper and said, "You've been approved." I couldn't believe it. I was coming to United States; it wasn't a fantasy anymore. I was happy, but confused.

We walked out of the winter and greeted my cousin outside; she was thrilled to hear the news. Everyone seemed happier than I was. I have to admit, I was in between. I wanted to go to this paradise everyone talks about, but I also wanted to be with my family. Ma hugged me and said, "*Niña, you're going to the U.S., I'm so excited!*" I gave her a confused smile and kept walking. My little brother didn't quite understand the situation and showed no feelings about it yet.

My dad sent money right away and I immediately got a plane ticket for March. My life was changing so fast that I wasn't sure if it was really happening.

My mom hosted a farewell party the night before my departure. Everyone wanted to take pictures with me and dance and have fun. I started to feel like backing up and not going anywhere, just continuing to live the life I had. But I kept my head high and smiled like it was the best day of my life.

Katherin with some of her teachers shortly before moving to the U.S.

The last time I saw Abu, it wasn't as happy and exciting as I had hoped it would be. I hugged her and told her not to be sad because I was going to live a good life. She told me that she is never sad over little things, that she knew I was going to be happy the first few days, but she was concerned about me being sad once I arrived to the United States because there was no coming back. Abu had always had a witch side to her personality: no matter what she said was going to happen, it happened, and that scared me a little because I didn't want to regret coming to the U.S. I got in the antique blue, Russian-made car and looked through the back window and waved goodbye to Abu. I could feel the sorrowful aura surrounding us when she didn't wave back, and I felt heartbroken and guilty.

Katherin at a swimming hole with her father and stepmother Martitee during a visit to Cuba from Louisville. She later moved to Louisville to live with them.

I left the next day at noon. The sun was bright and it shone upon my shoulder, saying a shallow goodbye. Everyone was crying like they were at a funeral, yet this was the beginning of my life. All my friends were there trying to smile while the tears came down their cheeks. My mom was devastated that her little girl was leaving but happy that her daughter had the ambition to pursue her dream. I hugged her tightly, crying, and didn't want to let go. She told me to stop crying because no one had died, that this was a joyful moment. As I stood on the stairs to the plane at the Manzanillo airport, I wanted to go back and never leave their side, to drop everything and put them under my wing, to never let go of the happiness I had, to run into my past's arms. Then my decision became final. I walked on the plane. I was all in.

A girl behind me looked straight into my eyes and said, "I see myself in you; you're like my reflection." Later on the plane she dried my tears and told me her own story of moving to the United States when she was younger. We became friends.

The plane landed in Miami. My dad, my stepmom Maritee, Tata (my paternal grandmother, who also lived in the U.S. now), and my little sister Karla were there waiting for me. My dad looked so different and Tata looked younger than she had last year when I saw her in Cuba, as if the U.S. had done her some good. My stepmom, whom I had met once on a visit she made to Cuba, looked the same, but that little girl she was holding was a new face to me. She seemed to cry all the time and looked like me when I was little. We bonded pretty quickly in the airport. They all hugged me and gave me gifts.

I was fascinated by the fact that the streets had lights. I immediately called my mom and told her about the shiny lights on the ground, about everyone having a car, and about the nice food. I spent an entire week in Miami enjoying the beaches and nice breeze. Everything was like my dad described it over the phone: the people looked elegant even in bikinis, and they all looked so happy that by glancing at them I could absorb the adrenaline in the air. My dad took me to the nicest places in Miami and even let me play in a pool with some old friends from Cuba. Everyone started asking me about Cuba and the people. They wanted to know if the pizzas were still five pesos each, and if people still gathered every Saturday at the beer brewing place. All their questions distracted me from missing my family.

I thought that Louisville was going to be the same, but instead of having a pool in the patio I had snow in my hair. When I arrived to the final destination I felt the need to cry and scream as loud as I could, yet there was no one to console me. The gloomy city of Louisville consumed me and the winter made me come back to reality. The first days I wanted to talk to my mom every day, but it is not like I had a job to pay the phone bills. So I went to my room and cried until I was dehydrated. The closest I was to my mom was through my stepdad Yoni, who had moved to the U.S. a month before I did. Sadly, he was living with his family in New Jersey, where he had to work two jobs in order to keep going and support our family in Cuba. I tried calling him when he had a break, but it was hard. I had to go to school in about one month. I spent that month crying myself to sleep and being sad all the time. Everything made me cry, even the stunning reflection of the moonlight. My dad wanted me to go out and make friends, but it was too difficult to accomplish. I didn't speak the language. I felt like a fish out of water. I wanted to go back home. I missed the presence of my mom, Yordancito, Yami, and Dayán.

When I started school, I thought that if I did the opposite of what my dad wanted me to do he would be mad at me and send me back to Cuba. He had told me I couldn't have a boyfriend because I was too young, so I started dating a guy I didn't even like. My dad was mad at me because I disobeyed his orders, yet he didn't sent me back to Cuba. He told me that I came to the U.S. to have a better future, and that no one forced me to come so I should deal with it. I was so mad, disappointed, and sad that I wanted to break things. So I did what I knew how to do best: I cried. I had to accept the fact that I wasn't going anywhere. I tried to be "normal" and enjoy school like those around me, even though I was considered too "nerdy" and "odd." I finally started to think of this as a vigorous thing that happens to a few people and I was one of the lucky ones because I had the chance to live it. I called my mom when I could and focused more on school than my own life.

Ma acted happy and like life was going just fine, which I later found out it was all fake. She did it so I wouldn't worry and feel worse. I didn't know until I went to Cuba two years later and Abu told me that my mom had cried every day and felt horrible for sending me away and that my mom couldn't bear the guilt. When Abu finished the story my heart broke, and all I wanted to do was hug Ma so tight that she wouldn't be able to breathe. Growing up with my mom was a blessing. Not having her by my side because an ocean of laws separated us was hard.

I thought my brother wasn't going to be affected by my departure. We always fought and said mean stuff to each other and we never said "I love you." I always thought we weren't as loving as siblings should be, but when I left he promised my mom he would not play or draw until I got back to Cuba. He gave up his favorite activities for me, for a hope that flew to the horizon and didn't come back. Every time my mom put him on the phone all he did was cry. It was too hard for him to talk to his long-gone sister that he might never get to see again. My radiant little brother was becoming a sorrowful little boy. He did not want to eat, take showers, or go to school. Ma did not know what to do with him so he could get better and go back to be that annoying brother I once had. So she took days off work and with some money she had saved she took him, his friends, and his cousins to his favorite place on Earth, Las Coloradas, a beautiful beach with clear blue water and white sand, surrounded by bright green palms. I had my part to play, too, which was to tell him I was having so much fun in La Yuma and that I went to all these alluring places and ate delicious food, and it seemed to make him feel better that I was doing great here.

When I came to the United States four years ago, the only English I knew was the most basic of greetings. I was told not to speak Spanish, my native language, and instead to speak a language in which I could barely make out the differences between the vowels. Suddenly I found myself lost in the colorful multitude of people passing by like planes. I had never thought about life being unfair since those who I love the most were unconditionally by my side, but I felt unfairness at that moment. I came to the realization that I wasn't the only one who felt this way. We all experience unfairness at some point in our lives. I understood why I was being asked to speak only English. I would never be able to speak English fluently if I didn't completely immerse myself in the language. Even if I didn't speak at the same level as some of my peers, the same rules applied to me. There are English speaking students who have to learn Spanish, so I thought they must feel the same way as I did. This did not prevent me from struggling.

I initially earned bad grades and my GPA dropped. My family accused me of not working hard enough to learn English. They questioned why I had such good grades in Cuba, but was doing poorly here. I couldn't find the words to explain to them how it felt to be forced to speak a language that was completely unfamiliar to me. They didn't understand how unfair it felt to me. Sometimes I wanted to scream for help but there was no one to hear me. Eventually, I learned to live with it. I thought that if other people could do this, than I was no exception. Little by little, I slowly began to learn English, and the more I learned, the easier it got. I've always considered myself a fast learner and pride myself on my ability to learn from both my failures and my successes. I've probably learned much more from my mistakes, my failures, and my struggles than I ever have from things that came easily to me because they show us our true character and allow us to grow.

While I was coping with the fact that I am a permanent resident in the U.S., my mom was finding new ways to be with me. Six months after I came to the United States, my mom came after me and risked her life. My brother Yordancito stayed in Cuba with Abu since he was too small to take such a risk. She got on a boat no bigger than fifteen feet and went to a *cayo*, or small island, near the Manzanillo coast, along with thirteen other people. The engine broke three times and they found themselves off course in the sea. Ten days went by and they were still in the same place. Merchant ships passed by them making huge waves, but none of them saw the tiny dot in the ocean. Finally, a Philippine-Irish merchant ship spotted them with a huge light and helped them out. They slept for three days in the ship's dorms. The captain talked to them and told them that he was going to leave them in the Gulf of Mexico because they weren't going far. There Mexican immigration officials took them into custody in vans, women in one and men in the other, to Ayucan, Mexico. She said that being treated like a criminal didn't feel good. There in jail they had to wait for permission to in Mexico. Twenty-one days later she got it and then immigration took them to a bus terminal in Veracruz, Mexico. That bus took them to Matamoros on the border with the United States. Then my mom went to New Jersey, where my stepdad Yoni was waiting for her. They later moved to Houston, where my mom's brothers lived and could help them. Yordancito still lives in Manzanillo with Abu, though my mother is working on the paperwork to bring him to the U.S.

I call Louisville home since I've lived here for about four years, in the house where I currently live. My memories as the new kid, as the nerd, as the Cuban girl with red hair, as prom princess are in that house. My room is decorated with faith and encouragement not only to myself but to the people who have the privilege to visit it. I have pictures of me and friends and family which is all under my name "Kat" on one wall, pictures of my favorite actors on the other along with an article about meeting the governor, who disappointed me. All over my room I have multicolored Christmas lights to give my room a sense of life. On the wall I have a gigantic picture of my worst *quinceañera* picture. (The photographer decided which photo should be the poster and my family and I didn't have a say in it.) In my closet I have eight colorful flowers made into a triangle. With some rhinestone stickers I spelled out a question on the door, "What should I wear?" I'm always asking myself this question. I struggle with it because society tells us to be a certain way and most people try to meet those standards, so I wanted to meet them too and not be "weird." Now I dress however I feel—feminism has saved me.

Next to my closet is my suitcase. It's maroon, my new favorite color. Inside I keep summer clothes and winter clothes, a pair of shoes, shampoo, conditioner, lotion, perfume, body wash, and in one of the compartments I have over fifty bus tickets. For as long as I can remember, I have always kept a packed suitcase in my room. I don't know why—perhaps because my life has been wrapped up and folded in a suitcase many times.

I thought my heart was going to leave my chest and walk away from me and get lost in the festive crowd. I was the happiest mortal in all of Havana. After moving to La Yuma three years before, I was finally returning to Cuba for my first visit. While I was on the plane I couldn't contain my excitement; I rubbed my hands on my lap, leaving traces of sweat on my red dress. Once we arrived everyone clapped gratefully and thanked the pilot. I was the first person off the plane. I was amazed by the hot climate and tropical feeling around me. I wanted to scream, dance, hug everyone, but I would look like a psychopath. So I opted to keep the excitement to myself and wait for my three-and-a-half-year-old sister Karla and my dad to get out of the plane.

Shortly after that, we went through a huge line so we could get our bags. Karla was frightened by all the people smiling at her. The extremely hot weather, the bright sun on our shoulders, and all the exhilaration seemed to torment her. Every kid in such a situation would cry, and that's exactly what she did. I took her to the restroom but she said that the bathrooms weren't purified enough to her liking. So I tried talking her out of her tantrum, which became even more embarrassing when I had to speak in English in front of some Cuban ladies in the room, most of them workers wearing maid-looking uniforms: navy blue and white, kind of short, hair up, making them look clean and neat. What would they think of me? I tried to look as Cuban as possible and my sister was ruining the possibility of finally fitting back into the community I wished to be part of.

My main problem is that I am not sure where I belong. Latinxs are always either too Latinx to fit in the American community or not Latinx enough for the community where we are supposed to belong. While I was talking to Karla beside the wash basin, she shamelessly peed herself even though she knew how to say she has to go to the toilet in both languages. Embarrassed, I took my sister's hand. I tried not to stress out because it wouldn't bring anything good, just more stress caused by stressing over the stress. I cleaned her up, changed her clothes and kept talking to her about Kit Kats, her favorite chocolates. Unluckily for us, we didn't have those in Cuba and my dad forgot to pack any. I was doomed. She kept crying.

After a while I managed to make her forget about it and think of something else. When we got out of the restroom her hair was a mess, her two dysfunctional pony tails were in a different place from where my stepmom had brushed them to be, dried tears were tattooed on her pale cheeks, and her dress was the only organized thing in her life. I fixed her hair as she said, "*¡No quiere pelo!*" which is a grammatically incorrect way of saying, "I don't want hair!"—she often mixed up "*quiero*" and "*quiere.*" She was yelling at me in both languages in front of everyone. She calmed down and, holding hands, we made our way to the unlimited and desperate line of people. After a few minutes we walked out of there with our bags in hand. I was really excited to see the outside, and so was my dad.

I felt like I was getting out of prison. There was a square fence and people who had just arrived were being released to be with loved ones shedding happy tears, falling in their son's arms, embracing their daughters' hair, looking at them like it would be the last time. And there we were, waiting for our

inspiration, hope, faith, whatever you want to call it: our family. I felt relieved when was able to distinguish my uncles from the huge herd surrounding us. I hugged them with joy, but parts of my heart were darkening. I wanted to see my mom's family, but they were in Manzanillo, too far for me to run into their arms. I wanted to see Abu and my brother but sadly they couldn't make it to La Havana for our arrival. Tio Felipe's car was waiting for us outside in the parking lot. The car was so small you could mistake it for a kid's toy car. It was bright orange and it didn't have windows, air conditioning, or music. The seats were really small. My sister kept glancing at it and when she got in the car she looked at me and said, "I don't like this car." I was so Americanized that I was embarrassed to get in that type of car and ride in the streets of Havana like it was the 1950s. All of a sudden I started laughing and all the shame went away. I was just glad I was there, alive and with my family.

Once we arrived to our destination, familiar faces beamed at me. Some new faces I had no idea existed also smiled at me. I began talking, getting to know the city I was born in. I found out that my childhood friends no longer lived there. More than ten years had passed—how could my egocentric heart think that they would still live there after such a long time?

I was there for four days. I preferred to be at my godmother's house, since she was always surrounded by kids my age and people who could still remember the childhood adventures we'd had together. We caught up on our lives and exchanged email addresses so I could write them.

We left La Havana in a rental car. This time we were going to the eastern part of Cuba. It took us an entire day to get there, since we traveled from one extreme point of the crocodile-shaped island to the other. As we traversed across the country, I noticed something I'd never noticed before: the fading of the accent. In Havana everyone talks like the letter "r" doesn't exist and it makes them sound cool. As we made our way east, people pronounced the letter "r" more and more clearly, until we got to the final destination where the Spanish language was spoken without shortcuts and was very clear to understand. I felt the words fading into the abyss as we explored the humid provinces.

When the "*Bienvenidos a Manzanillo*" billboard gave us a warm welcome, I suddenly noticed my hands getting cold and sweating. I was excited to finally be there; it wouldn't be long until I arrived at my beautiful town. As soon as I saw my house and my family and friends expecting me on the porch I started crying and ran into Abu's arms. She cried too, she who always assured me that she would never shed a tear for anyone, who hadn't even cried when her mother died: the strongest woman I'd ever met was crying. It made my melancholic chest jump and flutter since she was crying out of happiness for me. My little brother hugged me tight after my grandma released me from her cozy arms. He looked so different. I felt like I was looking at versions of all the people I love. I didn't think three years would make such an enormous change in them. Abu had more grey in her hair than the sky did. Her kind eyes were protected by a crumpled piece of skin. I couldn't believe that I was finally looking straight at them.

My little brother was so much taller and already had a girlfriend. It was my siblings' first time meeting each other. My little sister didn't care much because she was consumed with yelling and crying, but my brother was focused on her. "Hey Karlita, I'm your older brother Yordan. Do you want some cookies?" She looked at me as if asking for permission, which is unusual because she never listens to me. I told her, "Go get some cookies with your brother," hoping they would bond.

I proceeded with the warm hugs and cozy smiles until the sky decided to cry for me as well. I was free. I could dance, and scream, and act crazy. I was with my family, so anything was acceptable. I let my hair down, tossed my *chancletas* (flip flops) aside, grabbed my brother's hand danced in the rain with my neighbors and family. We were laughing and going house to house greeting other neighbors. I could taste the fresh rain running down my lips as I smiled at everyone passing by and staring at me for looking lighter skinned than the rest.

I felt weird at the beginning, since I thought my Spanish wasn't as good as I wanted it to be. As the days went by it was hard for me to think in Spanish and to try not to include in conversation those tiny English words that have become part of my daily routine: "okay," "so," "I mean," "lol."

In the United States I don't get to greet the sun every morning, so I looked like a snowflake in front of my tanned friends. I didn't notice how white I looked until I saw people staring, so I thought I should get tanned as fast as possible so no one would notice I came from La Yuma and think that because of that I have tons of money, which I don't. The next

The view from Katherin's family's old apartment in Manzanillo

day I got invited to a pool party nearby and thought, *Well, Katherin, this is your opportunity to look a bit like your old self.* So I spent all the time facing the sun, not knowing that laying on a beach bed with an American flag printed towel would make me seem even more superficial. I ended up getting sunburned. I was as pink as a pig, and my clothes bothered my skin, but I was with my family—sunburned, but I was with them.

I thought I was going to be treated differently by my own family since everyone who goes to Cuba and comes back tells that tale. Abu was still the same, and this made me glad. When I was in Cuba she used to throw *chancletas* at me if I did something wrong or

chase me throughout the entire neighborhood with a baseball bat in her hands. This time was no different. I was invited to my friend's *quinceañera* and Abu had told me not to come home past 12:00 a.m. I got carried away. My former classmate, who was the birthday girl, asked me if I wanted to be one of her ladies. In the tradition of *quinceañeras*, her "ladies" are supposed to be fourteen girls she cherishes and are about her age. They are each accompanied by a guy and the girls have to hold a dead candle on their hands along with a needle. The *quinceañera* has a lit candle and as the fourteen girls are lined up facing their "date" she lights up the rest of the candles and the ladies have to explode the balloon the guy is holding.

Luckily, I knew the guy I was holding onto; he was my neighbor and classmate.

With all the dancing, laughing, and catching up with the people at the party, I forgot what Abu had told me. When I got home at 3:00 a.m., I tried to sneak in by the window. I pulled off the old wood window shutters and slowly took off my shoes and placed them on the other side. Then I went through the window, trying not to wake anybody, and placed the wood shutters back on. Just when I thought I had gotten away with it I found Abu sitting on her loud rocking chair with a *chancleta* in her hand, waiting for me. I tried to explain but the *chancleta* was too fast—it flew and hit me in my torso. She started yelling, her voice relieved and angry at the same time. She said, "You know I worry when you come home late, and I tell you not to, you don't know what can happen to you. People know you came from the United States they'll try to rob your chains, rings, and everything! You have to be careful, *mija*. You're going to find me lying on the floor dead because I got a heart attack, and only then you'll feel guilty." You know, basic grandmother's sayings. I was glad she was still the same so I chuckled, hoping she didn't see me. As I was walking to the room I felt something hit me in the back of my head. It was her flip flop again. I loudly said, "Ouch!" and she hit me again with the other one and said, "You think that hurts? Try having grandchildren and them being irresponsible. You'll understand. Wait, are you laughing at what I said to you? Because if you are I'm going to hop on the horses!" When she said that I rapidly nodded because what she meant was that she was going to get angrier and be ready to hit me.

My own *quinceañera* party came up and that night I was the star of the show. I came in the room, wearing a blue, almost turquoise princess gown, and wearing make-up for the first time, and the room was adorned with blue and silver balloons and an amazing cake with lots of special dishes that I never got to taste. I had requested that decorations be blue, even though the anti-feminist women at the party thought it should've been pink or purple. When it was time for the shoe ceremony, my cousin Brayan took off my sandals and put some sparkly high heels on my feet. It symbolized that I was a woman now. I got up with his help because those heels were humongous. My dad grabbed my hand gently and asked me to dance the father-daughter dance. We moved our bodies back and forth slowly so I wouldn't step on him. Something I got from him is his very emotional character. We both softly cried as we smiled and danced.

Once the song was over my dad went to a corner and Abu came to where I was and gave me a bouquet of flowers. I looked at the red roses, at Abu, and back at the flowers, but I couldn't figure out why she gave me those flowers. Someone placed a video on the wall and I turned around. It was my mom. She was talking about how she would love to be there in such a special moment of my life but couldn't. She said that those roses meant her love for me. Again I cried, and so did everyone there. At the end she said, "*Felicidades, mi amor*. I love you." "I love you too, Ma," I replied, as if she could hear me. My brother came running to me, and I tangled him in my arms as strong as I could and whispered in his ear, "Everything's going to be fine. You'll see her again.

Everything's going to be fine; it's a party." He was still glued to my waist. I pulled him in front of me and kissed him on the cheek then hugged him again.

A big part of visiting Cuba is going to the beach where tourists reside, but I wanted to go the beach where Abu always took us. On one of the last days of my visit, Abu, my dad, Yordancito, Karla, Yami, Dayan, my cousins, and some aunts and uncles drove from Abu's house to that beach. Nothing fancy. Just a lonely, forgotten, and amazing place with nude sand clear water. There were a few rusty, sunken boats with millions of mussels attached to them. As I glanced at its waters I remember a time when Abu saved me from drowning in this exact spot. She sat on the edge of one of the rusty boats and recognized some friends who were the only other people on the beach. She started talking to them, and as I was playing in water I tripped on seaweed, then got entangled in my long hair and the float I was wearing. I could see Abu looking around her to locate me, and when she saw me struggling to come out of the water she pulled me up by my hair and said, "Katherin, you're always drowning. I still don't understand how you swallowed all that water when it was up to your waist." I didn't speak a word. She was right. When her friends left, we went to where our food was, in the sand. She had brought with us mango juice stored in an old water bottle and some bread with butter. As we ate, looking at the endless beach, she said, "When your mind is troubled or you have to make a big decision, you should sit by the ocean, observe it, hear its waves talk to you, and then you should know what to do.

Because *el mar* brings you peace and washes your problems away."

There's nothing about Manzanillo that I don't like. Even its darkest places are something I adore. I could write thousands of pages about every corner, every street, every monument, every amazing adventure I had there. I consider myself lucky to have been raised in a place where witches' spells are the most exciting technology. Manzanillo taught me that life will not always be fair, helped shape my feminist ideals, and taught me to love, to understand others, and to appreciate the little everyday things like walking with my mom to school, or sitting here on the beach with my siblings. Not only did Manzanillo show me a happy life, but it also taught me to learn from my mistakes, to be fierce and believe in my passions. Looking out at the sea with my beloved family members swimming in it, I wished I could take Manzanillo, fold it up, put it in my suitcase, and bring it back to Louisville. Then I realized I'd been carrying it in my heart ever since I left, and that it would always be with me.

Journey to La Yuma

YORDAN SOCIAS HERNANDEZ

The Cuban community I belong to has many stories. We all came to the United States with the same purpose: to have a better life and to help the loved ones we left behind. We took different paths to get here. Long ago, my neighbor Jesús was supposed to fly to Angola to help support communist forces there, but instead he flew his government plane to the U.S. seeking refuge. My neighbor and friend Donna went to South America and came over land all the way from the jungles of Ecuador to Louisville. Many others, including my parents, have risked their lives to get a share of the happiness every human deserves. They knew the risks they were taking, they knew that they might not make it, they knew that American society might not accept them. But they thought of the life their children would have if they had the opportunity to grow up in the U.S. We are all dreamers. I interviewed my dad about his journey. Here is what he told me.

—KATHERIN

Coming to the United States was something that just happened. I went to see my children in Manzanillo and *boom*, I decided to leave to try to help them and my family more. It was easier to emigrate from Manzanillo because there wasn't a lot of surveillance by the coast guard on the Eastern shore. I was thirty years old.

If we could have left on a real boat we would have, but it was a boat that we made. We didn't have any other choice. The boat was about ten feet long. The bottom of the boat was the roof of an ambulance, and it was surrounded by wood and plastic and glue. There were thirteen people on the boat, twelve men and one woman.

We left at about 3:00 a.m. and in two days we arrived at the Cayman Islands, Cayman Bravas to be exact. We arrived in the early morning and waited until the morning to get to the shore. The engine was falling apart; all of the sticks that were holding it were loose. We were crazy to ever get on that boat. We were able to fix it, and continue. The people of the island helped us with food and cigars, utilities to continue our journey.

From there we left to Sidney Island, which was supposed to take five days. When we left Cayman, the boat was full of food. Since it was only going to be five days, we ate everything we wanted. After five days, there was no food and we had not arrived either.

And then we started taking all the birds and seagulls hanging on the edge of the boat to eat them if things got worse. We had them in a cage until the hunger hit us really hard. But about two days later there was a storm and when we woke up there were a lot of small fish—those that you call flying fish—inside the boat, and that's how we fed ourselves. We were holding the sail by hand, which is crazy; without it the boat would not accelerate. Anyways, it was loose and we were holding it, plus the engine was on the highest power possible and the wind from the storm is what helped us arrive. If it wasn't for that we would not have arrived because the boat was falling apart.

We never found Sidney Island. It was a very small boat, and it would shake left and right and almost flip over at times. I had never gotten that far on a boat. The waves we would see coming from the boat were as tall as a ten foot building. I would think, *This is going to drown us.* But they weren't aggressive waves, just elevated. Imagine those same waves during the night, maybe five feet tall and belligerent—the bad ones, not like the regular ones. That constant movement from the sea, not everyone is able to put up with that. On a big boat you wouldn't be able to tell as much, you still feel the sea sickness but not as much, but on that small boat it really gets to you.

That's what made Angel, one of the people on the boat with us, get constant vomiting. He also had diarrhea, and became dehydrated and very weak. We could not take care of him since we were all in the same circumstance. This is very sad to say, but when you are in this type of situation all you care about is your own survival. Since so much water would come in the boat, he was just floating at the bottom of the boat. Also, the engine started falling apart and he hit his elbow with it and destroyed his arm—you could even see the bone. We tried to wrap it up, but he would have bowel and bladder incontinence. When he stopped moving, we decided that if he was dead we were going to throw him overboard. It was painful, but it had to be done; he was right in the middle of everyone. So we tried to get his pulse, and nothing. Then we took a feather from one of the birds we had caged to see if he was breathing, but he wasn't breathing. Two or three of us grabbed him by his arms and legs to throw him in the water, and he started moaning, trying to say, "I'm alive." He made it and survived. He survived! I will never forget him.

I would climb up the pole we had set up to look to see if I could see any land. Only one of the lenses of the binoculars worked. Every time I would say, "Land!" and it was a false alarm, people would get mad. One day I thought I had seen land, so I said to Yoan, "Yoan, land!" He told me come to down. I grabbed the steering wheel, and he got up there to look and said, "Yes, land!" We could already see the land through the binoculars, but two days later is when we arrived. Our boat actually sunk near shore.

This island belonged to Belize. It was a small island. Maybe half a mile long and about 300 meters wide. The name of the island is a bird that only lives on that island. When we went to tried to walk to shore, no one could stand up. We had been in that little boat for such a long time we could not stand on our own. We were starving. When we finally arrived, dragging ourselves to this small deck, there was a coconut tree. We ate a bunch of those coconuts.

We were met by four people, an old gentleman who was the lighthouse keeper, a security guy, and two divers. They didn't speak any Spanish, but they gave us food and treated us nicely, and we were there for a few days. It was a private island, where travelers get a tour by boat and are taken to feed the sharks and such things. We had to sweep the beach every day with these big brooms, leave these pretty lines for when the tourists came. When they came, we would have to hide in a cabin so they wouldn't see us. That little island was one of the best parts of the journey. It was beautiful because these fisherman would come from Belize, two black guys with dreads. They would come fish and clean the fish there on the dock later, and these big sharks would come by. They would come to eat the remains of the fish. Adrian and I grabbed a rope one day and we were able to catch a shark and bring it out of the water. It was a very big shark. We brought it out and then immediately released it back into the water. We had a good time with them during those three days. Then a guy sent by the owner of the island came by. He gave us fuel and all the necessary things so that we could go on.

Then we were on our way to Honduras. It was a two hour trip, but it took us two days because our boat's engine didn't work. We put in a different engine, but it didn't work either, so we threw it in the water. We had to row with some boards until we found some aboriginals from the zone between Honduras and Nicaragua and they helped us. They took us to their village. When we saw them at the seashore there were about fifty naked little kids. They grabbed us by our clothes and hands, and since we had never left Cuba and didn't know anything, we thought they were going to eat us. But those people were amazing. They helped us a lot. We were in their village for one or two days. Do you remember those Cuban history textbooks where they portrayed indigenous people living in thatched houses? Just like that. They sent each one of us to a different thatched house.

A day or two later, they gave us a guide and we spent three days walking through the jungle until we got to La Ceiba, a civilized city of Honduras. They took us to immigration officials, and they released us the next day and sent us to the fire station. We stayed at the fire station for fifteen days until some of our families and friends here in the U.S. got *coyotes*—people who smuggled people across the border to the U.S.—for us. But the *coyotes* didn't take us anywhere. They took us prisoners until our family members sent money. After they took our money, they sent another Cuban guy to get us, and he did the same thing. After he robbed us, we went to a convent. We were at the convent for a few days until the nuns told us we had to leave. At that point, we all had to separate, but I stuck together with my friends Yoan, Damaisis, and Adrian.

When we were crossing the border to Guatemala, things started to worsen. The police kidnapped the four of us and locked us in a house until our family in the U.S. sent money. I didn't have any family in the U.S., but others did. I think it was $1,000 for each person that we had to pay them before they released us. Right after we were released, another group of Guatemalan policeman kidnapped us and did the same to us. We got money sent to us, and once we paid them they let us go. Then we started walking toward the border with Mexico, and walked for three days and two nights. Every time there was a car we had to throw ourselves in the water, since every car around that zone was either the Zetas or the Maras, and they kidnap people. On the last night when we could see Mexico, we went to a house in the countryside and asked those people where was the line and they told us the line was where we were walking. It was like a street: one side Guatemala and the other Mexico.

The next day we crossed. We walked all the way to Villahermosa. We tried to turn ourselves in but they said they weren't accepting any customers that day. A woman and two men tried to kidnap us, threatening me and pointing at me with a gun and asking for money. But all we had was a water bottle. We were so hungry and tired. We told them we were not going to get in the car, that they could do anything to us, that we didn't have family in Mexico or the United States or anywhere, that we didn't have anything whatsoever. I don't know what happened—maybe God touched their hearts—but they let us go. Then some other kidnappers chased us. We started running to a church. The priest closed the door on my face and he smashed my fingers with the door. I still have the scars. Then we went to this old guy's house, where people we had in the U.S. had told us to go. He gave us shelter for about four days.

Then Yoan, Damaisis, and I went to turn ourselves in to immigration again so they could start the process so we could continue—Adrian didn't turn himself in; he went another way—and we were arrested for a month or so. In prison, we didn't use our soap. When the cleaning crew came by we exchanged the soaps for cigars, then sold the cigars for five pesos, 100 pesos for a pack of cigarettes. I had a girlfriend who was a security guard in front of the prison, where they sold soups, like Maruchan noodles. They had money but they didn't have coins, and I had a pillowcase full of coins—I looked like a missionary. I gave them the coins they wanted for paper money. That's how I spent my time there. Also we played cards and fanunga, a Cuban game.

After I got out and paid my fee, I went back to the prison because Yoan and Damaisis were still there. They told me I couldn't be there because they had released me. I rented myself a room in a motel nearby, so I could go visit Yoan the next morning to see how his process was going. He and Damaisis were already deported to Cuba.

The last kidnapping was there on the last point of control. The immigration security took my money, shoes, and everything. They tied me to a chair by my leg, but then he left somewhere, and I escaped. And that's when I crossed the border to the United States. I paid three dollars and then I crossed. But when I arrived to the United States' border, the immigration security didn't want to accept the phone number I had for a contact in the U.S.—Yoan's brother Yunior, who lived in Las Vegas. They asked for an address, but I didn't have it. They told me I needed one. I asked if I could call, and they said no, so I had to go

back to Matamoros, Mexico—the same place I had come from. I talked to the immigration security guy from Mexico and he let me use his phone. I called Yunior and he gave me the address, and I crossed again to Brownsville, Texas.

I was happy that I was finally free. From all the places I've seen in the U.S., Brownsville is one of the prettiest places. But there I had my first conflict with the police. When I was in Mexico, they told me to ask anybody on the streets for their phone so I could tell Yunior I was in the United States and tell him where I was so he could send me money to keep going. I didn't realize it at the time, but I looked horrible: I didn't have shoes on, my beard was long, I was dirty and stank—anybody would've been scared of me. The first person I saw was a woman. I signaled with my hand that I needed a phone and she pulled her phone and called the police. The policeman spoke Spanish, and when I explained things to him he laughed and let me use his phone. I called Yunior and explained to him where I was, and he sent me money to get something to eat and get a pair of shoes, because I was barefoot. The policeman took me to where I had to catch the bus.

Since it was so late, Yunior could not send me money that day. I had to stay outside. I met a homeless guy, an older man. He looked the same as me: had a beard, didn't have a good appearance. He took me to McDonald's. We had chicken nuggets and a drink. It was delicious. My only meal for almost a week. I will never forget that.

The next day I took the bus. That was another ordeal; I had to take five different buses to go to Las Vegas. When I received the money I had purchased some new clothes and had not thrown away the old ones. I just put them in a bag and placed it on the luggage compartment part of the bus at the bottom, because it was so stinky that I couldn't carry it on the bus. I only took it to keep it as a memory. Every time a connection came where another bus had to be taken, I didn't understand anything. I'd see that they were taking out the bags and try to go get my bag. I was running all over the terminal to see where my little bag had gone or would end up. That dirty bag! I'm not sure why they didn't throw it away. But it had the same sticker and everything as the other luggage.

I was so hungry. I had been scared to get off the bus, because what if it left me? On the second day I could no longer resist the hunger, and I got off at a gas station. I only had three dollars left. I saw a ham sandwich that was two dollars, and a drink was only one dollar. I grabbed them and started eating the sandwich before even making it to the register. When I went to pay, the lady said, "No, $3.18." I didn't understand anything. I gave her the three dollars because I thought it was two plus one equals three. "No, $3.18." Then the guy behind me said, "You are missing eighteen cents." I said, "I don't have any more." He told her I didn't have any more money, and the lady started making a scene. Then the guy took eighteen cents and gave it to the lady. It was so good and a tremendous relief when I ate. Then I stayed on the bus until we arrived at Las Vegas two and a half days later. Yunior was waiting for me in Las Vegas.

The United States government provided me with financial help. I was given $330 cash and $208 in food stamps. In the end, that didn't help me much because I had to give it all to the household that was sheltering me, and also take care of the little girl, clean the house, and cook. I was the housewife, because they worked at the casinos and didn't have time to take care of anything. They were helping me, so I was helping them. I got tired of it and had other friends that lived here in Kentucky. They called and said, "Hey, just come here," and I came here with them. I didn't have a single dollar. When I came to Kentucky, I started working as a driver for a therapy clinic near here. I have been living here almost ten years.

I brought my mom. I brought you. After Mom I brought my sister, then my niece. Now three more are coming. When they are all here, I'm going back. I have had enough of America, and I don't regret anything because from what I see my oldest daughter is on a good path. My other little girl is the most beautiful thing that ever existed, so I can't complain. I have had it good after everything that happened. It was worth the effort.

Warm Cuban Hugs Are a Fine Thing

YASLIN PUPO MORERA

My Spanish teacher, Yaslin Pupo, has been a huge help to us immigrant students. She has always given us her support and done the job of a parent countless times. Since many of my classmates, myself included, have faced the cruelty of not having our parents here due to deportation or other legal issues, Ms. Yaslin has tried her best to understand us and make us feel close to home. Here is part of her story.

—KATHERIN

I was born in Holguin, Cuba. I've been in the country for eleven years. I came here and I didn't know any English. I had a profession, teaching, and I knew how to do that, but in order to be able to do that, I needed to be able to have better control of the language. I had in my head practically everything I had ever studied in Cuba, where I had almost obtained a doctoral degree. I had a background in education and I had taught for quite awhile in a school where humanities were a part of the core curriculum. I had given courses in history and Spanish and I was well prepared to teach.

I studied English, among other things. It was quite a lot of work and quite a lot of effort. I went to Indiana University, I went to University of Louisville. But first I went to Jefferson Community and Technical College. I owe a great deal of debt to one of my teachers at JCTC, one of the ESL teachers, Mrs. Vicky Cummings, who was a faculty member there. She was a great help to me. She asked me, "Do you have all your documentation, all your certifications, all your credentials from Cuba?" I said, "Yes, I have my master's, my Ph.D., but the primary thing holding me back is my ability to speak English." Vicky tells me, "Let's take all these papers and send them to wherever they need to be sent, so you can go ahead and get certified to be an instructor. And in the meantime, Vicky offered me a job at Chapman Writing Center, which is a student writing lab at JCTC. I was a part-time work-study student making $7 an hour. I would finish my own classes and then go to the writing center and stay there to work with students as late as 9:00 at night. I spent all day there. What helped me learn English a lot was just listening to what the other students would say and trying to pick it up.

When all my paperwork had been properly processed, Vicky introduced me to the chief of Americana's Family Education Program and spoke on my behalf, vouching for my abilities, my personality, my sincerity, and things like that, along with the hard documentation. So everything was in place except for the ability to speak English very well, but nonetheless, that's how and when I first started to work at Americana Community Center. Even though my English was still not good, Vicky opened doors for me.

My students at Americana were those who had come as immigrants and refugees. After that, I began to teach in Americana's after-school program and summer program. I helped kids with their homework, especially kids who didn't know how to speak English. I have derived a great deal of satisfaction from this, and in fact, the English that I know, that I've learned, I owe a lot of it in part to what I've been able to pick up at Americana. It's just like a great big family.

Another school that helped me a lot was Young Elementary. I was at Young Elementary for four years and I feel a great respect for those who worked there alongside me. The teachers worked so very hard for the benefit of the students who were there at that school. It was really a lot of hard work, but it was satisfying. I spent four years there and I worked under Principal Mary Meyer Minyard. She was a very strong person, and helped me to learn many things. Among the things I learned from her was how to go about working in this country. She would tell me, "Yaslin, you do it this way, this way, this way," and I would just follow her and try to do what she said. After those four years, I came to

Iroquois High School. By then, I knew what my teaching style was going to be. I am extremely appreciative of Mary Meyer Minyard. She's the one who taught me how to get on with my work here in this country.

I had two children. They're twins. I had to work, study, maintain a household, and raise them as a single mother for several years. But it doesn't matter what happens to you, you have to make the effort to learn things, and you have to learn especially from the bad things. Because the bad things are going to show you how to make progress, how to be a better person. You learn to overcome, you learn that saying "I can't do something" is not a way out.

When I started regular Spanish classes, I would kiss my Cuban, Mexican, and Guatemalan students. And the American students would say, "Ooh, Ms. Yaslin, why are you doing that?" It's not the same culture. But now the American students say, "Ms. Yaslin, will you give me a hug today?" Warm Cuban hugs are a fine thing.

In Cuba, a teacher could physically touch a student, give a hug, a pat on the back, and here there are regulations that forbid that. I understand that, but I regret that that's the way it has to be. A hug tells a student that I care about them. That's important.

Thanksgiving is a time when you give thanks for good things. It's a time to be thankful for family, and basically, you guys are my family. It doesn't matter that your family is not here, your mother or your daddy, because I am here. I had a Thanksgiving party for everyone. Because it's so sad that so many of you are separated from your parents. Saying, "I thank you for being my student. I thank you for being my teacher," is the best we can do. Make food, and enjoy this Thanksgiving Day. We wrote out a bunch of invitations, and sent them to the other teachers. We all danced. We Cubans danced to Latin music, and the Americans danced to American music. Aunts and uncles and cousins cooked for you guys. They made flan, cold salad, Cuban food. They bought Cuban sweets, and I made the *congris*, and we made salad. And there was Mexican food, and there was Guatemalan food, and there was Salvadoran food. The Guatemalans made ceviche, which is made with raw fish with a bunch of lemons on it. I'm really grateful for all the Cuban shops we have around here, because we could go out and buy the ingredients we needed to make the Cuban foods. The Americans, more so than food, bought the other stuff—the decorations, paper plates, disposable cups. It was a special day. At the end, everybody was crying.

A'LEA MARIE SMITH

A Day and a Life

Brittany White

A Day and a Life

A'LEA MARIE SMITH

I wake up to my daughter Jae'dyce squirming in my arms, chewing her tongue and sucking her fingers. I lay her on my chest to take one last shot at putting her back to sleep, but she arches her back and screams a house-waking cry. I groggily get up and hear my back crack from this jail bench of a couch. Monday through Friday, Jae'dyce and I have the same repetitive schedule. At 5:00 sharp I say, "Come on, Jae'dyce, get up" and she peeks at me with her left eye, stretches her little bones, and cracks her back.

I lay Jae'dyce flat on her back for her morning diaper change. The wipes are running low and I remind myself to get more at the dollar store later. Jae'dyce stops crying now that I have given her my full attention. I put her in the crook of my arm and go to the kitchen to make her bottle with four ounces of water and two scoops of formula. I thank God I don't have to pay for it. We're in a program called W.I.C., aka Special Supplemental Nutrition for Women Infants and Children—a long name for a can of formula that would cost me twenty bucks. I can't afford that on my $8.25 per hour wages. I take a slow, deep breath and aggressively shake her bottle, then move her into a sitting position while she sucks on the bottle for dear life. "I have to go to work today after school," I whisper to her, already feeling the weight of being apart. Twelve hours is too long to be away from Jae'dyce.

Jae'dyce is fully awake and watching the bottle. "Good morning, beautiful," I say. She smiles, excited for her bottle. I bounce back on the couch, gazing at Jae'dyce as she smiles at me safely, knowing that her fist-sized stomach will soon be full with the vitamins and minerals that the formula gives her.

I turn my head to hear small feet scrambling towards me. It's my first child Jena, who is six years old now.

"You feeding my sister?" she asks.

I smile, and respond in a calm voice, "Yup. You hungry?"

Her beautiful bronze-brown hair is in pigtails, but I'm not allowed touch it now; it's an unspoken rule. Jena's eyes focus someplace else, towards the back of the house. She looks at me and says, "Is my Mama awake?" and for just a tiny moment I think she is talking about me. My buoyant mood declines rapidly and I break eye contact so she doesn't notice. I look back at the baby, adjust the warm bottle at her mouth. She clutches my fingers, her nails digging into my skin. I turn to Jena, my daughter, who calls another woman "mama." I sigh, and murmur, "I guess," as she happily skips to the back of the house.

Every day, I deal with burning guilt for passing up the opportunity to raise Jena. I pray that once she gets older, she'll understand my decision to give up custody to my guardian, not as an escape route, but as a plan to give her a better life; obviously not simple, but better. She'll understand that raising a child was too much for me to handle, that I was just too young.

I got pregnant with Jena when I was twelve years old.

My mother had just recently passed, and I missed her so much. When we were with her, she kept us all bundled up in a shell of protection, but after she died, time and trouble knocked the protective shell down. I had a twelve year old mind and a quickly developing woman's body. I wanted a mother. I wanted to be loved and guided. But when you're looking for love and you're not getting it anywhere else, you tend to go for whoever will give it to you: in this case, the fourteen-year-old boy who said that he loved me. He was the only one who gave that to me, so I attached myself to something that I could feel. That I could see and hold.

My guardian had become the only mother figure I could fall back on. We were in my guardian's room when I told her that I'd had sex. I felt the need to tell her. I wanted her to tell me to stop, that it wasn't right. "Well, having sex isn't bad as long as you know what your doing. Be safe," she said. Her niece and I just looked at her. I thought she was going to have a stroke when I told her. If our shoes had been reversed I would have slapped me right in the mouth, because I deserved it. I would have screamed and begged for me to stop. I didn't feel so protected anymore.

During my pregnancy there were women who said that they would be there, but when I needed them they weren't. At times like that, I begged for my mother to be with me again. I didn't understand why people treated me the way they did. I got little sympathy from anyone. I embarrassed my sister at school, and my brother didn't know what to tell our friends. Teenage boys a few years older than me would come on to me. I got treated like an adult but I was only twelve years old. I couldn't get a job. I didn't have anything or anyone. People truly could not get their minds to grip the fact that I was pregnant. I got a lot of rude and disgusted stares. People didn't care about my feelings. Even the nicest person in the world threw shade.

I was in the dark for nine months. Things were happening that I didn't understand. Milk leaked from my breasts. I panicked, thinking they were bleeding. My feet swelled, so I had to learn to lower my salt intake. My hair fell out. People were saying things that I didn't understand. They asked me to remember things that I'd never even thought about, like when my last period was or the exact day of sexual activity—things a normal twelve year old doesn't keep track of. I didn't even know what sexual activity was until I went to the doctor. The man and his nurse looked at me like I was crazy.

But when I rubbed my stomach, I thought about the life inside me. That's what she was: a life. She didn't ask to be here, and she deserved love and happiness and a fair chance. I wanted to run for the hills with her. Away from the worries. Away from everyone and everything. But I knew I was too young.

I knew I couldn't protect her, and during my whole pregnancy, I thought that I was giving her up for adoption. My guardian had parents lined up who wanted to adopt my child. I went to countless meetings and answered questions and thought it was all for me to be serious about what I wanted. I didn't want to give my child up for adoption: I was going to give my child away out of love.

I was in first period one day in sixth grade when I felt the contractions and figured out what they were. I tried to hold it in as much as I could but I had to leave school in an ambulance during third period. The adoptive parents met me at the hospital, but unfortunately it was a false alarm. I went home, but when the contractions were minutes apart I was screaming to get to the emergency room. If I'd have waited thirty minutes more, Jena would have been on the living room floor.

"This is actually happening," I thought to myself as another back-aching contraction hit. It's the type of hurt that has a climax and a falling action, like you're going up a painful rollercoaster. In your abdomen it feels like 1,000 bees stinging you at once. Your lower back feels like the site of a category five hurricane. I felt every pain and tear of tissue, but I didn't see anything, didn't want to. I couldn't tell you if there was blood or even if I cried. What I can tell you is that the sound that I heard next was the most beautiful sound to ever cross my ears. It sounded like heaven opening its gates for the first time. Her small cry was so adorable and warm it could make the devil tear up.

Jena was small. I gave birth to her maybe two weeks before the actual due date. She was about five pounds eight ounces. She had silky, jet black hair that shined like a diamond in the light, dark eyes, and smooth skin that felt warm and damp. Her skin was saggy and white. She looked like Benjamin Button's darker cousin. As soon as she was born the doctor put her on my chest. Nothing is as raw and real as the actual moment of meeting your child for the first time. The pain is over, and you're looking into

a stranger's eyes, knowing that—in the first minute this child has been in this world—you'll love this stranger with all your heart. You will protect this stranger, even if that means making a decision that you will regret for the rest of your life.

No one could ever be prepared to give away their child, but I was determined. I kissed her cheeks all night, and on the third day in the hospital, they took her away. When my stay was over and I was allowed to leave, I went one way and Jena went the other.

Then I was at home and the next few days went by in a blur. I didn't see my baby, but she was on my mind all day and all night. I called the family to check up on my child, but the parent and my guardian claimed it was inappropriate for me to do so. Jena consumed my thoughts like a vacuum.

Then I heard all of a sudden that my guardian had taken my baby back. I was not included in the conversation. I was confused. I woke up from my sleep to find out that my daughter was downstairs. I didn't get any heads up or hints that my guardian was bringing her home. Sadly she wasn't bringing her to me.

I felt very alone as my guardian let me know that she wanted to talk with me. This was not going to be an easy talk: I either had to leave and take my newborn baby with me, or stay and allow my guardian to raise her as a foster child. My guardian took all rights from me regarding my child.

I still slept with Jena every night. Soon she was calling me "Mama." She knew who I was, knew she came out of me and not my guardian, knew and understood the significance and importance of this. When my guardian realized the transition in my daughter's thinking, she stopped Jena from sleeping with me, and ordered her to stop calling me "Mama."

I was just grateful that I was there, though, and I looked at the bright side: she had not one person, but two very strong and loving people in her graces and on her team. That's two times the love. I'd rather watch my child prosper from the sidelines than damage her well being.

There is no definition of love. Love is not something you can develop overnight, or just something you stumble across. Love is like a sponge, and you soak up as much as you can. I watched and learned. I watched how my guardian dealt with Jena. I knew deep down that I was going to need that knowledge for another child, one I knew I could take good care of all by myself.

For a person who didn't go through it all, it would seem outrageous. You really don't know how you're getting through it, you just know you're heart is still beating. I just woke up every morning.

I'm pulled out of my memories as I'm snatching Jae'dyce's bottle from her mouth, panicking, raising her arms in the air. I pat her back aggressively to get the choking sounds to stop. My heart resurfaces from the icy waters of worry as her breathing returns to normal. She's always full but never satisfied.

"Slow down, Jae. The milk ain't goin' nowhere," I complain.

Jae'dyce looks at me and whines for her bottle, but I don't give it back until she screams, indicating to me that her lungs are breathing and distributing oxygen. I pat her back and struggle to get her to burp

at least once; I can't imagine getting her to burp twice, which is the correct way with a four-ounce bottle. I wonder if we'll be able to get a little more sleep before work when two toddlers (my sister's boys) loudly sprint in the room, screaming. I look at Jae'dyce wondering if the ruckus has affected her. My skin burns with envy because she is fast asleep, her small chest rising and falling gently. Watching the toddlers with sleepy eyes, I look back to my daughter and murmur, "I wish it was that easy for me."

Having a child makes the easiest things kind of complicated. I have to get Jae'dyce ready for daycare, so I go to pick out her clothes for the day, but she isn't fitting 0-3 months anymore which means the clothes she wore last week are no longer in service. I pick out my favorite outfit, a black and red polka dot onesie with black pants to match. The best part is her black and red booties with a lady bug print on it. I lay her back down and take off her shirt but struggle to put it over her head without pulling her hair. Her face grows red as she looks at me and I murmur an apology.

5:45 a.m. comes around a little bit too soon as I put Jae'dyce's snowsuit on. I couldn't afford to get us both a winter coat, and as we walk through the back door, the cold air bites at my sensitive teeth. I put Jae'dyce's hat on while I push her in her stroller. The sun hasn't come out yet. The trees are silent, nothing in the air. I walk as fast as I can to my TARC stop on the corner of Sutcliffe and 38th near my sister Anya's house. I lived with my guardian for six years before I turned eighteen and finally picked up the courage to leave. I was ready for the outside world. I left knowing that I could do anything I set my mind

A'lea's daughters, Jena and Jae'dyce

to and that the sun wasn't going to kill me. And I thought it was time to be connected with my biological siblings after several years of separation.

There is an elderly man smoking a cigarette beside me at the bus stop, so I move a few paces to the left, not wanting Jae'dyce to catch second hand smoke. It seems if you're not smoking, your sister or brother is, and I don't want Jae'dyce to grow up with temptation all around her. I go to school, provide education, and work to provide for my daughter.

I don't want Jae'dyce to grow up wondering where her next meal is, so I work twenty-five hours a week, after school, at Popeye's over on Preston Highway. I've worked there for a year and a half, but I don't have any loyalties. I walk in every day, look at my fellow employees and say, "Welcome to Popeye's." I put on a hair net, wash my hands and immediately get to work on the cash register, packing food, doing dishes, battering and flouring chicken and dropping it in the hottest, most used up grease, slowly so I wont get burned. People don't play about Popeye's chicken. For real. They go crazy over it. While I'm there I work my butt off, and when I get home I smell like chicken. It's hard work but it pays off.

I look down Broadway. The bus is nowhere in sight. Five minutes have gone by. If this first TARC is late it has a chain reaction: I'll get to my next bus stop late after I drop Jae'dyce off at daycare, and then miss the next TARC, and then I'm late to school. Some people think that my tardiness is the result of my laziness but it isn't. I've got to fuss with Jae'dyce at 5:00 in the morning. She's a child and sometimes she just isn't feeling it. Some things are out of my control.

The loud engine of the bus creeps up to the streetlight slowly. The tires slide against the ice along the concrete. The birds are silent, still asleep. Only crazy people are out this early in the cold. With Jae'dyce in her carseat in one hand, and her stroller in the other, I take my time struggling to get on the bus. Numerous men are waiting for me to get done and not one volunteers to help me. Chivalry these days.

After setting her stroller on the rail, I turn to pay my TARC fee: eighty cents for JCPS students. I insert a wrinkled old dollar into the machine, eager to get rid of it. I look up, expecting my transfer ticket. The driver is an elderly black man with a unattractive five o'clock shadow.

"You don't look like you're under eighteen to me," he says, not looking in my eyes, focusing on lower places. I put my arms around my chest and back away from him.

"I'm still in school," I claim.

He makes a small *hmph* sound while he gives me my transfer. I slam my body in the seat, upset at nasty people these days. People look at me and Jae'dyce. An old woman wearing shades with a Bible in her hands melts at the sight of my daughter. Jae'dyce loves the attention, of course, but I'm not in the mood to answer the same constant questions today. *How old is she? Is she teething? What's her name?* Don't forget the biggest one: *Is her father around?* The men always ask that one, and I politely answer, "No, are you offering? Because I'm taking baby daddy applications." Sometimes I am not that respectful.

One time Jae'dyce and I were on our way home, and an old rusty man with a limited number of teeth was smiling at her. I could practically see his tooth odor. Being the happy baby that she is, she fell out in laughter with the strange man's attention. He looked up at me and said, "Look at her, flirting with me!" I stopped him in his tracks from touching my daughter's polished face with his infected hands. I said, "No, my six-month-old is not flirting with you. Get away from us." I moved to the back of the bus. Although there have been times when I hated the TARC—the heat and the stench—there's also been times when I didn't want to leave or go home, when I wanted to stay forever.

For some reason I do all my heavy crying on the TARC. I was on my way home from middle school once, thinking about my baby at home. The brand new addition to the family who I couldn't touch or hug. When it was time to get off the bus, I didn't ring the bell. I sat there on the TARC and watched my house roll by. I just kept going until I was miles away from home, and I knew it was going to take forever for someone to notice. The day grew dark. It was peaceful. No one bothered me as I cried. But then an elderly black man sat beside me and gave me a tissue. He was wearing a black Kangol that didn't go with the black capris and wife beater he was sporting. He was insanely quiet, even when I wanted to talk. He stayed silent. It felt like I was talking to myself. I put my face in my hands. He took one of my heavy, sweat-filled hands in his and didn't let go until I had to leave. When I turned back to him, he didn't say goodbye, just looked ahead, waiting for the next stressed out girl he could make feel better. You come across all types of people riding the TARC, and you'll have all types of conversations. A friend of mine once said, "I'd rather tell my secrets to a stranger than to someone I know." I told that stranger all my secrets and I never saw him again after that.

We make a screeching stop in front of Jae'dyce's daycare. Gwennie Pooh's Daycare is a great place. The owner works with my schedule, and the children are heavily monitored. I come and sign her in and the ladies smile and reach for Jae'dyce. I happily let them. They are taking off her coat as I am walking towards the exit. Jae'dyce doesn't cry when I leave anymore. She's too drawn into the excitement of her classmates. I hate taking her to daycare because I miss her so much. Why can't Jae'dyce and I cuddle all day as I feed her soft chewy candy? Because I need to be educated to have a better life. Because I have to work so Jae'dyce has everything she needs. Because candy will cause her stomach to hurt. And last but not least, everyone expects me to fail. So I got to be on top of my game. I got to do everything right, even though I get tired.

Another TARC ride to go, and I'm downtown on Jefferson close to the courthouse before I finally get settled on the 6th Street bus. It's still dark outside but numerous people are out striding the streets, paper and cigarette butts blowing in the wind along with them. As we turn on 4th, I look east down Broadway toward Sheppard Square, the housing projects where I used to live when I was nine years old or so.

The memories start rushing at me all at once. I remember everything: the brown tile buildings, the mulch on the playground, clear blue skies and cotton candy clouds. I remember the giant silver boxing gloves statue centered in the heart of the community

A'lea's grandmother Paulie Woodford, her Aunt Shelby, and her mother Anita

in memory of the greatest of all time, Muhammad Ali, and the community center where my twin brother and I went for lunch and snacks when there was no food in the refrigerator. I remember lights hanging from people's doors, everyone smiling, the dandelions—those flowers you make wishes on—poking out from the concrete. I remember how the "candy store" was just someone's kitchen around the corner and long spring nights with cousins I haven't seen since then. Those were happy days. I was young, and my family was together.

We lived with eight people in a two bedroom apartment, the kind where the tube for the washers runs into the sink, and the dryer is outside. There was a big metal heater painted white connected to the wall that'd get really hot but didn't do any hard work. The place was immaculately clean. Sometimes when I walked in, I immediately felt the urge to cough because of the Pine Sol my mother aggressively mopped onto the floor. Through the window in my room I could see the gate to the little park, the slides where you'd either get burned alive going straight down or shocked in a whirlwind with static electricity.

I remember sitting down with my family at dinner time once in particular. My mother had filled our plates with taco salad—my favorite—and that night we watched *High School Musical 2*, which I'd been waiting forever to see.

"Is it on yet?" I asked my sister, my leg shaking.

"Why we got to watch this stupid movie anyway?" my brother mumbled. He wasn't into TV like me.

"Because Mama said I could."

"Yeah, but why we got to do it as a family?"

"Just sit down and eat," Mama said.

The sun was falling as the opening credits began. We munched on seasoned ground beef and tomatoes and we were all bundled up. Troy was singing his head off when my sister walked out of the room, and my brother was asleep by the time Gabriella got to her second song, "Gotta Go My Own Way." Mama and I were in tears. This song meant a lot to me. We had just left Georgia where my mother beat a Child Protective Services case, and I still didn't understand what was going on. All I knew is that we were finally back together. I didn't want to get split up again because I knew there's no going back and no do-overs.

By the end of the movie it was just me and Mama, which is just how I liked it. We never had alone time. I was up against her with the pillow in her lap. We laughed at the jokes and cried at the sadness. At the end, when everything worked out and the couple had their heartwarming kiss, Mama hugged me and gave me a kiss on my head, and we fell asleep there on the couch, just like that.

That's when my mother was at her healthiest point in life. She was stable, had money coming in, and we were happy. We were going to church at that time. At Dunamis World Outreach Church, the community would help us. When we got good grades the pastor would gives us money. The pastor's name was Shannon. I really enjoyed going to church with Mama. I don't know if I connected with God or anything—I just liked being around her. Mama always dressed up for church in black dresses that were flowy, never tight-fitting. I picture her clapping

Anya, A'lea, Anita, and Anthony

along with the loud drums and singing, her necklace and bracelet moving along with the beat. She'd smile and tell me to stand up with the rest of the congregation and we'd sing, "Never Would Have Made It." I liked this song most because when it came out of my mouth, I felt it. "I never would have made it without God," the ladies of the congregation sang, but all I could hear was my mother, because she felt it too.

Mama would leave in the middle of it all and go to the bathroom. She had a bad case of cigarette addiction and needed, "every cigarette she could puff," as she would say. She smoked Newport 100's. I always hear they're "the black cigarettes." She'd send me to the store to buy them and would always get upset when I couldn't get them for her. She'd come back from her smoke breaks, happier of course, and would rub my brother's head with the cigarette smoke in her wake.

My mama was huggable. Her eyes were as bright as polished mahogany. Mama had a huge smile like me and a big, loud laugh, as loud as the sun: you couldn't miss it. You know a laugh where you can look inside someone's mouth and it's dark and goes on for miles? Thats how big her laugh was: an unnecessarily loud ghetto laugh. The kind you dread hearing at a high school graduation. Well, now I'd beg for it.

When the bus turns onto Taylor Boulevard, the street gets bumpy. We pass up the Pic Pac at Central and Churchill Downs, and I think about all the memories I have of the South End, like when we lived in the now nonexistent Iroquois housing projects. I heard that they tore down the projects due to violence in the community. Or maybe it was financial issues. Regardless, they thought it was best if the buildings, and the people who lived there, were gone. So, the Iroquois projects are nothing but a memory for most people, but not to us. It was a home to people who didn't have one. The Iroquois projects were the building blocks of a young mother's life. It was a safe haven to those who were battered.

I remember it being quiet, the birds chirping, lizards laying on the concrete cracks in the ground, the homeless people waiting for the liquor store to open. I remember riding my bike and smacking against the rough texture of the red brick buildings, and I imagine the contractors demolishing them to dust. I wonder what was promised to the residents at the time. There's a farm right where they had the projects now. They replaced the projects with an organization to help the community. I wish I could say that I'm thankful, but even if you build an organization that helps the community, the projects are still gone, my memories are still gone, my home is gone. A place I could point out to my friends and say, "I lived there." It's sad, really.

Even though you had to look over your shoulder every corner you turned, the projects were a great place to live. Everyone knew each other. In the projects we looked after each other. If one neighbor didn't have sugar, the next one did, and eventually the whole hood had Kool-Aid. We made things happen. Yes, we fought and argued from time to time, but if you don't, y'all ain't really peoples. I chipped my first tooth at Iroquois. I learned how to make friends there, and I had my first fight on Derby Day.

Churchill Downs was way down the street, but still in walking distance, and the whole South End basically thought of the first Saturday in May as payday: some people would park cars, others sold food and beverages. On every corner you could smell the charcoal burning on the grill and my family would sell beverages on Taylor on Derby Day sometimes so Mama could pay the LG&E for that month. She'd always say she couldn't wait for rich white people to get wasted and spend their hard-earned money.

On this particular Derby Day, my mother and aunt went to Save-a-Lot to buy paper plates, leaving our sister—who wasn't great at surveillance—to watch us. My family and I weren't living in the Iroquois projects at the time. We were just visiting for the holiday. When my twin brother came back to the porch with food that didn't come from our party, I just had to follow. Anthony and I weren't familiar with anybody and didn't have friends there, but most of the adults around were not paying attention to us. I spotted the table of food and stuffed my pockets. My brother came up behind me drenched in water and red faced. I asked what was wrong.

"That girl keeps spraying me with the water," Anthony told me.

A little girl was having her birthday the same day, and she'd gotten angry at my brother. As we walked closer I realized that the little girl was dominating the water hose. She was unaware that my brother and I were kin, so I played it cool and let Anthony walk a few paces in front of me. I watched as my brother went to the middle of the crowd with sudden bravery.

"Can I play with the hose?" my brother asked as he let out his hand. The birthday girl smiled mischievously and moved her hand forward as if she was going to give it to him, but sprayed him along his pants instead. Everyone laughed around us; even my brother looked at the little girl with a grin. I quietly stepped out in front of him.

"If you spray my Bubby again, I will hurt you," I lightly promised.

Anthony's grin spread so big across his face that he looked like The Joker. It was silent around us. No one spoke a word. The little girl lifted the hose, looked me right in the eye, and accepted the challenge gladly. She was bigger than me, my forehead reaching only to the bottom of her eyebrows, and there were a lot of kids in the front yard. Adrenaline raced through my arteries but I didn't know what to do. I'd never fought before. *Will I win? Will everyone remember me losing?* My brother grew impatient and pushed me into her, and she fell into the dirt. I got up and looked around the small crowd. Their faces were in awe. I guessed the fight had started, so I began rapidly punching the air hoping it would successfully hit something or someone. Soon after we began sliding down the muddy hill. My Derby outfit was ruined and I knew that, regardless of the fact I was fighting for him, my brother was still going to snitch on me. That day I made a reputation for fighting neighborhood bullies.

Brittany White

Brittany was one of my mother's closest friends. She used to live on the hill between Hazelwood Elementary School and Save-A-Lot. Our family would visit her for holidays like Thanksgiving and Easter. I've known my aunt Brittany since I can remember. She has two little girls. Her eldest daughter Al'marie was named after me, A'lea Marie, and her youngest is named Anayah after my sister, Anya.

She is a very down to earth person, very smart and wise. She's competitive too—the kind of person you don't want to play Uno with. Brittany is honest and nice in most cases, but you don't want to get in her way: She plays NO games. She is loving and will sacrifice herself and everything she's got to help her family. I call her my fake real auntie. She's the sister that my mother never had. She is my role model. I wanted to interview her because she saw first hand what it was like in the projects. Also she was more present around the time my mother passed. She knows my mother's last moves and words, and I was curious to know what they were.

—A'LEA

I remember that Derby Day you're talking about. We all went shopping and got all the kids outfits. We weren't really going anywhere, but we dressed up for the cookout. I was at the store, and we pulled up right after it happened. Everybody ran up to the car like, "Mommy! Brittany! Guess what happened! A'lea beat this girl up!" That girl terrorized all the little kids in our courtyard. She bullied everybody, and she was the smallest one. She started it and she deserved it; A'lea got her.

I was out doing most of the shopping, and your mom was watching the kids and cooking that day. We were doing hair and everything that day. There was just a lot going on. Family stuff. We always had fun together. Had a good time spending time together.

That's when things were good in the projects. There were ups and downs, but we made the best out of everything, and we had a good time. I was going through rough times in my life and your mom kinda saved me. I'd rather have been in the projects than at home, and a lot of people didn't understand that. But when I went there, I felt nothing but love.

I had been waiting for it for awhile when I finally got a letter saying I got accepted. I was nervous to be on my own and raising my child in the projects. I'd been in the projects myself growing up, and I knew what it was like to live there. It was really like a battlefield all around me outside of my home. So my fear was raising a child there. I was afraid of raising a child around all of the violence and drugs.

But fortunately, I only had to live there for a year and a half before they started the process of tearing down the projects, and my building was the first to go. It was a stepping stone to get where I wanted to be, out on my own in my first apartment outside of the projects. It really helped me.

It was hard back then, but it was a great stepping-stone. Being a young mother out on my own for the first time, not knowing anything, helped me gain my independence, it helped me experience life, which I think is great. I wouldn't go back to the projects, but I look at it like a blessing. It was not where I was supposed to always be. But I would suggest anyone who needs that to utilize it. And not in a negative way, in a positive way as I did.

I didn't associate myself with a lot of people, not because I had anything against anybody, it was just the best thing for me. If you go there with the right mind-frame, and the right focus, then you can make it out and you can have a normal life. Some people get caught up in the lifestyle, and it becomes a part of them. The projects don't have to be who you are. I chose to utilize it to have a roof over me and my daughter's heads to get where I wanted to be.

People told me, *It's yours. You don't have to live with anyone else, you look at it like it's yours.* And I took that mind-frame.

After Iroquois, I moved to eastern Louisville. I got a three-bedroom apartment; a nice, almost new apartment. So, not only was I able to move out on my own, I got a very nice home. I was proud of myself for putting in the legwork to find something nice for me and my family.

It's not easy out here. I have struggled. I have been through a lot, but I am proud to be where I am, because it could be worse. I could still be in the projects. Some girls choose to take the Section 8 program. Some girls are too afraid to be on their own and have to pay real bills, and they chose to go to another project. But my mind-frame has always been, *this is not where I wanna be. This is not how I wanna raise my children.* This is what I have to go through, for them, so they don't have to experience that. Some people don't have that influence around them. Fortunately, I had your mother.

I met your mom in high school. I was best friends with your Aunty Shelby and on weekends, she was like, "I'm going to my sister's house, and sometimes she lets my friends come over." So my mom dropped me off, and it was kind of like I never left: I was basically adopted into your family. So I'm not your blood auntie, but I am your auntie. Your mother was the sister I never had. She meant a lot to me. She was one of my best friends and it still means a lot to me, and so do you and your siblings.

We bumped heads many a time in my young days. Me and your auntie Shelby were kind of rebellious, and we didn't listen when we should have listened.

Your mom used to get on us, but it was mainly about not making the mistakes that she made: being a teenage mother, living in the projects, and stuff like that. But guess who followed the trend. So, she tried to guide me in the right direction, and she tried to prevent me from going through some of the things she went through. She's played major part in my life.

Your mother was living with me when she first got sick. You were not there, you were living with your guardian. It was when she was trying to get you all back and going to the parenting classes. She was struggling, but she was doing it. I was young, but I wanted to motivate her. A lot of people didn't think that she was doing what she needed to do to get you all back, but she was. I took her to the classes, and then there were times where she would just not wanna go, but I would make sure she got there. She got really, really stressed out and she was smoking a lot of cigarettes, heavily. She was smoking two, three packs a day.

It eventually caught up to her and she got pneumonia. She got really sick and was coughing, but we thought it was a cold. One day, I was standing in the doorway of her bedroom, and as we were talking, she coughed into this towel, pulled it back, and then tried to hide it from me, but I saw blood. I said, "Anita, is that blood on the towel?" And she said, "No." I grabbed it and said, "Anita, it's blood. That's not good. You're going to the hospital." You know how I am, mother love. I can't help it. I called the ambulance, she went, and I said, "I'll come pick you up or whatever." She finally called and said, "They said I have pneumonia, but they're sending me home." So they sent her home, the same day, with pneumonia.

She comes home. She's continuing to smoke. I begged her to stop. She had a carton in her drawer in her room, so she ended up going back to the hospital two days later. She was coughing up blood again, and she wouldn't stop smoking, no matter what I said. She's like my big sister, so I couldn't tell her what to do.

I sent her back to the hospital, but this time, she didn't come back home. They said the pneumonia had gotten bad, her breathing was getting messed up. Two days had gone by and I got a phone call. They knocked Anita's teeth out to put a trach down her throat. I know you remember your mom, her tongue was kind of big and she couldn't breathe, really. So they had to knock her teeth out. She was so upset about that.

I went to go visit your mom before she got out of the hospital, and she was not the same person anymore. She could not talk, she could not communicate. She was trying to write down to me what she was saying, and it was all scribble-scrabble. So I'm teaching her, and me being a caregiver by trade, I've learned certain skills that help me communicate with people that have brain injuries. I was able to communicate with your mother, and that's my sister, so I know what she's trying to say.

She was very unhappy about the trach and having her teeth knocked out, but she was still happy to be here. She kept telling me thank you. Sort of letting me know I did what I was supposed to do. I felt like I could have done something else, you know? I could have done something better. A few months later, she died, and I lived with a lot of regrets for a long time, because the only thing I could think was, *If she was at my house, she would still be here.* You know?

It was very hard. I loved your mother. I know you know that. Your mother was not only my adopted sister, she was my youngest daughter's godmother. She meant a lot to me, and I wish I could have saved her, like she saved me. I am who I am, and your mother has a lot to do with that. I don't know all the things you were told. I've tried to tell you the truth. Your mother did fight to get you back. Your mother was trying her best to be who she needed to be for you, and I was trying my best to help her do that.

This is just my opinion: can't nobody tell you nothing if they haven't been through it. But I have, and there was a way out, and there was a light at the end of the tunnel. And you have one too, and I'm so proud of you. You are accomplishing greatness. You are beating all the obstacles that are against you. I always knew you would. I know who you are, and all the good things about your mother are in you. I'm serious.

Anita, her parents Mitchell and Paulie, and A'lea

Our lights were out all winter once. I called it the Russian Winter because it was so cold. We got electricity for the heater by plugging a cord into the light socket out in the stairwell hallway, which was illegal. The cold gave me good reason to hug up on Mama, though. It wasn't so bad because we were still together as a family. One morning the cops came and said if Mama didn't pay the LG&E bill and get the lights turned on or get us in a safe shelter with electricity, they would take us away. Mama chose the latter, packed the three of us on her hip, and ran for the hills. That's when we stayed with my guardian for the first time.

Over a few weeks, my mother changed. She was tired and she was sick, mentally and physically.

She didn't smile as much. She stopped taking her medicine. She became angry. I've never had much information about this time in our lives, and I've had to believe anything that made sense. I have been told that she went to Our Lady of Peace and while she was there, said some things she shouldn't have said, and that Child Protective Services snatched us out of school. That's how my twin brother, our big sister, and I ended up in foster care. We moved into a couple of different homes before we went back to live with my guardian. We were surrounded by people, but I felt like it was just me on this earth.

We started going to visitations with our mother after a couple of weeks. At the beginning, the social worker saw my unease. She knew I did not want to be there, but I did not want to be split up from the only family I had either. I prayed that my Mother would get better. It was good to see her, and I really felt at peace. But every session we had, I'd get upset because I knew I couldn't go home with her, and every week we were later and later for our visits.

The last time I saw my mother, we were in the visitation rooms in the Child Protective Services office; I knew because it said that outside the door. One would think CPS was more secretive, but I guess not. My stomach was in knots. I missed my mother dearly. The feeling was explosive. I looked over to my brother as we were in the elevator. He looked down, averting his eyes. I didn't understand why I felt so much animosity between my small family. I felt out for my sister's ghostly shadow but she didn't reach for me. The elevator made an annoyingly loud ding and opened its doors. My siblings' poor moods did not alter mine: I was extremely excited. There were so many questions to ask.

Before we entered the room, the social worker spoke, "You don't have to see her if you don't want to," she said. I wrinkled my nose. *She's wasting our time,* I thought. But my brother and sister nodded their heads. For some reason they didn't want to see her. They resented my mother. I could wait a thousand years for mother. Why couldn't they? My vision clouded with sadness as I threw my head down and finally entered the room, alone.

Mama had gained a little weight around the face. Her dark skin appeared pale and deeply over-heated. One other clue that Mama wasn't right was the hole in my mother's throat. It had white cloth around it. It formed mucus when she coughed.

The strong lines at the corner of her eyes grew when she saw me, as if her eyes were dim, then they brightened like the rising of the moon. I sat down on the yellow couch. I grabbed her hand.

"Are you okay, Mama?" I asked. She sniffled with tears in her eyes and whispered, "Yes." I smiled at her. And raised my hand to wipe her tear. I've never seen my mother like this. Broken and weak. A little fire sparked in my heart for her.

"Where's your brother and sister?" she asked. I looked down at my fingers rather than look into my mother's eyes.

"They're not coming."

"What?"

I repeated what I said and my mother's face fell into sadness.

"Where are they? They out there?" she points. I nod my head.

"ANTHONY MONTEZ LESHAWN!!!" she screamed. "ANYA LUCRETIA!!" Neither of them responded.

"Don't worry about them," I said, trying to calm her. "I'm here." With that her eyes averted from the door to me. My mother looked at me. Like *really* looked at me. She smiled.

"You been eating, girl?" At that point, I wasn't pregnant, but I was more developed since the last time she had seen me. I wrapped my arms around myself, and made a mental note to stop eating.

"How are you?" she asked. "Are they being nice to you?" I went the easy way out and answered the first.

"I'm doing fine." My mother and I looked at each other. I felt awkward. My mother started to smile again. "What?" I asked.

"Did you know a gay baby is born in every awkward silence?" I laughed at her confusion.

"Well good for that gay baby," I said. Our laughter died down, but the weight of the world remained. She started to cough. It sounded like a lawn mower scraping rust off a metal pole.

"Are you okay?"

I began to pat her back. She coughed inside of the used napkin then swatted my hand away and looked inside the napkin. I cringed lightly.

"Healthy as a horse," she responded as I frowned at her.

The action of declaring something untrue.

That's the definition of denial, and that's the emotion I felt when my mother died.

No one knew she was as sick as she was. I can picture her chain smoking her cigarettes, refusing to take her medicine. If she could have seen me, twelve years old and pregnant, the doctor wouldn't have needed to pull the plug: she'd have had a heart attack. That would've killed my mother.

As I walked through University of Louisville Hospital, a heaviness weighed on my shoulders and I was thinking, *This is not true. She's still with us.* I kept these repetitive thoughts in my head.

The first thing I noticed as we went in the room was the treacherous smell. I held my breath quietly, my nose naked and vulnerable to the stench. It smelled like death. I stepped closer to her and looked at my mother's swollen eyes. The desperate need to lay beside her was unbearable. The tubes went from her throat and arms to a machine on her

bedside. Her hands were balled into fists as if she was fighting to stay with us. As if she was fighting for us. I watched the machine control her breaths and I still didn't believe it.

At first the adults were arguing, debating if my mother should live. I thought the doctors would talk about doctor stuff, like charts and spreadsheets, but they were discussing my mother's life like it was simple. In the end, they pulled the plug. I thought the doctors were going to count down from three and turn off a switch, but I saw his hand move to the electrical socket. This caucasian man who possessed my mother's life in his hands didn't count down. He didn't even give us a warning. He literally pulled the plug.

You ever been so angry you saw red? Well, I saw white. Blank white. The type of white you get lost in. It was the total opposite of anger. It was sadness, betrayal. No one spoke. No one moved. No one dropped a tear. I watched in silence as her stomach fell for the last time. The little bit of heart that I had left was ripped from my chest. My fingers were numb. I wanted to punch something or someone. I couldn't breathe. I couldn't think.

When I was standing beside my mother's death bed, watching her life fade away, I was waiting for something magical to happen, like in movies when a person miraculously wakes up from a coma saying they heard Jesus tell them to wake up and spread His word. I thought she'd come back for us. I thought she would wake up and tell me how much she missed us and that we were going home with her and not our guardian. But that didn't happen. She didn't wake up. That day, when I turned my back on my mother, her heart wasn't beating anymore.

I looked at everyone and pulled my jacket closed to hide my now-obvious baby bump from my family. I was ready to leave. There was nothing for me there. My eyes blurred into the scene around me and I felt my chest squeeze. My mother was dead in front of me. Body still warm.

I turned toward the screaming. It was my auntie. Raw, horrific emotion radiated off her skin. I could feel it. The sadness in the room was at full capacity. Shelby sprawled on the floor, and three family members went to her aid. This whole "life" thing that God's got going on with us is bullshit. Humans are born into a world of pollution and poverty. People around you are slaving to give you a better life. But in the end we die. We just disappear.

I felt sluggish and weak. I felt numb. I didn't feel like A'lea. It's like I was looking at myself there on the hospital bed. Dead. People compare me to my mother a lot. My guardian says it as an insult; my family says it as a compliment. But, sometimes I just want to be me.

I gazed deeply around the small hospital room and saw that everyone in the room was panicking or had tears in their eyes. Everyone but me. I didn't feel that big outburst of emotion. When my mother died, I didn't cry. Nor did my brother or sister. We didn't cry because we weren't guilty. We never harmed her. We were just her kids.

That night while I lay in bed I thought about her and where that kind-hearted spirit was now. When I think about her, my skin gets warm as if her strong arms are around me, squeezing all the pain and ache, leaving nothing.

Time doesn't stop for anyone. The here and now is just a blur where I can see my mistakes, my achievements, my potential and all the bumps in the road, all the trial and error—everything in live detail.

Right now things are hard. There are decisions to be made.

Right now I'm trying, but some people don't see it.

Right now I see my goals at arm's reach.

Right now I am learning to be a mother, a sister, and a best friend.

Right now, to be all of these, I tell myself, "You have to learn to always be there. Keep showing yourself. Make yourself known and always show love. Give many hugs. Always say "I love you" no matter what, even when things are looking low and it's hard to smile. Just be around family. Be around the ones you love.

Right now I'm tired, and I'm tired of feeling tired.

Right now my feet feel like bricks everywhere I go. My eyelids the same.

Right now I'm raising a child. Sometimes I want to scream. Sometimes I want to cry. When she wakes up three times a night, I get angry, but I'm learning patience. When she cries now, I smile at her.

Right now a warm feeling comes to me every morning I wake up beside her.

Right now Jae'dyce is crawling. Scooting her butt off. She's fast.

Right now she is so pure. She is not judgmental.

Right now I will teach her all the things I know, and all the things I needed to know, but there are some things that a mother can't teach.

Right now, I'm praying: I'll be okay. If I'm okay, Jae'dyce and Jena are okay.

That's all I care about Right Now.

The 6th Street bus rides through the South End on Taylor Boulevard, Bicknell, and eventually the Outer Loop—"out where Wally World is," as my mother would say. This time it's a female driver, and the bus is packed. Kids sit on women's laps, people are hanging on handles attached to the silver rails. I squeeze between two men uncomfortably. It's funny when the bus is filled like this. Every time the bus halts to a stop we all sway in the direction that the bus is going. It's quiet. A lot of people to be on the TARC at 6:00 a.m., but at least we are all warm. The TARC stops in front of Iroquois High School. I take a big gulp of air. "Here we go," I say to myself.

I am not ecstatic to enter. Matter of fact I dread the moment. The lady at the front desk and I are on a first name basis, due to the number of tardies I have had over my high school career. I smile at Ms. Clara. She's black with shoulder length black hair with a pretty gray streak. She's been here as long as I have. Maybe longer. She doesn't pry about why I was late. She just smiles and tells me to have a nice day. That's why I like her.

"Better late than never," she says with a smile.

"Isn't that right," I mumble.

I've been at Iroquois since my freshman year, which seemed like a vacation getaway at the time. In the fifth grade, I was split up from my mom and then she died. That summer before sixth grade, I got pregnant. Seventh and eighth grade I was fighting the bullies who knew about it. So freshman year was like a fresh start for me: I wasn't ashamed anymore, no one knew I was in foster care, no one knew I had a three-year-old daughter. School was more than a learning center—it felt like home to me. It was peaceful.

Then, junior year, I got pregnant again. People noticed, and people talked—a lot—and it got to me. But I took up for myself, and I got to understand who A'lea really was and where my life was headed. My personality and attitude got stronger. I made friends with the people who didn't have friends. We had a clique consisting of the school's American rejects: the weirdos, the freaks, and the girl who got pregnant at twelve.

I have had ups and downs, but these have been the best years of my life. Iroquois High School is much like the projects: we are thick like glue. We stick together. We are united as one. Stereotypes and statistics have given my school a bad name. We are known for a reputation that's slowly deteriorating. The first thing my guardian said when she found out I was going to Iroquois was, "You're too smart for that school." It's unfair, yet inevitable. Although our test scores haven't been all the way on point, our school's behavior has been at its all time best, with fewer and fewer fights each semester. With the decision of limited dress code last year, our staff and students' relationship is at its tightest. We have this invisible mutual agreement for peace, and it works. Teachers do everything in their power to help you prepare for college. They're pretty tough people working at a school that is denigrated constantly, but they come anyway and keep trying.

But Iroquois should be the school known for our ever changing colors. We are the most diverse school in all of Kentucky, and lots of different languages are spoken here. That should stand for something. We have international students from over 100 different countries. When we are packed in the hallway, I see afros, hair picks, I see so many skin colors moving at the same time and direction. Tan skin, brown skin, white skin. The smell of fresh flat irons. Hair spray. Hair glue. I see jerseys and pom poms, I see posters for fundraisers and club meetings. We all become a blur at once.

We have a day called Hijab Day where females of all colors and sizes have a chance to see how beautiful they look in Muslim attire. There was much love in the air and females did not want to take the scarves off. International students have all year to participate in American activities, and all day outside of school to see our traditions. But we celebrate them with one day, International Day. International Day has gained so much popularity over the years that even people who consistently miss school show up for this event. There is no school that I know of that has a whole day devoted to people of international origin. On International Day, students represent their country and offer their traditional food, express their art, show their flags, and explain their traditions, break them down so we can understand them. They even let us steal a few recipes.

This year people performed different dances from around the globe—from hip hop to K-pop to Indian styles. The dances were amazing. It took everything in my power not to get up there and dance with them. It was their time to shine and everyone was filled with so much energy. They stomped their feet to the music, clapping and jumping around, smiles on their faces, love and memories in their eyes. These traditional dances were so good. When your hear that hips don't lie, think of this moment, because oh baby their hips

were not lying. It could convince you that Beyonce needed lessons.

This year I got a henna tattoo. Henna is an ink that African, Middle Eastern, and Indian people use to decorate their skin. The good part is it doesn't hurt. It may itch a little after, but it's pain free. Once it dries you can peel it off and the art stays for days. The woman who did my first henna tattoo was very slow with her hands. She was of African descent and wore a reddish orange hijab with matching skirt. She must've done her own henna tattoo because it looked similar to mine. Her whole sleeve was occupied by the ink. I focused on her hands so I wouldn't be distracted by the other things going on around me. She took her time, regardless of the long line behind me, and she was gentle, made me feel special and calm.

Sometimes people from other countries grow shy and only hang out with other international students. But that day they opened up too. Shared their food and told their secrets. We should be able to trust them. The are like our foreign allies. International Day is when you learn where your friends come from, what they had to endure to get all the way over. It's the day we learn from each other, respect our friends' past and history. Everyone is different, but everyone is the same: we all woke up this morning, brushed our teeth. We are all equal. And that is the truth in God's eyes too.

I am graduating from Iroquois in May, and it feels like the biggest achievement I have ever made. Senior year, my goals were to make my schedule firm in order to raise my child correctly while juggling my job and school, to be honored with the award of Who's Who—an outstanding student award—and also to graduate with my class. I achieved all of this. I feel truly blessed. It makes me want to do more. What more can I do? What more does God have in store for me? There's a whole world out there. Graduating on time with fellow peers will bring me one step closer to ultimate victory: having a good prosperous life with no financial problems, and no family drama. This whole systematic thing that the world calls happiness: I want that.

At freshman orientation four years ago, college was the first thing we talked about, and has been pretty much every day after that. But I don't understand why our mentors feel the need to stress college on a student who is scared of her own shadow. Life is moving way too fast. Everyone says, "Go to college. Get a career. Get a husband. Live your life. Don't screw it up." Sometimes they scare us by describing how difficult college is. And the dropout rate discourages us most of all. If those people didn't make it, how can I? Student loans are the straw that broke the camel's back. With everything life puts on our backs, a lump of debt is not needed. A human being should think twice about putting themselves in a situation like that, and sometimes I feel like we shouldn't have to go through all that. I don't feel like walking uphill to get to a pond. I just want to get to the pond.

Sometimes I feel like I'm going to college just because people want me to, because I'm the only one in my family right now that is so close. I don't know what I want to study or who I want to be. I'm going to college so they can help me with that. So I won't feel trapped or misguided. So I won't have to sit in a classroom knowing I don't understand the subject. I

was forced in high school to do that. This time I have a chance to say what I desire to learn. I want to feel confident and proud that I am there.

Everyone and everything is a mentor or role model to me right now: my sister and brother, my mother and her short life, less fortunate people living on the streets. I understand that I have come a long way. I grew up fast. There's nothing I can do now but keep moving forward. I don't always know how I'm going to succeed, but I do have a life routine: every night, I think about the next day and how it's going to go. I think about what I need to get done, and then I handle my responsibilities. When I know what I want, I know what I can accomplish. If you can visualize yourself achieving it, then it will happen.

Sleep on the floor with your child for three months on an air bed as useful as its broken down pump, and you tend to make promises you know you'll keep. Jae'dyce and I needed space. At first I was looking for a regular old apartment, but then I realized I couldn't afford a regular old apartment. A friend of mine recommended me to New Directions Housing Corporation. I went there and put in an application and they told me that they would call me when they had a place. Five months later I got the call and I was moved in the next day.

So I finally have a place I can call my own. The wait was long, and there were nights I couldn't take it: living with people is kind of hard. You have to learn to respect each other's space. I remember crying and was fed up with a lot of people's ways. But now I have my own space, and I don't have to share. I can do as I please when I want. It feels good. I waited, and the Lord answered my prayers.

There are all types of non-profit organizations that are there just to help women like Brittany and me, and I took advantage. Income-based housing is a blessing. They help you build on your financial situation so you can build your future. History repeats itself. My mother and her mother both started at the bottom, on income-based housing, food stamps, etc. Mama also shed sweat and tears to take care of us, and I'll do the same. I saw my mother cry. More than a child is supposed to see.

New Directions Housing Corporation has given me a huge opportunity by renting me an income-based apartment that I can afford. This program is giving me a kickstart in life. I tried not to cry tears of joy when New Directions called me and informed me that a unit was available—a two bedroom apartment in Shawnee. The lady who did my application showed me the apartment the next day and I loved it on the spot. I had the money upfront and I moved in that same day. Sure, it's small, but it's my home and my comfort. It's mine and no one else's. I can decorate my living room, cook or burn food if I want. I have a warm bed to go home to and food in the refrigerator. I love when I get home and lie down, just me and Jae'dyce. Now I can be safe and comfortable. Jae'dyce has her own space. She can crawl around and will soon begin to walk. I feel like I've been handed this amazing opportunity.

I walked Jae'dyce around the apartment pointing at things and saying, "Repeat after me: everything that belongs to me now belongs to you." I made her understand that this is her home too. It's just us.

No one else. I asked her how that felt for it just to be us all the time. She smiled at me. Having this great chance in life has made me think about what's next. About my future with what I want to do in life. My mind is at peace now that I have a home. It means that I can work on other things, like furthering my education and taking care of Jae'dyce.

I was invited to the New Directions Housing Corporation's Family Festival. They sent me a letter in the mail. I appreciate that not only do they offer safe housing but that they have events and invite their tenants. I felt like my landlord didn't forget about me once I signed the lease. It was my first invitation to any event, so I was super excited.

At the event they had free food, games, a bounce house, and door prizes for literally any kid that came. Kids were everywhere. I brought my eldest daughter Jena, Jae'dyce, and three other kids I was babysitting that weekend. It felt like a field trip with all the kids I had.

Jae'dyce's face was red due to the heat, which really troubled me. I kept her inside where the food was, had her rest for a while to cool off. I served all the kids food first. The event served hamburgers and hot dogs, including the condiments. They also had pineapple, watermelon, baked beans and potato salad.

During this event I felt an inner peace for just a few moments. Happiness was all around me. I had no troubles. The sun was shining in my face and both of my daughters were there with me. I felt at peace with the world. I was surrounded by my neighbors, who I trusted. I reflected on these last several months of my life. The lowest months of my life. I remember times I was screaming for God to take it all way. But one thing I did learn is that the unfortunate things in my life are like an ocean. My problems, my demons, the struggles of motherhood. Everything. There was land somewhere and I was dead set on finding it. I didn't give up. I kept fighting those whispers in my ear that doubted me. I woke up every day. God intended for me to survive.

I felt overwhelmed with the feeling to cry happy tears as I looked at my children enjoying themselves. Jena carried Jae'dyce around and I remembered when I had nothing to offer her, not even a mother's instinct. But now I have a shelter. An education. I have everything a regular mother can offer their daughter. And this filled my heart with so much happiness.

I don't have money to take her to Louisville's finest attractions, which can sadden any hard-working mother. But I packed five kids on my hip and took the bus six miles away to participate in a family festival. Towards the end, there were too many toys and not enough kids, so they where just giving the toys out and every child was happy beyond belief. Then it started to rain just before we headed to our bus. The toy that Jena won was pretty big—a plastic kitchen set with dishes included—so I carried that on top of Jae'dyce's stroller with her inside it. One of the two-year-olds got tired, so I put him at the bottom of the stroller where storage space was available. It might have looked ghetto with kids of all colors and sizes with me, but they had some fun, and we all deserved that.

MEHWISH ZAMINKAN

We Were Stronger

Returning Their Share

We Were Stronger

MEHWISH ZAMINKAN

When I was five years old, I went to live with my grandma in the village of Bazira, Pakistan, far away from where my mother, sister, and twin brothers lived in Islamabad. When my uncle moved to Saudi Arabia with his kids and wife, my mom started to worry about my grandma living in that big house all by herself. My mom asked my grandma to come and live with us in Islamabad, but she had lived in the village of Bazira for her whole life. How could she leave her beautiful house, her garden, her cows, and those beautiful fields and farms where she used to plant potatoes, wheat, watermelons, radishes, carrots, corn, green tea, and mint? She would never want to leave her village where she grew up, made a home, and started her own small farm. But my mom was still worried about her. If she got sick, who would take care of her? Who would help her with cooking, going to market, or reading important government papers? One day when they were having lunch at my grandma's house, my mom told my grandma, who I called Amma, that she would let me live with her.

Amma's house was a big wide open house with six bedrooms, one bathroom, a kitchen, and a garage. Across from the house, she owned a field where she would cultivate crops such as wheat, sugar cane, and mustard. Behind the house, she also had her own personal garden, where she would cultivate vegetables, fruits, and medicinal herbs. Amma had gray, shiny, almond eyes that looked like diamonds. She gave me the nickname Peshu, which means Kitty in Pashto. She raised me, and gave me so much love that I almost forgot about my siblings in Islamabad.

The thing I liked most about life in Bazira was that it was calm. The people of Bazira were very hard working. Some grew crops, some sold cow's milk, some made pickles or cheese at home and sold them, some did other things. Life was full of hands-on work. You never saw technology such as computers or smartphones. You wouldn't see cars very often; only a few rich people or the governor of the village had them. The life there was very natural. The food we ate was fresh and homemade, the vegetables were homegrown, the major water sources were wells. There was no tap water. There was no industrial smoke and pollution. If someone in the neighborhood did not have anything, people would share their food with neighbors. If any of them had a wedding or ran out of money or food, there was a community of rich people who would donate money to them. Bazira was a land of love, brotherhood, caring, and sharing—a land of happiness.

The Kamar Khel River

My favorite season was the hot, humid summer. There was a lot of load-shedding, which meant that there was not always electricity in the village, making it difficult for a lot of us to sleep well. But I would go to Kamar Khel, the small river a few miles from Amma's house, and spend summer afternoons under the shade of trees on its banks, enjoying the natural air conditioning there. All the women and young girls would sit on one side of the river and the men and young boys would sit on the other side. People would relieve their stress and worries and share their problems with each other. I would sit in the river for a long time and let the water flow around my limbs, drinking away my laziness and the heat from my body. While I did this, Amma would fish. She was very good at fishing. For lunch, Amma would take out some roasted chicken on top of fried rice with some *achar*, a pickle she made. I would enjoy this delicious lunch while sitting on the stones. When we were back home, Amma would cook the freshly-caught fish for dinner, and it would be delicious.

I was a girl with so many dreams of doing something in my life, not just to live life like a typical housewife. I was the best student in my entire school. I was the bossy one, and my friends were scared of me, but if someone fought my friends I would fight them back. We went to Attock Grammar School, which was the source of getting a better education for a lot of girls in Bazira.

I was very close with six girls: Yusra, Hamra, Nadia, Sobia, and my best friends, Khuzaima and Ayesha. We would walk to school together—there were no cars or buses. The only transportation were *tangas*, light carriages drawn by horses that moved so slowly that they were not allowed in the cities. In the morning we walked to school through fields full of crops, and our uniforms would get wet with the dew. We would have to wear niqabs, which covered our whole face except our eyes, because in the villages it was very shameful not to; if you didn't follow the rules, you had to face the consequences from your parents and the *misharan*, which means "leaders" in Pashto, the language we spoke in the village. I started to wear a shawl or *chadri* when I was in sixth or seventh grade because once a girl reached puberty she had to cover herself. She could get banished if she refused the rules of the *mishar* and village elders. There were consequences for everything because it reflected upon the parents' reputation and also the village's reputation.

In the morning we used to gather at Khuzaima's house and then we would leave together. We six girls were together everywhere. One day we were coming back from school, and on the way back there were some boys who we called *lofaran*, which means "they who avoid work." They did not have any work to do. They did not go school. Their job was just to interrupt girls and try to make their image look bad. This was one of the most unjust rules in villages in that part of Pakistan: no matter how bad a guy behaved there often was no consequence for him, and if something happened, everyone blamed the girl, even if she didn't give a damn about the guy. Girls were blamed for

everything, so they took every step very carefully. They were afraid that no one would marry them if someone snitched or spread news in the village. Whenever we saw those *lofar* boys, I would tell my friends not to be scared of them, that we were not girls who should be quiet and listen to what they told us.

One day there was one boy who really bothered my friend Khuzaima. He stopped her and said some nasty words, "*Lag mata ogora jannat ba darta oakham*"—"look at me once, and I will show you heaven." I took off my shoes and threw them at his face and made him embarrassed. None of his friends even looked up at us after that. They were also scared because Amma was well-known as a really strict and strong lady. They knew she would tell the *misharan* in the village, and that the *misharan* really respected her.

Amma taught me not to follow any rules, to raise my voice and stand with truth. She raised me in a very conservative way, but she also taught me how to speak up for myself. The kind of life expected of women was very different from men. No girls got education beyond the tenth grade. They could not get postsecondary education. By the age of seventeen or eighteen, a girl was married and maybe already had kids because the village society made it impossible for almost every girl to work like boys to become something. But Amma taught me not to be scared of any boy and not to live like a normal village girl. Pashtun culture is very strict about the rules and regulations for girls. They would do anything for their *nang*, or honor, and a family's girls are considered as fragile as rose petals. If a boy even looks at their sisters or girls or wives, this is considered an insult, and they will kill the boy. In the villages, it is very common to see guns in Pashtun houses. If a girl and a boy fall in love and males in the girl's family find out about it somehow, then it's the last day for that boy, because no marriage happens like that in Pashtun culture. Your family has to pick a boy for you, though they will ask you if you agree with that marriage. You can't go on a date with a boy openly because girls are considered the family's pride. A man would kill his sister, daughter, or wife and also would kill the boy if he heard anything bad about him.

On the other hand, Pashtun people have the best hospitality and a never-ending love for their guests. If a guest comes to their house, they can stay for months if they want. Pashtun people would never say a word or tell the guest that they have to go. Pashtun culture is very open-handed in spending money on guests. Even if they have to borrow money from another Pashtun family in order to feed their guests, they will enthusiastically cook homemade, fresh, and delicious food for them. They will take their guests to the beautiful places in their village and do all the fun activities, such as taking them to Pashtun concerts at night. They will also pack fresh vegetables, fruits, and herbs for their guests to take home with them so they will remember them and come back again.

Every morning at 5:00 or 6:00, teenage girls would go to the Bandra, a big well where everyone would go for water. People used that water for cleaning and cooking, and for the plantation. Even though we had a well in our house, my friends and I would take pitchers to the Bandra every weekend to fill

Arfin and Tauskhan Zaminkhan in the house where they lived when Mehwish was born

Arfin with baby Mehwish

with fresh water for those who didn't have a well in their own houses. I wanted to get some fresh air and to spend time with my friends Kanat, Ayesha, Amna, Yusra, and the funniest one, Gulfareen. We would sing together "*Sta da gati gati stargi tabahi da tabahi*" while we went to the well on those breezy and refreshing mornings. On the way, there were small shops and one local stall where Kaka Jamal sold necklaces, rings and friendship bracelets that he had made from flowers, especially roses. I would always get twenty rupees from Amma to buy one of the flower bracelets for my friends. Gulfareen always made Kaka Jamal give her two bracelets for free. She would say, "Kaka Jamal, we always come from far away to buy bracelets from you, because we love you and the way you make the bracelets, and you should give us at least two bracelets for free."

"I will give you two just because you come from far away and you entertain everyone," Kaka Jamal would say.

Kianat, the quiet and honest one, said to Gulfareen, "Don't do that. He is poor and wants to sell these to make money for his family."

Kaka Jamal would just laugh at us and he would tell Kianat, "I'll get more money from her next time she comes."

"You will see. I will get the bracelets the same price I got them today," said Gulfareen.

While they were talking back and forth I told Kaka Jamal, "We are like your daughters. Do you charge your daughters?"

He would call me Chalaki—the clever one—and say, "You always say something that makes me quiet." That's how I would get so many bracelets for free

and some for half price. With the money that we had left, we would buy delicious *malahi*, or popsicles, from an old man who made them in his home, and those were the best *malahi* in the whole wide world. The memories I made with my friends left a special mark in my heart that is still there today.

My mom and siblings sometimes came from Islamabad and visited me at Amma's on the weekends. I would take my siblings and cousin to the mountain area because I knew almost everything about my village. Amma had a garden where she planted fruits, vegetables, and roses. I would help her with watering all the plants. My brothers would pick the ripe fruits and put them in the basket. My sister Maria would cut the extra and distracting bushes that grew around the plants. After picking all the fruits and vegetables we would wash them and put them in baskets, and Amma put them in bags for my mom to take with her back to Islamabad. For our lunch, Amma would cook the fresh vegetables with some rice or grilled chicken, or sometimes Amma cooked vegetable soup. I would cut fruits in a big bowl then serve them as a dessert.

The most beautiful nights would be when we would have a big family feast, usually during summer break or winter break or for special events like Eid. My uncles, aunt, and my mom would gather and have their conversation while sitting in the backyard and enjoying tea with some homemade cookies, candies, cakes, sweet dishes, and donuts. We kids would laugh and play in the field outside of the house. Amma would give glasses of fresh cow's milk to all the kids before we went to sleep.

I really miss those moments, but I don't think they will ever return.

During the holy month of Ramadan, Muslims dedicate their spirits and their time to the one and only Allah and are obligated to fast every day from dawn to sunset. Fasting requires abstinence from food and water and, most importantly, it requires worshiping as much as you can. Because in this month the spiritual reward is double that of other months, it is very important to do as many good things as you can. The Quran says, "Everything you do in this month, do very carefully because in this month your deeds can take you to heaven or to hell." Everyone forgets about their conflicts and rivalries before the night of the first fast.

During Ramadan, the village of Bazira becomes very calm. At 3:00 a.m. everyone gets up and prepares for Sehri—the pre-dawn meal before starting the fast each day. The imams walk up to the top of the minarets of their mosques and announce over loudspeakers, "Get up, everyone. It's Sehri time." Then everyone gets up and prepares food for Sehri. Bazira's people usually eat rice pudding with some honey and dried fruit on top for Sehri. Some people eat bread that has been cut into small cubes and mixed with fresh, homemade cows' butter. Some people drink banana shakes made with honey, dates, flax seeds, dried nuts, and crushed ice. These shakes hydrate you and keep you full for a long time. Some people prefer a yogurt drink because it is cold and doesn't make your stomach burn. It makes you feel fresh.

There is no one in Bazira's streets during the afternoon during Ramadan. They stay in their homes or pray in the mosque and then sleep until 4:00 p.m. because they have no energy at all and they want to sleep, especially when Ramadan happens during the

hot summer like it did during my years in Bazira. When everyone wakes up in the late afternoon, they all start preparing food and setting things up for Iftar, the closing of the fast. Small food stalls and local shops set up at 5:00 p.m. and people start selling *pakoras, samosas, kebabs*, fruit *chaats*, and *sharbatas*. Everyone waits for the call to end the fast at sunset and then eats all the delicious food that they cooked all day long with their family and relatives. Every night before going to sleep, people say a special prayer called *Taraweeh* that lasts thirty minutes. People repeat the same thing over and over for thirty days. It is a very precious month in Islam; you sacrifice a lot of your free time and dedicate it to Allah. You stay away from the normal things you do every day when you are not fasting.

My first fast was when I was twelve years old, and though I was very excited to fast, the whole day was very hard for me because I didn't eat anything. I just drank the yogurt drink. The good thing was that I slept the whole day, and all I did was take a shower again and again because of the summer heat and because it felt better to feel fresh. Because of the heat, I couldn't walk barefoot on the floor of Amma's house or my skin would burn. The sun's rays were very strong, and most of the crops dried out and died. Those poor farmers who worked so hard while fasting during that hot Ramadan!

There was always a shortage of food, but the good thing about this holy month was that no matter who you were—poor or rich, Punjabi or Pashtun—everyone really cared about each other. During this month everyone tries their best to do good deeds. No one in our village would refuse you if you asked for something. People got low on food, but wealthy villagers would also have a lot of food that they had stored and saved. During Ramadan, I never saw a single person in Bazira who had no clothes or food for their Iftar time or Sehri time, because the Quran says true Muslims, especially if they are rich, have to give one quarter of their wealth to poor and needy people.

When Ramadan is about to finish, a lot of people start preparing for Eid-al-Fitr, the holiday that marks the end of the holy month. People go shopping from 10:00 a.m. to 3:00 p.m. to find things that they need for Eid. I really miss those stalls that sell bangles, henna, jewelry, clothes, shoes, and other gifts. Eid-al-Fitr is my favorite holiday because of the feelings we all get when we've done something very difficult: starving ourselves, doing worship, and not doing any bad things.

By the time I was a teenager, the Taliban were ruling the people in the neighboring country Afghanistan, and had started to come over to villages in the northern part of Pakistan near the border with Afghanistan. We had heard rumors, but we never imagined that they would come to Bazira. One day I was sitting in the classroom and gunmen from the Taliban—their faces covered, wearing all black—entered our classroom and threatened everyone, saying that no girls could come to school anymore. Their voices were heavy and terrible as a storm. We were all shaking and hoping that we wouldn't pass out in front of them. They wanted to talk to us face to face, so they told our teachers not to stay in class

with us. We sat quietly in our chairs, listened to their awful voices, and hoped for death to come early so we wouldn't have to go through all the cruelty of the Taliban. We couldn't make eye contact because that would be considered as challenging them. We hid our faces behind our scarves because we did not want to be recognized.

They were using Islam in the wrong way, telling us that in Islam it said that a girl should stay at home taking care of the parents and husbands. "Women are meant to stay at home, and no matter where they reach, they are women, and women can't be like men," they said. "They cannot rule the world. Only men can. They can't bring babies into the world and grow the generation without a man."

When the Taliban left the room we were shocked, scared and hopeless. We hugged each other tightly and kept our voices low, fearing that they were still in school. Tears were running down our faces like a shower tap. We remembered the memories that we had all made together, such as participating in school activities, working hard, and being competitive with each other about grades, having lunch together, attending school conferences, going to weddings together. We hadn't imagined that this would be the last day in our lives that we would see each other. Our teacher came to our room, and when we saw her we got emotional and started crying again. She told us, "We love our girls more than anything, but we don't have a choice and we want the best for you all. We don't want to risk keeping the school open because we would be killed for sure, and we don't want your families to see that. It's better to be alive and live with your love ones than to die."

As we left school, the teachers hugged us and we walked to our homes and looked back at our school and the tears came to the edges of our eyes. "What just happened?" we asked each other. On the way home we exchanged phone numbers and hugged for longer than we ever had. We waved our hands and didn't know if this would be the last time we would ever see each other. When I got home Amma was sitting near the well and pouring water from the bucket, washing clothes. "*Salam*," she said.

I was really quiet, my voice was changed, and my eyes were red and puffy.

Amma said, "Did they come to your school today?"

Amma opened her arms and I ran into them like a small kid. I hugged her, crying and sobbing and angry and cursing at the Taliban. Amma was wearing a white shawl, and I stained it with kajal, the black eyeliner I was wearing. My tears were mixing with the kajal and streaking it down my cheeks. It looked like someone did Halloween make-up on my face.

When a tsunami comes, it destroys everything and the crops die before they are ready to harvest. That's what happened to the girls of Bazira: they were getting ready to sparkle and blossom, then the Taliban took over my village. They took innocent children from their parents, kids who had dreams to become doctors and engineers, and taught them to use guns instead of pens. The kids had no other choice. They were told to choose a side: get killed or become Taliban. They took over people's property. The Taliban banned girls' education and bombed hundreds of schools. They told every girl's parents to

stop their girls from getting an education or their whole family would be killed. Many innocent girls were married forcefully.

The government was so weak that they couldn't do anything. Every day we heard and saw and felt bombs exploding and tanks firing their guns in nearby villages. Many of the local red mud homes were destroyed by bombs or by the tremors they caused, and many people's farm animals ran away or were cut loose from their ropes. The whole world—the fields, the roadsides, and the sky—all felt gray to me.

I was suffering and I was desperate for education. I still could not believe that I was banned from school. It was killing me to no longer have my everyday morning routine at school, time with my friends and teachers, my homework routine at night, and the competition with my friends about who would score higher on our exams. Every time I would go to my room and look at my uniform, my backpack, my books, my notebooks, and my school shoes, I would cry.

The markets were closed, and women and girls were not allowed to leave the house except to go to the madrasa, an Islamic religious school where we spent three or four hours a day learning how to recite the Quran by heart.

My friends and I thought our dreams were crushed. We were very close with the woman who had been our Islamic studies teacher before the Taliban shut down our school. When we told her that we did not want to give up our education, she started a secret school in her tiny mud house. I told Amma about the secret school. At first she said, "What would I say to your parents if something happened to you? They would never forgive me if you got hurt." I usually got my way with her, though, and finally she gave me permission.

My teacher, my friends, and I text messaged each other in Punjabi because the Taliban did not understand that language. We went to school two or three days a week. We always learned a lot on Fridays because almost every man and boy was busy praying in the mosque that day.

We left our phones at home whenever we walked to the secret school. We held the Quran close to our chest instead of carrying school books. Whenever I passed by a boy or a man in the street, my heart beat ten times faster, my forehead started sweating, and my throat dried up. *What if he is a spy for the Taliban? What would happen to my family? What would happen to my friends? What would they do to me?* Every day in the news we heard about girls getting caught going to school and being shot.

My teacher's house had a fireplace in the corner of the kitchen where she would cook food since there was no gas in the village. The small bathroom did not have a sink or a mirror. We would spread a cloth on the cold mud floor before sitting down, but the house would get messy when it stormed—mud and leaves everywhere—and our clothes would get dirty and our feet would get muddy. There were only two books for each subject, which we would share among six girls. We would keep our voices very low.

The Taliban were strong, but we were stronger. They were smart, but we were smarter. They were ignorant and we had the power of a pen, the power of education, which no one would ever be able to take away from us.

I was very worried about everything going on in my beautiful Bazira. Things were getting worse and my mom was freaking out in Islamabad as she watched the news about what was going on in our part of the country. She developed a heart condition and her health was getting worse and worse. She was fainting again and again, and was admitted to the hospital several times. Amma and I didn't tell my mom that I was going to a secret school because it would have made her even more worried.

After two and a half months of living under Taliban control, Amma told my uncle, who was a rickshaw driver in Bazira, that she wanted him to take me to Islamabad because she could no longer stand seeing my mom suffering as much as she was. He agreed to take me, and a friend of his agreed to let him borrow his car for the journey.

I packed my belongings to get ready for leaving Bazira. We were going to leave at night because in the daytime the Taliban could recognize us and ask a lot of questions. They had people on duty all day and night at checkpoints because they knew that girls wanted to escape to other parts of the country to get their education. My uncle told me to dress up like an old lady, so I wore Amma's shabby clothes. Amma later told my mom that when I was leaving Bazira that night with my uncle, she was certain that it would be the last time she would ever see me because she thought that the Taliban would catch me. I had never seen Amma crying like she did that night, so weak and sad and alone.

We left at midnight. When we were going through security checkpoints, my heart was beating very fast. My uncle had told me to act like I was sick,

Landscape near Bazira. Mehwish's grandmother Maroo Jan grew fields of wheat like this in front of her house in Bazira.

so I was holding my stomach and turning my head on the left side of the seat so that the guard could not see my face. A guy who was covering his face, wearing a black *shalwar kameez*, and carrying a heavy gun asked for my uncle's driver's license and asked the reason why we were traveling. My uncle said that his wife—meaning me—was sick and had very bad stomach pain. Finally, we passed through the checkpoints. I felt relieved that Allah gave me a new life.

It was five hours of driving, and while my uncle was driving I slept. It was 5:00 a.m. when we arrived in Islamabad. I immediately noticed the huge change in the environment just by looking at all the lights, the cars moving at high speed, and those tall buildings. Finally, we arrived at the house. My mom's hugs were never-ending. She called my aunt, who lived a few blocks away, to celebrate that I had made it safely to Islamabad. We started a *Khatam-e-Quran*: we invited women from the neighborhood to our house and read thirty *paras*, or lessons from the Quran, to show Allah that we were thankful. Then we cooked homemade sweets such as *kheer*, *badam ka halwa*, sweet rice in multiple colors, *ladoo*, custard, and *burfi*.

But nothing looked good to me. The food was not real food. In Bazira, Amma made her own tandoor oven out of mud and made all bread from scratch. In Islamabad, we didn't make our own bread—we just bought it from shops. I was used to drinking water fresh from the well. My siblings would go to restaurants to get fast food. I got food poisoning.

I missed the old days in Bazira when I would help Amma in the fields and help her with the garden. I missed Attock Grammar School and my friends there. The house was way smaller than Amma's house in Bazira and there were roofs on everything—no open courtyard like Amma's house. In Bazira, we had dirt floors, but in Islamabad the floors were tile. There were no scorpions in our house in Islamabad, but in Bazira Amma had to kill them every day. In Bazira we didn't have electricity all the time because of load-shedding—Amma would light a lantern and carry it around when that happened—but here they always had electricity. The house in Islamabad had air conditioning, whereas in Bazira if we were hot we would sleep out in the courtyard on *charpai*, cots woven from the bark of a local tree. In Islamabad, the children would play in the streets and it was really chaotic like I had never seen before. The smoke of the restaurants and everything was just making me freak out, and I felt like I was in prison.

When I moved to Islamabad, the main thing I was not used to was sleeping in a different place. In Bazira I used to sleep in the same room with Amma. I missed her supernatural bedtime stories, her warm hugs, and the unconditional love that she would shower me with. I missed the smell of Amma when she would cuddle me every night. I missed the mornings that she would wake me up to pray Fajr, the prayer that Muslims do before dawn, and I missed the breakfast she would make right after she would milk the cow, which included tea she made from that fresh milk. I also missed the calmness of the village, getting up early in the morning, and taking the fresh air into my lungs.

All the changes I had been through made me so sick that I got really weak. I stopped eating for a while; nothing looked good. I wanted to go back to my beloved Bazira. Amma would come and see me in Islamabad three days a week because she missed me and was worried about my health. She would come in the morning and would spend the whole day with me and then at 5:00 p.m. drive all the way back to Bazira to sleep at her house because she was concerned about the *lofar* boys who would steal her jewelry or livestock or food if she wasn't there. Amma was really smart. She chose daytime to spend with me because during daytime people are outside working in fields, doing their work, and people can't sneak into other people's houses. Amma would bring me fresh milk, yogurt, butter, vegetables, fruits, and herbs from her garden while I was really sick and my stomach was not used to the city food. She would make soup, cook fresh bread, and bring some fresh tea that she had picked from her garden.

Things were getting normal and I was getting well, so Amma started coming once a week instead of three days, but we would still always talk on the phone every night through our family friend Uncle Jamal, who had a phone. Uncle Jamal was also the person who used to read my dad's letters to my mom when my dad was working as a sailor. Amma had never used a phone in her life. Amma was happy and every night she ended the call with say, "*Alhamdulillah*"—thank the Lord.

After a month and half I went to school and registered for classes. It was difficult because in cities they had a computer system where they kept the records of your grades, but they couldn't find my records from back in Bazira. Finally, I started to adjust to the environment and was able to go to the same school as Maria. I started my school there in Islamabad and I worked harder and harder because

I was not a quitter. Maria taught me how the school system worked in Islamabad. She was the expert and she helped me with everything. We were sisters but grew up in very different environments and we had way different experiences and beliefs and dreams. She grew up in the city and her mind was very liberal while mine was very conservative.

Even though I was close to my mom, I hated the life there and couldn't adjust. My fellow students would stare at me. I would get bullied a lot in and out of school just because of my conservative clothing, my strong Pashtun accent, and the rustic food that I ate. Maria and her friends would wear jeans and *kurta* and didn't cover their hair, but I still wore *shalwar kameez* and a shawl, which was a more conservative way of dressing. They would make fun of me for my village superstitions: that crossing a black cat brought bad luck, that washing clothes on Friday would bring sadness and poverty, that a loose hair falling to the ground while brushing it meant that a guest would be coming to the house that day. They would tease me by calling me Auntie because they thought I was so old fashioned. All the resources were in Islamabad but I couldn't feel relief. I hated my life at that time because everything was so different for me and I still couldn't embrace the change that I was living in.

Life in Islamabad went at a very fast pace compared to life in Bazira. There, I would go to school, then go to the madrasa, then come home and help Amma, and then do homework in the evening. In Islamabad, I would go to school, and after school I went to a tuition academy, a place where Mom paid for tutoring to help me catch up academically

Mehwish with a teacher at Army Public School in Islamabad

because my schooling in Bazira was not as strong as the schooling in Islamabad. I would come back from the tuition academy and then go straight to the kitchen to eat something because I had not eaten anything the whole day. After that, I would go to my room to study more until 1:00 a.m. I would fall asleep with books on my face. Mom would bring warm milk for me and put it on the table, and put a blanket on me. Life got busier and busier every day in Islamabad, and I kept pushing myself to improve.

In my culture, if you are the oldest son you have a lot of responsibilities. In Islamabad, I started to take those responsibilities on my shoulders because I had no older brother. I took mom to the hospital when she had appointments. Our family was applying to

move to the United States, where my dad was now living; whenever we received a document from the Embassy I would read it to Mom, and I would go with her to the post office to send documents to the United States. Mom had always wanted to move to a Western country so that we could have better opportunities than we would have in Pakistan. After years as a sailor, my father had moved to Louisville, Kentucky, U.S.A., to work at the Brown Hotel. Once he got his permanent resident status, he applied to bring the rest of us to the U.S. to join him. Fifteen months after I made the big move from Bazira to Islamabad, I made an even bigger move—from Pakistan to the U.S.

Mom had wanted to move to a Western country ever since she was a girl. Although she grew up in a very small village, she was always independent and had big dreams of living inside her. When she was little, she was not allowed to go to school. But she wanted to go school and she loved when her friends would have books in their hands. So she sneakily went to school with her friends. In the village, there was no gas for cooking, so people would collect bushes to make fire. My mom told her mother that she was going to collect bushes, but she went with her friends to school instead. She sat in class, and when the teacher asked who she was, she said that she was a visitor. She fell in love with the environment, the books, the uniforms, the teachers, and the pens. On the way back home, she collected bushes.

When she got back home from school, she made a backpack for herself from some leftover fabric. She was very excited and she thought she would be able to convince her brothers and mom to let her go to school. She asked Amma if she could enroll in school. She told Amma that she wouldn't have to worry about the school fees because she would be able to manage by sewing clothes for her friends and neighbors.

Amma and her brothers told her that people would think bad about our family. My Pashtun Amma was very strict and pride was everything to her, more important than her daughter's goals and dreams. My mom's father had died six months before she was born, so he was not there to stand up for her and protect her. Amma was scared that someone might start rumors that her daughter was going to school to do *haram* things—things considered evil in Islam—like having a relationship with a boy who has no *nikkah*, or Muslim marriage, with her. She was worried that someone might do something to her daughter.

My mom told her mother that she accepted this, but the next day she snuck to school with her friends again. Her brother went to the school, pulled her out, and brought my mother home because he was angry that she had lied to the family. She never went to school again.

After that, she started to work jobs to make money at a young age. She cleaned the house of a lady in the village who was an expert tailor in exchange for sewing lessons. Then my mom started sewing clothes for people and she saved up to buy a second-hand TV to learn Urdu by watching Pakistani drama serials. Urdu is the national language of Pakistan, but people living in Bazira speak Pashto. In cities and schools, however, no one knows Pashto. My mom would sometimes go to a nearby town called Attock to buy things, and everyone in Attock would talk in Urdu. Even though she was mad at her mother and brothers for not letting her go to school for the rest of her life, she did not want other people to make fun of her ancestors and her mom and brothers.

My mom married my dad when she was seventeen years old. He was fifteen years older than her. I lived with Mom when I was very young. My parents had a house in the village until they moved to Islamabad a few years later, right after the birth of my sister Maria, when I was two. Before Maria, I was the only child and at that time my parents were living in Bazira a few blocks away from Amma's house. When I was young my dad went to work as a sailor on an Australian ship. He sold one of the houses that his parents had left to him when they died. When he sold that house, my dad asked my mom, "What do you want me to do with the money?" My dad really did not want to leave my mom alone at home. My mom was very fond of the idea of going to live in a Western country because their living conditions in Bazira were very poor and she was very tired of everything, so she told him, "If you want to see me live happily, just go outside of Pakistan—somewhere where my kids can have bright futures."

My dad left my mom with 150 Pakistani rupees and left in search of better work for his wife and his kid. He went to Karachi to work for his old school friend Javed as a waiter in his hotel. Javed knew some people at the Thailand Embassy, and he told my dad that there were some visas for Thailand which they were offering for people willing to work for an Australian ship line. My dad was very happy and he somehow was able to manage the money and bought a ticket to Bangkok and started to work for the Australian ship line. There was no direct way to use phone lines in Bazira, so my dad sent a letter for my mom and Amma. Because my mom and Amma could not read, he sent the letter to his friend Uncle Jamal. It took a month for that letter to be delivered to my mom. My mom was crying with happiness because my dad also sent two thousand Pakistani rupees.

She wanted to save the money that my dad was sending to her and use it to work on our house, and to use the money she got from sewing clothes to pay for private school. She bought a sewing machine from one of her friends for a low price because it was having some problems. She took that sewing machine to a repair person who fixed it for 100 Pakistani rupees. She was happy that she was now able to sew more clothes. She would work until midnight at her sewing machine and would sleep at Amma's house at night because unemployment and poverty made people to do horrible things such as kidnapping and stealing, and my dad was worried about her being alone at night.

Her biggest dream was to go to a Western country where her kids could raise their voices and become whatever they wanted. Whenever she talked about this at her friends' houses they would say, "Arfin has lost her mind," because they thought that her dream of going to another country would never be a reality. But they were wrong.

When I first came to the United States, it was another big adjustment for me because it was a whole different country: new people, a new culture, and a new language. When I got to New York on our way to Louisville, I was so shocked because the hotel we stayed in was so amazing. Through the hotel windows I could see the tall buildings, people with dogs, and different lifestyles, a coffee in one hand and talking on the phone with another. I thanked Allah for giving me a life that was going to be full of opportunity. When I looked at the buildings and the people across the street from our hotel, I remembered the bombs and bullets hitting the schools and houses in Bazira, the smoke, the dust and ashes covering the roads. I took a deep breath, looked at the sky, and said, "Oh, Allah, bring peace to my beloved Bazira, and my beloved Pakistan."

The United States does not recognize how names are structured in our culture. We traditionally only go by one name. We don't really have last names the way people in the U.S. do. When people like us apply for American visas, the visa document will list our name as our last name and list our first name as FNU, which stands for "first name unknown." Whole families will have different last names and the same FNU first name on our new documentation. FNU is printed on visas and then trickles down to every other official document: green card, driver's license, car insurance, bank accounts. But we think of our last name as the name of our tribe, or our grandfather's name, or place of birth: in my family's case, Zaminkhan.

When I moved to the United States, my legal name became "FNU Mehwish," not "Mehwish Zaminkhan." It made me feel like someone had taken my identity. Whenever a teacher would call me "FNU," I would correct them: "FNU is not my real name; my real name is Mehwish." Sometimes I would get tired of correcting people. Sometimes I would get mad. When I would go to the hospital with my mom and my sister and the nurse would call, "FNU," the three of us would get confused because we didn't know which FNU they meant: my mom, Arfin, my sister, Maria, or me. When I got books from the school library, the librarian would get confused. She would ask, "Are you FNU Maria or FNU Mehwish?" FNU made me embarrassed everywhere I went. Blushing would make my face red like a tomato or beetroot. I wanted the earth to open up and swallow me whole, but there was no rescue from this embarrassment. It was absolute torture. It just made me feel really sad when I realized that Mehwish was not my name anymore. At home I was Mehwish, but in public I was FNU.

My mom could not open a bank account. She went to the office where you have to make your identity card and she asked them if they could put her real name on it. She showed her marriage certificate, which in Islam is called *nikah nama,* but the official said, "Sorry, we can't put it in that name unless you go to court, change your last name to Zaminkhan, and have it signed by the judge." My mom almost gave up on changing the name because it takes hundreds of dollars and you have to get a lawyer, which Mom could not afford. She was sick and did not have a job, so she thought that she would have to live with that name for the rest of her life.

In school people would ask me when and how I got the name FNU, and I would just say I didn't know or say that the school put our names backward in the computer system. I gave up on giving explanations to people and I hated the fact that Maria and I had the same classes because they would confuse us FNUs and I would get embarrassed in front of our classmates.

Your name is your identity. It was miserable facing the problem of being FNU wherever I went.

My first two years in the U.S. were the hardest because I was adjusting to a new country with new people around me and learning a new language. I started going to Iroquois Public Library and got involved in the English Conversation Club there. I also participated in the youth and teen programs for refugees and immigrants at Americana Community Center. I was very excited and curious about life in the United States and was enrolled at the Newcomer Academy for two months before being transferred to Iroquois High School, where Maria and I both started as freshmen.

My sister and I would go everywhere together because she didn't have her Islamabad friends with her, and our relationship got stronger and stronger every day. People started asking us if we were twins. Finally, I was able to get really good grades and I started to make new friends and I started to assimilate into American culture. The girl who had never left home without covering her face, who had never worn jeans and Western-style shirt and hijab in her life started to wear pants, shirts, and hijab, which covers the hair but not the face.

In the United States, I saw my mom asking her neighbors to take her to the grocery and taking buses in severe snow and severe hot weather because no one in our family could drive. My dad had multiple surgeries for his eyes, Mom couldn't speak English, and my siblings were not old enough to get a license. So I learned how to drive, got my license, and became the family driver. I took my mom to the hospital, and I would pick my brothers from school whenever they would stay after for soccer practice. I would help them with their homework and stay up late to study so I could do well in high school and go to a good college without my parents having to pay out of their pockets for my tuition. They worked hard and sacrificed a lot just to bring us here, so that we siblings could have a good future and better opportunities.

When I was a senior at Iroquois High School, I went to the Kentucky United Nations Assembly (KUNA), a three day leadership conference at the Galt House where your school's team represents a country and looks for a solution to a problem that your country faces—like the real United Nations does. We arrived around 1:30 p.m. and got our room keys, our resolution books, and our name tags. We all wore Vietnamese cultural attire (I wore an *áo dài*) and visited the booths and the watched the performances and the parade of nations. After that first day was over, we went to out rooms and slept. The second day of KUNA was Business Day. I woke up and put on my royal blue and black business suit, my royal blue turban, and my royal blue watch. The day was chaotic because of the meetings in the committees and summits which included debates and votes to pass or deny the resolutions. I got my breakfast and headed to my first meeting.

At the end of that day, we had a ceremony where we lit candles and the KUNA student officers talked about Syrian kids. While I was sitting with my friends listening to these really emotional speeches, I received a text from a number in Pakistan. It said, "Hi, this is Gazala, your friend. Did you forget about me?" It was one of my old classmates from Bazira. I couldn't believe that it was her. I had not talked to

Mehwish with classmate Tam Le at KUNA

her in years. She sent me her picture and there was a cute little boy sitting next to her. I told Gazala that I was so sorry, I had been in a meeting and couldn't pick up. She told me, "Thank Allah you picked up the phone." I asked her how she got my phone number and she told me that she got it from my cousin. She asked me, "How are you feeling and when will you come back to Pakistan?" I told her, "*Inshallah,* soon. Who is that small boy next to you?" She replied, "That's my son." I thought she was joking, but she was serious. She said that she got married in 2014, the year I moved to the United States. I was concerned, and tears trickled down my face because I was remembering all the memories we had when we were in the school in Bazira—our laughs, our tears whenever we would miss a question on an exam, the togetherness on the Chand Raat—the night before Eid—where we classmates would do henna for each other, going to each other's houses to collect gifts of money from elders, and sneaking into other people's fields to make trouble.

"Send me your picture, Mehwish," she said. I sent her a picture of me wearing business clothes, a watch, and makeup, and she told me that I was lucky that I got to the United States. "At least you are not like me, Mehwish: being married, taking care of kids, and doing whatever my husband tells me," she said. I asked her how she got married and she said that the Taliban made her parents worry about her future, so they had made her marry a boy she had never met. She'd had no choice but to marry him, or she would have hurt her parents' reputation in the village. In the pictures she sent, she was sitting in a small kitchen which had walls that were made of mud, with no cabinets or drawers for utensils or spices. She told me she had no access to gas, so she had to go to the field behind her house to collect bushes to make a fire so she could cook food for her family. She had to work as a tailor to earn money for her kids' clothes and her husband had to work as a farmer in the fields. She had to keep her mouth shut, and she did not have the right to make her own life decisions.

That is exactly what would have happened to me if I had not been lucky enough to leave Bazira, pass through those scary checkpoints, and make my way to Islamabad. My education would have stopped before I even finished high school and I would not have had access to college because the elders didn't believe in spending so much time on educating a girl when she would just end up getting married. If I was there right now, I would be making babies, taking care of kids and my husband, listening to whatever my husband said, and I would not have the choice to leave. If my husband were to divorce me, that would devastate my parents and the people of the village would think that I was not a good enough wife or that I had an affair with someone else. Here I am in the United States, finishing high school with honors, entering college, and having no fear that the Taliban or anyone else can stop me from going to school and chasing my dreams.

Returning Their Share

DR. MUHAMMAD BABAR CHEEMA

Dr. Babar is a physician who practices internal medicine and geriatric medicine. He is a local interfaith and peace advocate who strives to bring people together by breaking down man-made barriers. He is the president of Muslim Americans for Compassion and a board member of a lot of local organizations in Louisville. I wanted to interview him because he is Pakistani-American, because I am interested in a medical career, and because I wanted to know about his life and about his experiences as a civic leader in Louisville. One day I would like be a leader in my community the way that Dr. Babar is.

—MEHWISH

Pakistan before the Afghan war was a tolerant country. But after Afghanistan, the country changed, extremism was on the rise, the foundations of that nation were destroyed. People are more religious now in *their* sense, but they've gone away from their spirituality. Everything has become *haram* for them. Mullahs have done their narrow interpretations of the Quran. It's not the interpretation of Prophet Muhammad. This phenomenon is not unique to Islam, either. In Medieval Europe, they did the exact same things. There was a guy, Servetus, in the 16th century, around Martin Luther's time. The only thing the poor guy was saying was that we need to treat Jews and Muslims nicely because those were also people of faith, and they hung him for that.

You need to keep the religious right on hold. If you empower them, they take over and it's always their way or the highway. As I'm growing older in life, I believe there is no one way to God. Every human soul has their own thought process, their own feelings, and their own way to reach the Almighty. The mullahs, rabbis, and priests will all tell you the only way to salvation is go through their path. But life is much bigger. America gave me a chance to look outside the bubble that was created by Pakistan's religious establishment and media and reflect on my own faith tradition. I believe that I'm a better Muslim, more true to the essence of my faith, because of America. That is the biggest gift of America, not any economic benefit or anything else but just giving me this feeling. The essence of any faith tradition is love, compassion, and how you treat other people, your fellow beings.

I came here as an exchange visitor. There is a visa category called a J1 visa. It's a training visa, basically. I did training in New York. There was a path to citizenship if you served in the inner cities where the American doctors did not want to go, so after my training I took that path and served in the inner city in Buffalo. But that hospital filed for bankruptcy while my citizenship papers were being processed. My wife was a U.S. citizen, so I applied through her. That's how I got here.

We moved to Louisville in 2004. Around when we were going to have our boys, I started thinking about my life, reflecting on what kind of world my boys were going to grow up into. There were more and more terrorist attacks, more and more hatred— all those things were spreading around. I started reflecting that we need to bring some sanity because, quite frankly, it was not fun to be Muslim and a person of Pakistani descent in current-day America. I thought that biggest problem with Islam was the religious establishment. They had moved away from human service, which is the essence of Islam. The Holy Quran says if you help anybody, you're not doing any favor—you are just returning their share to them. That was the life of the Prophet Muhammad. He wasn't just sitting in a mosque and preaching. He was out in the community taking care of and helping people. So we decided that that's what route we would follow, too. We have the Association of Physicians of Pakistani Descent of Kentucky and Indiana. I was its president. We started partnering with local nonprofits. There is Dare to Care, which is a food pantry, big in town. There is the Center for Women and Families, which is for women of domestic abuse.

We have Home of the Innocents, for youth at risk. We volunteered with them, we spoke to the mission. A tornado happened in Indiana, so we took a team of volunteers from the Islamic Center, fifty or sixty people. We cleaned people's houses, the fields, all those things. We did a lot of grassroots work.

Eventually, we started the non-profit organization Pakistani American Alliance for Compassion and Education. That's a long name, so we changed the name to Muslim Americans for Compassion. I'm not going to go into detail about the projects, but we did a lot of local work. In March and April 2017, we started a group we called Love from Louisville. We sent a container full of supplies to Greece for

Syrian refugees, in collaboration with Jesuit Refugee Services. We thought that when we had done this thing for the Syrian refugees, we should do a similar kind of effort for our own people. When Hurricane Harvey devastated Houston, we took a lead, the local Islamic centers and the churches and synagogues, and then we collected donations. We sent forty pallets of baby supplies and other supplies to Houston. Our group that took a major lead in that.

I wish you had a chance to see America before 9/11. Such a feeling of freedom. Nobody cared what you looked like or how you worshipped. There was no fear. After 9/11, Muslims were under a microscope. And then the media perception of Islam is all through the actions of ISIS and those people. There was a poll by Pew two or three years back that found that people who knew a Muslim have a favorable opinion of Islam. I think more than seventy percent had a favorable opinion if they knew one Muslim and if they did not know a Muslim, it was less than twenty percent. It's the human relationships. Your class fellows, they know about you, but their parents may have different perceptions. After 9/11, Islam in America was on trial. It was unfortunate, the political factors there. All the hijackers were from Saudi Arabia, but nobody got after Saudi Arabia. Everybody was after Afghanistan and Iraq because we need cheap Saudi oil. The irony is that this war on terror has made us more unsafe than we were at that time, unfortunately.

Then the next phase is now the Trump era. It's even worse than 9/11. I did not feel this crazy after 9/11. Now it's even worse. The people who have their own inner fears, and who have no exposure to people who look different from them, are drawn to the same kind of politics which they do in Pakistan. They divide people to advance their agenda, and our leaders are doing the same thing. In America, some people among Caucasian population fears that the country's been taken over by Black people or the Latinos or the Muslims. Those fears were highlighted by President Trump. Now, America is on that route which Pakistan got on after Afghanistan. This really scares me. America is a special place and right now America is at a crossroads. When you unleash this phenomenon of extremism, this genie, you cannot put it back in bottle easily. Even if President Trump is not re-elected, this phenomenon is not going to go easily. It's going to take us two, three decades. There are going to be a lot of sacrifices in this country before this phenomenon goes away. Before 9/11, nobody cared if you were wearing the hijab or not. Now when I see people wearing the hijab and I look at the looks the people are giving them, there is a difference there.

Somebody put graffiti on our Louisville Islamic Center, and a thousand citizens gathered together and they all painted it. That was the best spiritual feeling I ever had in my life. Part of the graffiti was the Star of David, a Jewish sign, and I'm proud that not a single Muslim said, "Oh, the Jews did this to us." It was just some kid who did that, and when we did our press conference I just said, "If you are listening to me, please join us in clean-up on Friday. We all make mistakes in life. We don't want this mistake to surround you further. We have nothing but forgiveness and prayers for you." My heart tells me that person was there at the clean-up. That is the Islamic spirit, that's what Prophet Muhammad would have done. His life stories are full of that. We could have gone the other direction and gotten angry, but we used this opportunity to bring people together.

We were trying to establish a Muslim cemetery here because the cemeteries are very expensive. A lot of Muslims in this city are from Somalia and Bosnia, and came as refugees twenty or thirty years ago. They can't afford that. Islamic burials are very environmentally friendly, because we don't use any artificial dyes or anything. We just bury the piece of cloth. We were looking into some land just next to Louisville in Bullitt County. There were only three houses close by, but when the zoning commission hearing came, almost eighty people showed up. They said, "We don't want Muslims here." Somebody said, "It's an insult to my grandfather, who fought in the Second World War." I wanted to stand up and tell him that *my* grandfather also fought in the Second World War. They refused us. Four to one. But then the nuns called me from Loretto and said, "You can have whatever land you want. We have thousands of acres here." But that was too far way for us. We got another place within the city. At the meeting to discuss the proposal, we went as an interfaith coalition. There were a couple of people who had some objections. One of my friends who was Executive Director of Council of Churches, spoke there and she said, "Thousands of years ago, Prophet Abraham negotiated with the Hittites about a burial place for his wife, Sarah, and loved ones." She said, "Now, today, the children of Abraham are here, and they're asking a place for their loved ones. I hope you will not deny them." And she had tears in her eyes. We got a piece of land, next to one cemetery here. We use one of the local funeral homes.

In your life, whenever any adversity comes, any tragedy, think positive. The Civil Rights Division of U.S. Department of Justice from Washington, D.C., contacted us when we were refused in Bullitt County. They said, "We can pursue a lawsuit for you guys, because this is not America." But I told our board, "Listen, we are trying to establish ourselves here to our positive work of service. If we go to a lawsuit, it's a negative thing, and we should not get into a negative thing. We should stay positive." We held an open house at the Islamic Center and invited people from Bullitt County to know more about Islam. No one showed up, but we did this gesture. We did not file a civil rights lawsuit. I imagine that it increased our respect within the city. People thought that, "Man, that was very compassionate." We told them, "We are a city of compassion. Islam is a compassionate religion. Why should we do a lawsuit? There are other pieces of land here and we will go through a reconciliation." Always think positive.

MARIA ZAMINKAN

Opening Act

Now the Gloves Are Off

Opening Act

MARIA ZAMINKHAN

I grew up in Islamabad, Pakistan. It was a wonderful place: big buildings, noisy streets, traffic like New York, but greenery everywhere. Everyone was busy chasing their dreams. For most of my childhood I lived in a three-story house with my mom, younger brothers, and older cousins. It was a really big dream house. It had a gigantic maroon gate where you entered the house, the floors were gray glass tiles, and everything was so stylish. It had a lot of rooms, even a basement, but my favorites were the study room and balcony. Our house had a big garden, swings, and play courts for sports. We had a lot of plants with different kinds of flowers and fruits. As a little kid, I loved living in the big city, but I was lost emotionally. I was so alone a lot of the time. There was no one close I could talk to. My older sister Mehwish lived far away in the village of Bazira, where my mom had sent her to live with our grandmother. And my dad had left home to work as a sailor to support our family.

I remember the last time I saw my dad in Pakistan. My dad, mom, brothers, four cousins, two uncles, and my auntie were having breakfast. The smell of different foods made me so hungry, and I wanted to swim in the big jug of mango juice. That breakfast was different from the usual breakfast of omelets, tea, and toast. We had plenty of food on that long wooden table: donuts, omelets, paratha, halwa, tea, juice, fruits, cake, salad, fries, ketchup, sauce, kebabs, rice, chicken, biryani, and more. My cousins went to the basement to get long deep metal pots for cooking. The wood was wet, so the fire was smoking. People coughed and their eyes got red and watery, but they laughed at the same time because it wasn't new for them. There were different types of vegetables: spinach, broccoli, cauliflower, cucumbers, tomatoes, onions, green, red, and yellow peppers, zucchini, mushrooms, carrots, radishes, eggplant, and so much more.

Every member of my family was busy collecting things for my dad—traveling food, a bag for his clothes, shiny, pointy new shoes. I started wondering if we might have a birthday, but no one had a birthday on that day. Everybody was doing their own work, and I was a lost kid with my upper lip covered with milk, standing in the middle of the house, looking around with big owl-eyes. My mom was busy making dough for bread. White flour mixed with water was on her hands, on her clothes, and on the ground. When she put her hair back, it got covered with it, and her nose had a little dough on it too. She looked like a child playing in mud. She said, "Let me get you ready for school." I made a confused face and asked her, "Is Dad going somewhere?" She dropped my hand, then looked at me with brown diamond eyes. "Why? Did someone tell you something?" I said, "No, Mom. I was just wondering." Her fake happiness came across her face again.

"Oh, no. He just wants to clean the house, and he's looking for his stuff." I knew whenever Mom or Dad was trying to hide something from me. They couldn't look me in the eyes, their excuse wouldn't make sense or would be off topic, and they'd rub their thumbs when they pretended to tell the truth.

"Mom, so we dress up like professionals?" I said. "With new shoes shining like stars and with new socks? A tie for men, a handkerchief in their pocket, their hair combed up, and strong cologne that's filling the room? Why is Dad wearing these clothes and cleaning the house and getting a bag full of clothes and some documents in a folder?" I gave her a look of disappointment, let go of her hand, and ran toward the balcony.

The balcony was the only place where I could feel myself and talk to myself. It had kept me calm in hard times. I always felt so relaxed when I went to my peaceful place. I was deep in thought about what was going on when I heard emotional crying. I crept into the room near the balcony. I found my dad, wearing shiny, pointy shoes and a soft, grey handkerchief in his pocket, crying and murmuring to himself.

I was scared and asked, "Are you all right?" Dad wiped his face then held me up high and hugged me. I could see the leftover tears near his brown, pained eyes. I asked, "Are you going somewhere?"

He looked me in the eyes and said, "Yes, hon."

"How can you leave me?" I said. "I need you when I get tired and want to sleep in your arms. I need you to go to parent-teacher conferences with me. I want to let my friends know that my dad is the best and how proud he is of me."

He held me close to his chest and said, "Baby, I am going for you, your mom, and your siblings, so you guys never have to work or miss your studies. Having to think about getting food can distract you from your education."

I told him that I could solve this problem and to wait there. I slipped out of his hands and went to the closet. I grabbed my piggy bank and handed it to him. "I won't buy anything when I go to the market." I said, "I can live on this money. Then you don't have to go anywhere."

He smiled and said, "How long will that money feed you?" He started putting bills in the piggy bank. I stopped him with my hand, took the money, and, with the pen from his pocket wrote *D-A-D* in squiggly handwriting on it. I said, "I will keep this money till the day we meet again, *inshallah*." I kissed him on the forehead and hugged him tight and let my tears flow like a river as he held me in his arms.

I locked the piggy bank in an old suitcase in the closet in my room in Pakistan and put the key in a framed photo of my family. That suitcase is still in that house, which is now occupied by my cousins and their families. Those bills might still have the smell of Dad's cologne. I didn't see him again until almost ten years later, in the Louisville airport.

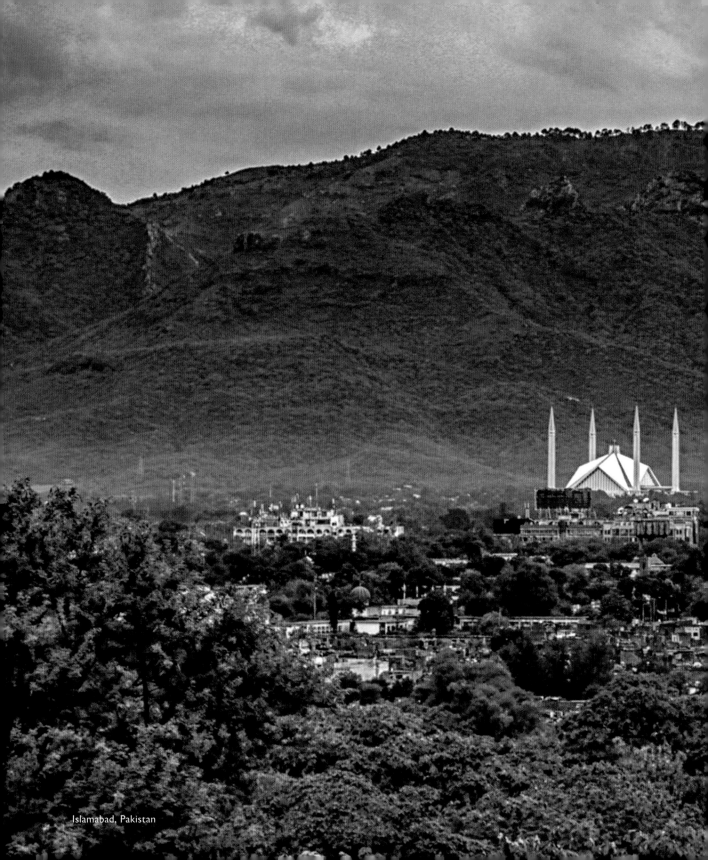

Islamabad, Pakistan

Maria's mother Arfin as a young woman

Throughout my childhood in Islamabad, Mom was ill with a heart condition because of all her worries about Dad and Mehwish living far away from us. Every morning, she would talk on the phone with Dad, and every evening she would talk on the phone with Mehwish and my grandmother. She had a hard time being apart from Mehwish and worried about her all the time. She also worried about paying our bills. All of this worrying sometimes caused her to pass out. To help out, three of my older cousins, all women in their twenties, stayed at our house, and their kids stayed with us too.

In Pakistan, I was around my whole family, but I never felt connected to them. I was just a kid running around. I never experienced my mom's love, my sister's help, my brothers' teasing, or my dad's late night stories. I was all alone, by myself in my room. I barely saw my sister and my brothers. My best friends were my dolls. I never got to sit and talk about my day with my family. Mom would always be worried about Mehwish, but she would never really get troubled about me. She knew that she was near me. I'm not blaming Mom for that. It was the situation she was put in. I would be alone talking to myself most of the time. I felt so connected with my friends rather than my family. Sometimes I felt I was invisible at home. Sometimes I would go to a friend's house directly from school and would sleep over there because I felt loved while in their home, in the middle of a huge family.

When Dad was in the United States, he would send money to Mom and she would spend it on our studies. Even though we weren't army kids, I was able to attend a private army school because we paid double the tuition. Mom loved that school because it had a high standard of study and a good environment. I had made a lot of friends at my school, and I was the root of my friend group. They all would gather around me, give me gifts on special occasions. They would bring food from their home in their lunch boxes and share with me, even though some afternoons I would forget mine. Every morning these girls would line up near the principal's office waiting for me so they all could start the class. I had respect, friends, and happiness.

But there were two girls, Aiza and Nima, who were different from those others. They didn't join my group at first. They ignored me many times and would get so mad when I would get cheers from my girls. Then one day I was going home in a cab like I always did, and I saw them walking on the street talking to each other. It was very hot and sunny, and I could tell by the way they were walking that they were tired. As I was waiting in the car at a crosswalk, Nima sat on the side of the street and pulled out a lunch box and mango juice. They sat in middle of nowhere, free from every problem, and shared food with each other. Looking at them, their love for each other bloomed in my heart. It reminded me of Mehwish and my eyes got a little wet. I told the driver to stop near these girls. He said, "It's not safe and I can't stop in middle of nowhere. Your mom didn't give me permission to do that." It made me a little angry and I said, "I'm telling you to stop for my friends or otherwise I'll tell Mom you didn't come to pick me on time." The driver stopped near them, and as my window rolled down they turned around and looked at me. I said, "You want to come with me? I can drop you at your houses. It's hot here and it is dangerous to walk like this."

"No thanks," they said. "We can't take help from strangers. We don't even know you."

I said, "You can trust me."

Nima whispered in Aiza's ear and said, "We usually don't take rides from strangers, but you don't seem like you could be a threat to us." I opened the passenger door and let them in. Aiza sat in the middle next to me, and Nima sat next to her. The whole way we would look at each other and didn't have courage to start a conversation. As we were driving, the radio station FM94 was in the background, playing music from Pakistani movies. When the driver asked,

"Who should I drop first?" they both said, "Drop us at my house."

The driver parked the car in the parking lot. Nima opened the door and got her stuff like she knew what she was doing. Aiza giggled and said, "But we don't know your name." I said, "My name is Maria." Aiza said thanks and hugged me before leaving. Nima looked at her and also said thanks. By their accent, I could tell that they were Pashtun like me. I rolled the window up and the driver headed to my house.

This moment just melted me. I wanted to go to a friend's house like this, but every day was the same: come home, stay in my room, do homework, eat alone, and sleep. My family was so protective of me and where I went, so they put a lot of security around me. I would never walk alone outside of school or my house. I always had someone by my side, a bodyguard that Mom paid for with money that Dad had sent home. Not a lot of my friends had that kind of safety. Seeing my peers not having what I did made me feel upset. Kids were being kidnapped just because there was no one to speak up for them. I was the same as them, coming to the same school, but because of my social class, kids thought I was spoiled by my parents and arrogant. But it wasn't true.

I went home a little later than usual, so my family had already eaten. My cousins were talking with Mom and my cousin Samreen said, "Take a fresh bath and I'll bring your food upstairs." I said okay and went to my room. I took a bath, changed and waited for food. There was a knock on my door, and Samreen brought chicken biryani with salad and lassi, a yogurt drink. She spread a cloth on the floor and put the food on it. She left the room and I ate alone, thinking that Aiza and Nima had it better than me because they had someone to share their food with them.

I put the leftover food on the table so there was a possibility that someone would come take the dishes. I snuggled into my bed and drew the blinds so I could think straight. I slept for a while, then woke myself up because I had to do my homework. When I finished my work, I went to the balcony and leaned over it. I could see little tiny people down on the streets buying groceries and playing. Noises of little kids, people on bikes laughing and racing. It was all going in slow motion. They all looked so happy, and I wondered if they were happier than me. Did they have dreams that they wanted to accomplish like me? I didn't know if the future I had created for myself in my head would ever be real.

I stood there until the sun went down and made the world dark all over. I closed the curtains and went back to my room. I sat on my bed and looked out at the stars. Then I heard footsteps. Mom opened the door and chuckled, "Look who is still up. I haven't seen you all day." She kissed me on my forehead. "I'm just so distracted with everything. Your dad and your sister are not here. I have to take care of everything, including bills. The stuff that men do, I'm doing it. I don't ever get to give you or your brothers time. I'm sorry. You know I will always love you." And then she hugged me. "Okay, now go to bed, and let me look over your brothers." Mom left and closed the door. Those two or three minutes of Mom sitting with me made me feel so loved.

Every day, students from each grade would do the pledge on stage in front of the whole school, and I was usually the one to do it. All my friends were lining up and I went on stage. The bell rang and they closed the school gate, which meant whoever came in late got punished by having their hands hit with sticks. As I was doing the pledge, my eyes went to the line where the late students came in and I saw Aiza and Nima at the end of the line, worried and talking to each other.

After the pledge everyone went to their classes and I went to get a drink of water. As I was going, the principal called, "Maria, can you come here?" I was his favorite student. He said, "I have to attend an urgent meeting." He handed me the sticks, told me to hit the tardy students on the hands, and left. I didn't want to do it, but I had to. I started hitting them even though I didn't want to. I tried to hit all of them gently, and when I get to Aiza and Nima, they looked at me with such sad faces. They put their hands out and I had to hit them like I hit the others.

My heart was screaming inside, but I somehow held my anger in and put the sticks in the office and went to class. Aiza and Nima came in and I was trying to find a way to talk to them, but before I did, they both came to me and Aiza said, "Can you be our best friend?" Then Nima said, "She means, can you make space in your heart for us?" I was more than happy to do this and said, "First of all, I'm sorry that I had to hit you, but I didn't have any choice." Aiza said, "That's the thing I like about you. You treat everyone equally, and that's what brought us to you." We all chuckled and then I said, "I want us to be like sisters." Nima and Aiza said, "Of course!"

From that moment on, we became best friends. They would ride with me to school every morning, and ride back with me on my way home. We shared lunches with each other. We were such close friends that my other friends got a little uncomfortable when they were around me. They didn't like it because they didn't want me to have other best friends. So, eventually, I went to talk to them.

"I thought you were our friend. You're going to be with those two girls who were always mean to you?" they all said.

"My mom always says I come to school to learn something, make friends, and make her proud. Allah gave us big hearts. We can forgive and love everyone. I don't want anyone to fight over me. I want to be with all of you. You guys make my day, and if you divide yourselves from me, it will only hurt me more."

Nima and Aiza were drinking water nearby, so I called them over before saying, "Shake hands among each other to start new a beginning." They all did, and we were all cool. So we went into the cafeteria, and we all ate together. When the bell rang at the end of the day, we all hugged each other. They all said, "*Allah hafiz*" and left with their moms, dads, or guardians who picked them up.

Aiza, Nima, and I got in my driver's car and talked about what we would do after we got home. Nima said, "I'm going to a family reception for my newly married cousin and her husband, and Aiza is going with me."

"Why don't you go with us?" Aiza said. "It will be fun. We will eat, play, and probably get some money from the bride's family. Let's go to your house. I'll

ask your mom about it, and then we'll go to Nima's house to get ready."

When the driver dropped us off at my home, Nima and Aiza went to Mom, who was cutting up a salad for the family lunch. Nima said, "*Assalamu alaikum*, auntie. I am Maria's friend."

"*Walaikum assalam*, beta. How are you?" Mom said.

"Auntie, we are okay, and we are going to a wedding reception for my family, and as we don't have homework we were wondering if Maria could go with us," Aiza said.

Mom pushed her lips together, "Well, that's very sweet of you. Why don't you guys stay for lunch, and I'll pack her stuff."

So they stayed for lunch and my cousin went upstairs to pack an outfit that would be appropriate for a wedding. We ate a big feast together and I felt so happy. When we were about to leave, Mom came and hugged all of us. As we sat in the cab and went to Nima's home, I didn't even know what clothes my cousin had packed for me.

Nima's home was located in a neighborhood of narrow, bumpy dirt roads, with no trees or gardens. Some of the buildings were made of mud. When the cab stopped, Nima and Aiza started picking themselves up from their seats, which made me realize we had arrived. Nima's house was beautiful, even though it wasn't that big. Its bricks showed that the house was quite old. Its peeling colors were off-white, dark brown, and black in the corners. The main door was wooden and had flowers planted around it. The house had two bedrooms, one bathroom, and a basement. Aiza's mom was visiting Nima's mom, and Nima ran toward kitchen where they were and said, "Mom, I have new friend who will go with me to the reception." And Aiza went toward the other woman and said, "Mom, I ate really good food at Maria's house. Her mom is so nice, she makes really good food, and she takes care of us." Aiza and Nima introduced me to their moms. Nima's mom smiled and said, "Welcome to our dusty home. You might not be used to things like chickens running around or smoke throughout the home because of cooking food."

"No, no. I love your home," I said.

Nima's mom said, "Take her to your room and I will bring something for you to eat. Until then, change your clothes, and give Maria your clothes so she can feel relaxed. It's hot, and the electricity is gone for a while. Fans won't work."

We went in her room, which had three beds in it and was dark. Nima opened the curtains and there was one window, which Aiza opened. Nima's mom brought biryani and cold mango juice in plastic cups for us and put on the table and said, "Maria, if you need anything, let us know." I smiled and thanked her. Nima handed me her comfy clothes and we took turns taking baths and changing because there was only one bathroom. They let me go first. Even though things were different—dirt floors, thatched roof, only one small light dimly lighting each room —there was so much love in that house that I wanted to live like this.

Nima and Aiza said, "Let us see your outfit for tonight." I got the bag that my cousin packed and took out a purple tailor-made anarkali dress with purple leggings and a neck scarf. They said "Wow!

It's so beautiful! More beautiful than ours. You will look so cute in it.

I said, "Let me see what you guys are wearing." Nima got an off-white dress out of her closet and sky-blue dress for Aiza. They were very cute dresses, but they looked handmade. Nima said, "My mom made these for us." They said we should change, but before they got up I said, "I don't want to wear my outfit." It wouldn't feel right because mine was made by my tailor and looked perfect.

Nima's mom came in. She had changed her clothes too and asked if we needed anything. Nima said, "Mom, we might have to look for a dress for Maria. She doesn't want to wear the one she brought. Her mom said, "Wait. I started a dress for you guys for Eid and it's almost finished. I just have to make some final stitches. You two change, and I will go finish it really quick." And she left us with joy. Aiza and Nima said, "Yay! We will match today." And they went to another room and changed one by one. They did ponytails for each other and Aiza said, "We will prepare you, too. With my pocket money I have been buying plastic princess crowns." I smiled because I felt so good when I was around people who shared everything even when they had nothing.

Nima brought the dress and said, "Sorry it took so long." It was elegant because the love of her mom was so visible in it. I wanted to pause that moment. I felt like someone cared about me and had time for me. I didn't feel alone. I ran toward her and hugged her. It made me cry.

I grabbed the dress and changed. Nima said, "It feels like it was made for you." I loved it. Nima and Aiza helped me with my hair, and in a few minutes we were ready. We had so much fun that night, and I finally got outside of my box and got to know people from different families, with different ideas. It was such a nice time.

We got to know each other very well. On most days, the three of us would go to Nima's or Aiza's or my house. We would play games like *chindorai* (hopscotch) and Feet Together, walk all around our neighborhoods, do our homework together, and eat dinner together. We were inseparable. I was so happy to have such close friends.

It was a beautiful autumn afternoon. I heard children laughing and playing, the sound of swings, birds, trains, and cars. Mom and I decided to go to a nearby shopping mall to get school uniforms and school materials. Mom wanted my twin brothers to go with us so they could get fresh air and buy something for themselves, but she couldn't convince them. She allowed them to stay to play cricket. I told Mom that I wanted to play cricket with my brothers. My decision spoiled Mom's mood, but she didn't let me see it. I gave Mom a big hug and gave her my best smile.

My brothers, my cousins, and their friends on the other side of the house shouted, "Maria, come on!" I ran toward them and said, "I'm ready! Let's play!" My cousins whispered in my ear, "Maria, they are so good." I said that we were going to win, *inshallah*, because if I had told them the truth—that we couldn't win—they might have lost their hope and not played with courage, passion, heart, confidence, and love.

The game started when our team put wickets at the end of their pitch. They were doing so well, making at least four to six runs in every round. We got so tired picking up the ball and running. They got out with a score of 38 points total, so our team had to score 39 points to win. We got a five-minute break before we had to start batting. In the beginning, our players were not playing well, but they warmed up and we scored 28 points with one batter left. Guess who the last player was? It was me, the girl who knew nothing about the game and who was playing for the first time. I was so nervous, but my team cheered for me.

I was better at cricket than I thought. I hit the ball, ran to the wicket and back. I made some runs to tie the score, and needed one more run for my team to win. I walked toward the wickets uncomfortably, held the bat in my right hand, took my stance, and took a deep breath. I had that feeling that all eyes were on me, like every move I made was being watched. I held the bat more strongly and locked my eyes on the lime-green ball coming toward me. I hit the ball so high that it went on our roof.

I put the bat down and looked at all of them, waiting for them to say, "You wait here. We can get it," but there was only silence. I asked them who should get the ball. They all nodded and made themselves look lazy, whispering in each other's ears.

"What are you guys waiting for?" I asked.

"There are women on the other side of the house," they said, "so if we climb onto the roof they might not like it." That made sense. We were surrounded by a conservative culture that gives so much protection to women, and it is disrespectful when you climb on roofs and there are women on the other side; they might not be wearing their hijab, or they might be wearing pajamas or half-sleeved clothes. I told them I would go get it.

I went up to the wall on the outside of my house that I used to climb up to pick berries from the roof. On the roof, I walked over a little distance until I got to the place where we figured the ball had landed. It was fall. Yellow leaves were all over the ground. The view was so gorgeous and colorful from up there. It was hard to find the ball on the roof because of the leaves, and the wind was blowing my hair into my face. I turned around so the wind wouldn't bother me, and I saw the ball and went for it. The moment I picked it up, I called to them loudly. They all ran toward me. "Did you get the ball?" I smiled and threw it to them. They caught it and went back to playing.

I called to them, but they didn't hear me over the noise of the construction that was happening there: the pounding of a jackhammer, a loudly idling cement truck, a grinding concrete maker. The weather was getting a little rough and the sand from the roof got in my eyes. I was all alone on that side of the house. I was getting a little scared. I went from one roof to another, and then I had to decide to take the stairs or climb down the wall. I chose the short cut. I put my feet on the wall and started coming down by shuffling my feet and using my hands to help. I was wearing purple flip flops and my feet slipped. With shaking hands, I held on to the wall. My heart was pumping hard. Workers had just finished bricking this new wall, and it was kind of dry, but not completely. I fell down and so did the wall, right on top of me.

I was facing downward when I hit the ground. It felt like someone had broken my head with a hammer: it ached and was wet, and the cold wind on it hurt. My eyebrows crinkled up like a wave from the pain. My mouth was bleeding. My arms were under the rocks. My eyelids got heavy. My body wanted to rest, and I didn't have enough energy to hold my body up anymore. I went unconscious.

The others came back to look for me. When my brothers saw me unconscious on the ground, they yelled for our cousins. My brothers and cousins hurried and tried to wake me up. My cousins carried me on their backs to the hospital because it was close to our house and because the street near our house was so narrow that it would take too much time to take the car out of the garage, turn it around, and put me in it. People came out from their homes, and a small curious crowd was getting bigger behind us.

I was so injured. My head was bleeding, my whole body was covered in scratches and bruises, and my hair was covered in cement. The doctor checked me immediately, then said, "She has already lost a lot of blood, and now I have to stitch her head." The nurse switched me from one bed to another because the pillow and the bed sheet under my head were covered with blood. The doctor did his work and told the nurse to observe me in his absence. The doctor told my brothers and cousins that I had gotten twelve stitches, that I had to get a lot of rest, and that I would be okay after some time.

My brothers called Mom, who, I later found out, fainted from fear of losing me. That same day, one of our neighbors had fallen from their roof and died. Mom hurried to the hospital. I was weak and felt like someone was stopping me from breathing. I was covered with bandages on my arms, head, feet, and more.

Later, when they brought me to the house, my family cried and prayed all day and night. That day was so important for me because I think I got a second chance at life because of my family's prayers. I gained consciousness after eight hours. Everyone was sleeping around my bed. I felt so lucky to be with them. I was looking for water and when I moved the pillow and I found a plastic packet containing my hair that had been cut. Mom had left it there so I could see it because she knew how much it meant to me. I fell to pieces when I went to the mirror and saw my long, straight, hair had been cut: my head didn't have hair on the place where I got stitches. But my family didn't let me break apart.

No one ate anything, slept, or went anywhere. My whole body was so sore and pale and covered with scars and bandages. When I moved my hand, I felt someone holding it for a long time because it got a little sweaty and warm. I rolled my eyes to my left without moving my body, and it was Mom. Mom and my siblings were with me and supported me at that time. When my brother saw me looking at Mom, he came and hugged me and gave a tiny shout of happiness, and this made everyone wake up. They had tears in their eyes. I got so many hugs that I didn't know what to do and feel. Right at that moment they decided to give *sadka* (to give food and other things to poor people) as a way to thank God. All my relatives came and asked about my health. They fed me simple food like bread and warm soup to dip it in. I never felt alone for a minute.

Maria (left) with her mother and siblings in front of Faisal Mosque in Islamabad

After five days, I was sent to the hospital to get the stitches removed. The blood was dry, so Mom told me I should take a shower. When I put water on my head, a lot of blood flowed. I got scared. Mom helped me. My brothers and cousins came to me and apologized. I told them that it wasn't their fault. And I got a good lesson: my family would always support me. That autumn changed my life. I was like a dead leaf, but my family brought me back to life again.

Dad spent years of his life as a seaman. Traveling around the world and seeing new cultures and meeting a lot of people was a unique opportunity that not everybody gets. He started his journey from

Karachi, Pakistan, and from there he went to Dubai, then to Australia, and then to America. Those are the places where Dad stayed the longest and where he made a community and felt at home, but he saw almost the whole world and learned every culture. Dad asked what country Mom liked and she said the United States, so Dad went there. When he arrived in the U.S., he liked the freedom, people's behavior toward immigrants, the weather, the culture, and the beauty. After all his travels, our destiny was finally in the U.S.

One day Mom was talking to Dad, and he told her something, but we didn't hear it because the call was not on speaker. We thought an incident had happened because Mom had a mixed expression. When she finished talking with him, she called us into the living room and said that in a week we would be leaving for America. There was complete silence. We could even hear birds chirping. Suddenly we all laughed with excitement, but I could feel that Mom was a little upset. She went to her room and took out the family photo album, stopped at grandma's photo, and started crying because it was such a quick change. I brought a cup of water and gave it to her. She looked so emotional, and why wouldn't she be? She would be leaving her family behind. We all were so happy because we would finally get to see our dad, but sad because we had to leave all our cousins and our dear grandma. "No one knows if we'll meet again or not!" she said. My grandma was sick, and no daughter can leave her mom within a week. After I calmed her down, all of my cousins and my grandma surprised us by standing outside the door.

The week passed and everyone had their jobs like packing, shopping, cooking, and cleaning. The day before we left, Aiza and Nima both skipped the whole day of school just to celebrate some last moments with me. They bought me a lot of gifts and we had a really good time. We went all over parks with both of our families cooking barbecue chicken, steaks, biryani, kabab, and chapati.

We were at the airport when I hugged them one last time. They were crying and would not let me go. Would things be different when I came back to my homeland after some years? Would we even see each other again? Would our love and friendship survive? All over the airport, I saw other families crying, some with giant smiles on their faces, some families getting separated and others getting reunited. Some people just looked confused and lost.

Soon I was in a crowd full of people waiting for me to move forward in line. I looked at Aiza and Nima. Before I went through security, I told them that we would always be connected and that I would send them stuff from the U.S.: dolls, chocolates, gum, and more. They giggled and said they would send clothes from Pakistan, and we said goodbye. As my family passed through security, we all were crying and sobbing. Crowds of people blocked our way to my beloved giant family until we couldn't see them anymore.

We felt so nervous to start our whole new life, the life we had all been waiting for. The moment had arrived. I asked one of my brothers, "Can you imagine? We are going to see Dad! We are going to America, the place where everything is possible and where we can be away from all problems. We will live in tall buildings, sleep in big beds in our own rooms, which will be full of balloons and teddy bears. We will ride in cars and stay up late seeing stars from our window and making wishes. We will be able to play in snow and do a lot of shopping. I will wear jeans all the time. I'll go to school freely, work on my career. I cannot wait to get there."

My brother Hamad said, "Hmm. Seems like you have planned out everything, but who knows how it will end up when you get there? You might be happy and everything you imagine about America will be true, or it might not."

We didn't notice what was around us because we were lost in the thought of being in America with our dad. Mom got our documents ready, and we got on the airplane. Even though I am scared of heights, I sat in the window seat so I could see my country for one last time. Our plane took off and all I could see were clouds. We arrived in Louisville on March 7, 2014. We were coming to an entirely new world, and everything felt so different.

Mehwish and I wore the same clothes: blue shirts and blue jeans, black leggings, and similar hijabs. Mom looked so excited. All of our eyes were looking for someone special. Then Mom's eyes stopped in one direction. We all froze. Dad was wearing a black business suit with polished shoes, combed hair, and a great smile on his face. It was like we were all in a movie, and it felt like I was going in slow motion as I ran to hug Dad. Mom got tears in her eyes. Dad was so happy because he felt like he had solved a puzzle by bringing us here.

When we entered our new house, it was decorated with balloons and teddy bears, and food was prepared. When I closed the door, I didn't want to let that happy moment go. I took out my phone and took a picture of Dad for the first time. Our family was completed, and we started the life I had dreamed of since I was a kid.

In Pakistan, I spent almost all day with Aiza and Nima and not much time with my family. Now in the United States, I was far away from Aiza and Nima and was spending a lot of time with them. Mehwish, my parents, and my brothers were all in the same situation: we were out of place and felt a little lost in a new country. I got to know my sister Mehwish much better during this time. We had the same classes in school, and we talked with each other all the time. We really bonded and felt like sisters for the first time. Mom also gave me more attention than ever before and we started having long talks that made us closer.

When I first got to the U.S., I would talk over Skype with Aiza and Nima almost every day before school. But over time, we talked less frequently: once a week, then every couple of weeks, then once a month. Then Mehwish forgot the password for her phone, and we lost the ability to communicate on Skype for a while. When our family got an iPad, I couldn't remember the contact information for Aiza or Nima.

One morning I came into the kitchen late. My family was making toast and sitting on the couch drinking tea. The smell of cooking mixed with the cologne when my brother passed by me made me feel like I should've gotten up earlier. Walking barefoot on the carpet felt like a layer of soft grass under my feet. Mom was talking on the phone to my uncle and cousins in Pakistan, describing how everything was going in the U.S. and talking about how much she missed the traditional weddings, food, and their people. I had my head on her shoulder and she was playing with my hair as I scrolled through my pictures on my phone. Mehwish put the breakfast on the table for me. My morning was going more than perfectly.

I went to help Mehwish in the kitchen with lunch for the day and left my phone on the table. My brother came through the room, his cologne spreading as we walked, and he said, "Who's phone is that? Someone is calling." The number said PAKISTAN, and when I answered it, the person on the other end of the line did not introduce herself; she was just crying and I couldn't make out her words. I didn't know what was happening, so I hung up. After about five minutes, I called back because I was curious. This time, she identified herself: it was Aiza's mom. She started crying again. She asked about my family and life in the U.S. When I asked about her family, she said they were well. I asked if I could speak to Aiza, and she didn't say anything. I asked again, and she said, "I heard you. I just don't know how to tell you this." Then she told me that Aiza had died.

My heart shattered. I froze. I couldn't talk, couldn't move. My hands shook and I felt blurry. I started screaming. Mehwish and Mom came from the living room as the phone fell from my hand. Mom picked it up and got the news from Aiza's mom. I didn't know what was happening around me, couldn't feel the ground beneath my feet. I said, "When did that happen?" She said, "It's been four or five days. She got tuberculosis." I screamed so much that I passed out for a while. I just couldn't admit that she was not with me anymore.

Mom tried to comfort her and said that if she needed any help, we would always be there with her. After they hung up, we all were crying. Mehwish held me close to her chest, patting my shoulder and saying that everything would be okay. I knew nothing would be the same. I regretted that I hadn't talked to Aiza. I thought of the last time I had seen her, and I wished I was in Islamabad, but we didn't even have green cards yet and couldn't go back. I felt guilty.

I could see in Mom's eyes the fear of losing any of us. She said she would send some money for *zaqat* for the poor. I wished I could see Aiza again, give her the gifts she had asked for, hug her, tell her she would be okay, tell her that I would always remember her and could take her pain away. I would never, ever forget her. When I returned to Pakistan I would leave those gifts in the cemetery. I would be her voice, so passionate about education. I would be a daughter to Aiza's mom.

Although I lost my good friend, after a while I got more social in school, doing after school activities and making a lot of new friends. I started going to the Iroquois Library and Americana Community Center to participate in activities and met a lot of good people there. Mehwish and I became very close. I was getting good grades. My English was improving. I was adjusting well to life in the U.S. But still there were tough moments.

About two years after arriving in the U.S., there was a time when I felt nervous, confused, and like I just didn't belong. It was at the airport on a school trip to the Holocaust Museum in Washington, D.C. I was wearing a yellow summer shirt with jeans and a hijab. All around me people were gathering their luggage. My teacher told me, Mehwish, and one other student who was Muslim to not to say "Allah" anywhere in the airport. We got our tickets, then one of the security guards stared at Mehwish and me with suspicion and doubt. He asked for our IDs and passports, and two more security guards, both women, came from far off and stopped us in the middle of other people. They took us into a small white room.

They told us to sit down. They told us they were given permission to search us because we were wearing hijabs, and they touched the outside of our hijabs. Then they even made us take our hijabs off. Then they touched our hair, telling us that they had to make sure that we weren't hiding anything there. I felt so disappointed. After this, they asked to see our documents. They held my passport and green card. Both listed "Maria" as my last name, but one of them listed my first name as "FNU" and the other listed it as "No Given Name." They spoke into a walkie-talkie to call in someone else to look at the documents, and that person typed some things into an iPad. Then that person called another person, and they kept calling more people. One person made calls to the Social Security office to make sure that our social security numbers were real. I got more and more uncomfortable. They kept us for an hour. All of my friends and my teacher were waiting for us. I felt like we shouldn't be there, but I also knew they were following orders from above. I felt so depressed because of the way we were treated differently from the others. They judged us because of what we were wearing, and what we believed in.

When we moved to America together, I got my family back, something I had always wanted. I got my sister back. Without her, I had felt incomplete. I had my brothers, who laughed at my silly jokes, and my dad, who I had always wanted to be with when our family was feeling rough. I had my mom, who gave me so much love. Unlike in Islamabad, I got to listen to her childhood stories, and we did lunches and dinners together.

Mom made a lot of sacrifices for us. In Pakistan, she borrowed money from people for our tuition, and worked in people's houses to make money for our uniforms, lunch boxes, bags, pencils, and books. She is my mentor and my best friend from whom I can't hide any secrets. I love her more than anything in my life. Not everyone in Pakistan sends their girls to school, but she sent me to school because she loves me and did not want to take any rights from me just because I am a girl.

I was in the kitchen with her once when she had cooked biryani, but I didn't want rice so I told Mom to teach me how to cook chicken handi with chapati. It was just one of those days when I was really craving handi. She told me to do all the chopping for the recipe: onions, tomatoes, cilantro, chilies, etc. I sat on a chair, put all the vegetables in a deep bowl, and started cutting, and she started cooking the recipe by adding them in a cooking pot. She asked me, "Beta, can you check if the teapot has tea? If it does, can you bring it to me? I feel a little headache." I brought her some tea and biscuits on a plate and served it.

I wanted to know how Mom managed to live in a society where life gives more opportunities to men than women. I asked Mom about why she let other people get in the way of her dreams.

She took a deep breath and said, "Honey, what do you know about life and people around you? You think we got to make decisions like you guys do? People are not nice. They can tear you apart with their talking." It was so quiet around us. There is an idiom in my language that says, *da khamoshi da deer loii tofan rawasto ishara kai, chi kum zan sara bah her seh yosii*: when everything is quiet, it is the sign of storms to come. The sun's rays were coming from the crack of the window and Mom dipped a biscuit in her tea for so long that it broke off into the cup. She was lost somewhere in deep thought.

"Why do you always try to avoid whenever I ask you what's wrong?" I said.

She held my hand said, "I know. I'll spit it out." And then gave me a hug. "There are some parts of my life that I can't forget, even if I wanted to, and I don't have the courage to talk to anyone about it because it hurts. And even if I did tell someone, nothing is going to change. In my child-hood, I didn't ask for princess dresses or toys on my birthday. I just wanted a normal life like you guys have. I wanted to be a girl who woke up every morning with an alarm and got excited to go to school and learn something. I didn't need a cute dress to wear; I would sew it for myself, because I knew how to. I didn't need money for transpor-

tation; I would walk from home to school. All I needed was support."

"Your grandmother was living in a society where they did what everybody else did. They didn't question their thinking: women should be at home doing housework. On the other hand, men could do anything. They could stay out late, go anywhere they want, and go to school if they wanted. No forcing them to stay home. No telling them what to wear, what not to do. Men live their lives without questioning, and if you ask a man why, they will blame beliefs, culture, traditions, religion, and customs that say that women are meant to stay at home and do housework for men. But they will do anything to keep it continuing." Tears were making their way from her eyes. "I had a dream about being something one day so I could help my family with money. If I was educated, I would not have to put pressure on you or your siblings to take me places or explain things for me. But I live with it every day. I wish there was a way to fix it, but there is nothing I can do."

My mom grew up poor in a village in Pakistan where everything is very conservative. Both of my uncles were sent to school to get an education, but my mom was not. Instead, she started sewing clothes. People would come to her with clothes to sew for weddings or for their homes, and she would stay up all night working. All around the village, people started coming because her sewing was very clean and not expensive.

Her work gave her hope again, and she started buying school supplies and books with that money. She went to school with her friends sneakily. She went to the classroom, saw people learning, thinking differently, and that made her so happy.

When she came home from school, her brother had ruined her happiness by snitching on her. Her mother was so shaken. She thought she was going to lose my mom. Because if people found out, they would talk behind her and my grandmother's backs. My mom felt like someone had taken the ground from under her feet. She was so scared about what would happen next.

My grandparents took her to a room they called "the Conversation Room" where they would go to discuss crops, make decisions, or discuss something serious that they wanted to keep secret. The room was huge, and quiet, and dark. As they were talking in the room, their voices got louder and louder, then my mom slammed the door open and came out from the room. My auntie went to her and asked her what happened. She didn't answer. She started biting her tiny nails and didn't even look at my auntie. My grandparents came from the room with mysterious stress and worried feelings and said that, after today, my mom would never go to school again because they lived in a society where girls didn't go to school, but stayed in the home and married and started a family.

My mom angrily threw her bag in a tub full of water near her and didn't say a word. She spent all day in her room crying, laying on the cold marble floor not eating anything. The next morning she got up before anyone else. She went to my uncles and asked them why she couldn't get an education. It wasn't her fault that she was a girl. She asked, "What is the future of girls in the village? Arranged marriages and starting a family are not enough. Boys can go anywhere and get as much education as they want." My uncle felt sad, but explained to my mom, "We can't go against our society. If today you go to school, other girls will look at you and go to school. Then the village elders will blame us. So leave everything the way it is. We will give you all of our love but can't give you permission to do that."

My mom felt disappointed and sat on the porch. She thought, *What if because of me something happens to my family?* She couldn't tolerate it, so she called everyone in the house and said, "If I try to become who I want, you all will leave me. So I will stay at home and do housework. No more dreams of school, of being something different."

Like Mom, I started wanting to do something different from what my culture expected when I was a young woman. I started wanting to take off my hijab. I really respected my religion, and I didn't want to weaken my beliefs. But I didn't want to live according to the stereotypes of Middle Eastern countries: that if you are a girl, you should be limited, you should be quiet even when you feel that something is wrong, that you should not stand up for yourself and for other Muslims, that you should wear the hijab even though in reality it's not required by Islam.

I didn't miss anything about Pakistan, except myself. I missed who I was there. I'd had the freedom to be myself, to do everything except get a good education. In America, I could get a good education, but I didn't have the freedom of doing anything else. In Pakistan, no one had cared if I wore a hijab. It wasn't a priority because I was living in a liberal environment in Islamabad. But in the U.S., Mom made me wear a hijab because she was scared that my family in Pakistan would think that I was getting away from my culture, becoming more American.

One day I was going to University of Louisville's campus with Mehwish for a campus tour. I thought, *Now it is my time to take off my hijab, to do what I like maybe just for a while*, because all my life I had been doing what other people, tradition, and culture wanted me to do. I sat in the passenger seat thinking about how it would impact my image in society and my friends' hearts for me. Would changing my appearance make me a bad person? I did not want to tell Mehwish. We would get in a big argument and we were on the highway, and a distraction would not have been good for us. So I waited for us to get to campus.

As we entered the university, my heart pumped faster and faster. As I looked at the students from the car window, I felt like I was one of them, but maybe I wasn't completely. Mehwish parked the car and we got out. I held my breath, moved my hand toward my head, and took my hijab and underscarf off, letting the wind blow through my hair. In that moment I felt like I had never felt before. The small happiness I dreamed of was finally coming true, little by little. I felt so freed and so like myself when I took it off, like I was in control of time, of the universe.

But when Mehwish turned around and saw me, she was so shocked that she looked at me like I was a different person. "Why do you do this? How could you make this decision alone? Do you know what will happen if Mom or Dad finds out about this? They will kick you out of the house, or stop talking to you, and if I take your side, they will kick me out of the house too!"

"Please, Mehwish," I said. "You know how I am, so help me cover this up. I will make Mom and Dad happy, just please let me enjoy myself and do what I want. I've never had much love since I was born. I am not blaming you. I can live with it, and I love all of you so much, but doing what I like is loving myself. It at least gives me reason to be happy for myself."

She nodded but was not that happy with it. "No matter what you do, I will always be with you. Just don't make childish choices. If you take your hijab off, there is no difference between you and an American."

We went through all the doors and came to the orientation. I ran my hand in my hair, and I felt happy and free. It was like breaking the chains of our culture. I was forming into the shape of the Maria I had known four years ago. It had taken long enough to come out of the darkest cave into the light.

Since I was young, I had always spoken up for myself, and I could never let people's beliefs and traditions control my actions, so I made an appointment for a haircut. It was such a hard decision and I was so scared because I knew that Mom had told Mehwish that if she did anything like that she wouldn't have space for her in her heart because it's not good and people would talk badly about us. I knew Mom wouldn't calm down easily, but I also knew she loved me more than anything. On one side was what I liked and would bring me happiness, and on the other side I was burdened with all those cultural and traditional views of my people.

The next day, I couldn't keep it inside anymore. Mehwish gave me a look and said, "Spit it out." I told her I made a salon appointment at 4:00 and asked her to drop me at the salon after school. She turned around. "You made it anyway? I told you yesterday to forget about whatever is happening in your mind."

"Mishi, I don't know what to do. I already made the appointment, so will you go with me or should I go on the bus?"

She said, "Are you kidding me? You never ride a bus. Quit making me feel guilty. Fine, I'll take you." I hugged her because I knew it was so hard for Mehwish to handle5 two sides, and she loved both of us. She smiled and said, "Let's leave at 3:30. And don't worry, I'll try to get everything smooth and good."

I was really nervous when we arrived at the salon. I took a deep breath and put a fake smile on my face and stepped inside holding Mehwish's hand. The place had a lot of accessories for different hair textures and lengths: combs, shampoos, colors, hair sprays, blow dryers, scissors, straighteners, brushes, bowls.

Mehwish asked the guy how long it was going to take and he said two to three hours because of how long my hair was and because they would be dyeing it. Mehwish made a disappointed face because earlier Mom had called and we had told her that we had stayed after school and then would be dropping off my friends, but that wouldn't take so long. Mehwish was worried about what we were going to say if Mom called again. For me she had to lie over and over again, and I didn't like that.

As we talked to the guy at the salon, I uncovered my hair, which came down to my knees. I had been growing it since childhood. Mom had trimmed my hair but never cut it since I was fourteen. I had the longest hair in my family when I left Pakistan. Having long hair as a kid and the longest hair in my whole family meant a lot to Mom. She didn't want me to cut my hair because she wanted to feel the pleasure of someone giving me compliments.

Within seconds, the length of my hair was separated from me. I didn't know if I should be happy to finally get what I wanted, or sad because this was the first time in my life I had done something so big without my beautiful Mom. I hadn't wanted to take that away from her, but if I had brought her with me she would have been stressed out, and her health was not that good those days. She already worried that our family was breaking apart, that we were not giving each other as much time as we needed to, and because of that had fainted so many times that the doctor told us strictly not to give her any stress. These thoughts were a bundle of circuits exploding in my head, and the smell of the dye was just making it worse.

When he massaged mint shampoo into my hair, it made me feel much better. I closed my eyes and thought about positive vibes. When I woke up after a while, I looked like a completely different person: I was blonde. I asked him to make it a little darker and he said it would take a little more time to let the hair get the new color, then wash and blow dry it. My bangs had to be cut and layered, then he washed it again then started making small curls and when I looked in the mirror, it gave me a whole new style.

Outside it was getting darker. The guy took pictures of me before and after for his profile, and then Mehwish—my selfie queen sister—took dozens of pictures of me in different poses. Mehwish paid for me, which made me so emotional and expanded the space for my sister in my heart.

When we arrived home, Mehwish told me to go straight to my room so I didn't get stuck answering questions. "I will handle it. Keep your scarf on your head until you go to sleep," she said. We entered the house and everybody was watching a Pakistani TV show.

"*Asalam-o-alaikum,* Mom. *Asalam-o-alaikum,* Dad," we said.

"*Walaikum assalam,*" they answered. Mom looked away from the TV and said, "You guys are late, I thought the schools didn't let students stay later than 7:00?"

Mehwish winked at me. "Everyone stayed today because we are far behind on our schedule so we had to do some work," she said.

"Oh, okay. I was just worried. Did they give you any food? I cooked biryani, chapati, and chicken karai. I will put dinner out for you both, but first go to your room and change into your pajamas."

Before Mehwish headed to her room, Mom asked, "Is Maria okay? She just went straight to room without saying anything or complaining about food."

"She's okay, just feeling tired," Mehwish replied.

"Okay. I was just wondering if maybe she was mad at me. Let me set dinner for you both."

Mehwish came into the room and closed the door. She saw me crying. "I feel so guilty," I said. "I can't keep it in anymore. I'm telling Mom."

I rushed to go outside, but she held me back and said, "If I were you, I would not tell her now. She's in such a good mood. Don't ruin it. Just let her live that moment." I hugged Mehwish as she patted me on my shoulder. "It's okay, we will get through it together," she said.

I locked the door and took my scarf off and looked closely at myself in mirror. I loved this image of me. I was a different person now, and I could make my own decisions. I wondered if people were going to see me as I was before.

The next morning, in the car, I looked all around just to make sure no family members were around, and then I moved my hand to my head and removed my hijab. I fixed my hair in the car mirror, putting it in a side hairstyle. The whole way, Mehwish didn't talk to me. I looked out the window and watched until finally we arrived at my friend's house. When she got inside the car with us, she said, "OMG, Maria, why aren't you covering your hair?" I turned myself around in the passenger seat, looked her in the eye and said, "I like myself like this. It's always been my choice to wear a hijab or not."

When I got out of the car at school the wind was blowing my hair and I turned around to see all my friends and teachers in shock. I felt like time had frozen. I waved my hand at all of them. They all smiled, and I could hear my Muslim friends murmuring behind me. "You look so different. Not saying you look bad, but when you have the hijab on you were so recognizable, you were like one of us. Why did you take it off? It's *haram*—it's a sin when any man sees you."

It pissed me off. I looked at one of the girl's saying these things and told her, "Oh yeah? If that is true, then why is it that I can see your side bangs? Every male can see it too. That isn't *haram*? Me not wearing a hijab is none of your concern. I didn't wear it in

Pakistan because I didn't want to, and after coming here, I took it off by my choice. I can wear hijab any day and any time I want to. Maybe tomorrow I will, who knows? But it's my choice alone, and I especially won't take advice from a person who's doing the same thing as me in this case. Even if your bangs are short, it's the same as my hair."

But most of my friends gave me positive compliments. "You just changed your style. You are still the same Maria, our friend, and we would be fools if we judged our friend for what she wanted. You do look cute both ways, with or without a hijab." They told me that I can do whatever I like, and they gave me hugs.

When we arrived home, Mom was making food for us and Dad was helping her for the first time in a long time. We stepped inside, and our mother welcomed us. She said, "You guys came just in time. How is everything going?" We giggled and gave a big hug to both of them.

I felt so bad because I had never lied to Mom about anything, even small things. I hope even my worst enemy never feels the pain I was feeling, because lying to your loved ones is so hard. I had no idea how she'd react after learning about my haircut, or that I'd been lying to her about it for days, but I couldn't keep anyone in the dark anymore. Telling the truth is hard, but the more I hid it, the harder it would get for me to discuss. I decided to tell her.

I asked Mom if we could go for a walk. I wanted her to be alone when I talked to her. We went for a walk and were talking, and then I finally said, "I want to tell you something, but first, tell me you won't get mad."

She said, "I won't."

I said, "I really wanted to get a haircut. I got tired of my long hair and wanted to try something different, so on Friday I cut my hair. I also dyed it, and while I know you will love it, I also know you told me not to because you like long hair. But I will grow it out again. I found happiness in it, and I loved it. I made an appointment for that day and went when you were at work."

I was about to continue, but she slapped me.

"You didn't even ask me before making this decision? You hid it from me? Yes, I am mad! You broke my heart, not because you got a haircut, but because you kept it hidden. How did you get there, and who took you?"

I thought if I said Mishi directly, she would get mad at her as well, so I said, "Mom, I went with some of my friends. They were going there, so I went with them in their car."

Because it was dark, Dad sent Mehwish to keep us company. Mom started yelling and crying, so we decided to take her home. As I held out my hand for hers, she pushed me back and went with Mehwish.

I wiped my tears with the long side of my scarf and I went inside the house. I heard the sounds of Mom sobbing and Mehwish defending herself. Mom said, "She doesn't appreciate what I have done for her! She always does what she likes. Why did she do this to me? She hurt my heart so bad." She had been crying, and her light skin was getting as red as ketchup. Her eyelashes were wet like a field of long grass after a rain, and her eyes were red and full of rage. It felt like she was crying for everything that upset her: not going back to Pakistan to see her mom, not getting educated, having no family here.

Maria with her parents at the Festival of Faiths

I wanted to go to Mom and try to explain or give her a hug, but her shaking body made me nervous. Everyone was so depressed. Mehwish pulled me to her side and whispered, "Go to your room before everything gets worse with your presence." I went to my room and closed the door and started crying. I waited a while and was staring blankly at the door when the sound of footsteps awoke my mind. The door opened, and Mehwish said Mom was feeling a little better now, and that it would be good if I stayed away from this until things cooled down. Thinking back on it now, I wished I had taken things more carefully and tried a different way of telling my secret. Mom's health got worse because I chose to be something other than my family wanted.

Weeks turned into months and things were tense at home. Every day I would cover my hair when I left home, trying to make things a little better. I tried to be a good daughter, sister, and friend. I did what they wanted me to do in front of them but still took off my hijab on my time. My life was like a movie in which I was changing roles every day: in the morning I was the Maria my family wanted, and the moment I was in the distance, I became the Maria I wanted to be. I hoped they wouldn't ever overlap; otherwise, things could get bad.

Mehwish and I talked with Mom one day. We told her that the Festival of Faiths was coming up. We explained that it was a ceremony where people from all over the place came to observe, learn, and show love by respecting all cultures, traditions, and beliefs. It would be a big day for us because we would share our stories on stage in front of people and celebrate the sacrifices she and Dad had made for us. We told her that all families would be coming and that we would really love if our family would sit and cheer for us. She said, "Of course. I've been sad lately, but that doesn't mean I stopped caring about my kids. I am not sure about Dad—he is not an easy person to convince—but I will make it happen." She smiled, and her eyes shone.

I had been practicing my speech for a week. Every night I would stand in front of the mirror to practice my speech with my hair open so I could feel perfect in front of a lot of people. But my family would be there, too, so I knew there was no way I would be able to leave my hair open.

The day came and everyone was happy. That night, when I was going with them, I wore the hijab, but not completely covered. I had my bangs out and a high ponytail. I decided to compromise because I wanted my family to have good time, and I didn't want any other drama. Our speeches went really well —so well that we got a standing ovation from the audience. It felt incredible. Mom and Dad were so proud of Mehwish and me. They had tears in their eyes seeing where we are now compared to where we were in past. We hugged them, took family pictures, and got a lot of compliments from my family, friends, teachers, and a lot of people in the audience who I didn't know.

As we all were walking home, Mom said, "You didn't wear the hijab how you used to in school." It shook me, and I didn't want to end the night with sadness, so I told her, "Mom, I tried to do it like that, but it didn't go with my outfit and my style." Mom said, "Well, you look cute either way," and gave me a kiss on my cheek. So things were better than before.

After that night, Dad was close to us again, just like before, going shopping, eating meals with us, and talking together after so long. It made Mom so happy because she always wanted us to be together and love each other. We were all getting more connected and I really hoped that she wouldn't find out I wasn't wearing a hijab to school. I realized that the more I talked about my hair and the hijab in front of Mom and Dad, the more it would cause problems in their relationship and ours. I had my family back after so long, and I couldn't take any chances of ruining it.

My graduation was a very big day for me and for my family. Mom was the most excited one. She ran around getting out dresses, matching sandals, flowers, and gifts for us. She called my cousins and uncles in Pakistan to let them know it was our graduation. I hadn't seen her that happy for anything. We started the morning with so many hugs, so much love and

happiness—everything was perfect.

I wanted to talk to Mom about not wearing a hijab, but I was scared because I didn't want to ruin our graduation and her celebration. I had been helping her all day, waiting for the right moment to talk to her. Mom was in her room smiling at our picture from freshman year. "You guys came so far. I cannot believe those years have passed so quickly," she said.

I sat near her, playing with her hair, and said, "Mom, what are you going to give me today?"

"It's a surprise, but you can ask me anything you want," she said.

"A lot of things can fall under the *anything* category."

"You can ask anything of me that I can provide you with," she said.

"I want something from you, but I'm not sure you can give it to me," I told her. "It would be my best gift ever."

"That's vague. Tell me what you want," she said.

"I will tell you, Mom, but if you cannot give it to me, I will still be okay with it."

"Now you're scaring me. Ask me what you want. I will try my hardest to give it to you."

I took a deep breath and said, "You know I have been waiting for this day for four years. I have been seeing people doing all kinds of stuff with their hair, and the graduation cap looks so good with open hair. Today is my graduation, and I would be really happy if you would let me take my hijab off, just for today. That's the present I want from you. Nothing else."

Mom looked around, not sure what to say. Then she looked back at that freshman picture of me and said, "You know, I never thought you would ask this for your present, but it is your day today, and you deserve so much more than that. I wish I could do more for you. Yes, you can for today, but please, when you leave the house, cover your hair—you know your dad."

I hugged her tightly. I could not believe what I'd heard. I told her that it was a perfect gift from my perfect mom. I ran toward the living room and asked Mehwish, "What style should I do for my hair?"

Mehwish whispered, "Please don't do it today. Mom is going with us!"

"I know. I am leaving my hair out with Mom's permission." She looked confused and said it was no time to joke. I told her I was for real and to go ask Mom.

Mehwish went to the room and asked. Mom said, "It is a big day for her, let her enjoy," then looked at me and said, "Curl your hair. It will look so cute, just like a Barbie doll."

I was so happy. When we were about to leave, Mom handed me the hijab and said, "Wear it until we get to the car." I wore it, and Dad tapped me and Mehwish on shoulder and said, "Your mom can cheer enough for the both of us. Always keep going forward," and he hugged us.

We went to Iroquois Amphitheater, where we took pictures wearing our medals, award pins, and sashes. I walked proudly with my hair open on my big day, celebrating the way I had dreamed of. After I got my diploma, Mom handed me flowers, kissed me on my cheeks, and hugged me, and I cried from happiness. She said, "I am so proud to be your mother. My sacrifices weren't pointless."

I felt the love I had always wanted in Pakistan.

As a child, I played a lot in the river. When I got tired and my body got sore, all I wanted to do was rest along the water. I would put my feet half in the water, half out on the soft sand that stuck to my body. I also loved making small, cute sand houses by the river. I would get some sand in my hand and start working on how it would look. First, I would give it the shape of a house, then I created more of it, then I decorated it with small, multi-colored rocks from the shore. When we were leaving, big swells of water would come in. I would try to block them, putting myself in front of the house I created, but the water was rough. The next moment, I would look back, and the house wasn't there.

As I was growing up, I built my home in Pakistan on good memories. The pillars were the friendships, the bricks were cherished moments that time forgot, the cement was my family, and the roof was the hope that I held onto. The lights seemed dim because deep down I still felt like I was missing something. I wanted to have closer relationships with my family and fewer restrictions on my career goals. Once I came to the U.S., I started to see things in new ways and I built a better home that was stronger. One of the changes in my home was that it was decorated with culture and traditions inherited from my family. Every time I step inside, the lights seem brighter because my family is by my side, and the clouds of desolation above my roof are disappearing. This time there is nothing that can wash away my home.

Now the Gloves Are Off

REENA PARACHA

Interviewing Reena Paracha was an amazing experience. Before interviewing her, I only knew a little about her: I knew that she is an activist, and that she is from Pakistan. We come from the same country but very different backgrounds. She is such a courageous woman and speaks out if she does not agree with something. Even though I've decided not to wear the hijab, I respect how she recently started wearing the hijab. She is so inspiring—a successful, independent Muslim woman who speaks for justice with confidence and power.

—MARIA

My story is different than a lot of people who are coming over here as immigrants or refugees. I grew up incredibly privileged. My family is considered one of the more wealthy families in Pakistan. I grew up in a household where political repression was not tolerated and girls' education was important. I came here because I married an American.

In 2001, we were living in Hershey, Pennsylvania, where my husband had a one year fellowship for interventional cardiology. When 9/11 happened, my husband was attending a training in Chicago. He called me up from his hotel that morning and said, "Turn the TV on." I was like, "What do you mean?" And he said, "Turn the TV on." So I went and turned the TV on and I saw the buildings come down, and my heart sank and I immediately heard, "Islamic terrorists." My immediate reaction was, *How could they know this so fast? How is that even possible?* Any intelligent person would question that.

My husband said, "Go and do the groceries with the kids as much as you can, because we don't know what's going to happen." When I was walking towards my car, the woman who worked in the office for the condos where we were staying came out and looked at me and yelled, "Crawl back under the rock that you came out of!" I was pregnant, I had two children, I had my car keys and a diaper bag on me. I didn't know if she was going to throw something at me. I didn't know if she was going to do something to me. I was so fearful that I froze. Then I got into my car and locked the door and started crying. I was just, like, *Why am I being attacked for what happened?* At that time, I didn't wear the hijab, but everybody in our complex knew that we were Muslim because we observed Ramadan, we prayed, and my kids had very distinct Muslim names. The kids and I used to go to the pool, and sometimes I had a religious book in my hand while the kids were swimming.

But we had a young man who lived right next door to us, a gay man. He knocked on my door and said, "I can do any grocery shopping that you want." That was big. He realized that there was going to be backlash because gay people had endured backlash for so many years that he just automatically knew that I was going to need help. For the three days it took my husband to come back home, this neighbor was the person that I thought, *at least he's right next door to me, and he knows I exist and will know if something happens.*

The second person who was really spectacular for me was a nurse who worked with my husband. She immediately called me up and said, "I can come stay with you," because she realized what was happening nationwide. She ended up doing all the groceries for me. I stayed indoors for three days.

When my husband's friend saw the planes crashing, he immediately thought that something big was about to happen. So he ran and got a rental car, because he knew that there was no way that a flight was going to take off. He and my husband and two others drove from Chicago all the way to Hershey, Pennsylvania, which took a long time. They were stopped a lot of times; there was a lot of security on the highways, there were four brown people in the car, so you can imagine. "Why are you going? Where are you going? Where are you coming from? Are you sure you're a doctor?"—they had to answer to all that stuff.

Pre-9/11 I was even more of a different human being than I was post-9/11. Pre-9/11, Reena Paracha did not understand what was happening to the black people. Reena Paracha was buying into the narrative that had been pedaled for years and years about the

black people, in certain respects. Not vocally, but in the back of my mind, unconsciously saying perhaps there's some truth to it. Post-9/11, when stuff started happening to *us*, is when we realized we were *not* a post-racial society, that what had been happening to black people was now going to happen to us. That's what opened our eyes to the struggle of the black person. Still, our eyes are not open: there is still racism within the Muslim community against black people. Going back home, I see the Shia-Sunni split. That has always bothered me. I don't believe in minorities being subjugated. I've always spoken up against that. I've always seen my family speak up against it. I think what I'm doing now is literally an extension of what I was doing back home.

A lot of times I've been asked, "Why do you wear the hijab? Is that not repressive?" What most people don't understand is that I *chose* to wear the hijab. That's not an oppression, it's actually exercising my right to do what I want to do. I am the only person in my family who wears the hijab. I've never been told not to do something. My father's only concern was the backlash I would get here. He was afraid for me. He was afraid of the rise of Islamophobia, what the perception of me covering myself would be. It shocked a lot of our friends when I started to cover myself. One of the people I know point blank said to me, "You are doing this in retaliation," which was offensive to me. Retaliation to what? Her thing was that it was a retaliation to the Trump election. Well, I was covering myself *before* the Trump election. Did I lose a lot of friends when I started to cover my head? Yes, I lost *all* of my friends when I started covering my head. I think they were uncomfortable around me. I think they couldn't figure out what was happening to me, and instead of asking me a question they chose to make a judgment about me. I would say ninety percent of the people we socialized with voted for Trump, despite the fact that they knew us, and knew how it was affecting our children and how it was affecting our lives and day-to-day interactions, just going to the grocery store or filling up our gas or walking into a mall. And they still chose to vote Trump. Now they are, in certain respects, hiding their affiliations, but at that moment, they were openly supporting him.

All my friends that I socialize with now are newer friends. I have been covering my head regularly for two years now. I'm not saying that I'm not making a political statement. I am also making a political statement. I am sending this message out that a strong Muslim brown woman can choose to cover or uncover herself and does not need permission from anyone around her to do that.

My son was driving at that time of the 2016 election, but he couldn't vote yet. One of his very good friends was old enough to vote and was excited to vote, and my son drove him to the polling station. The kid goes in—he was wearing a sweatshirt—goes in, votes, comes out, takes the sweatshirt off. Underneath it said "Trump 2016" on it. It shook my son to his core. He couldn't believe that this was his friend, this 18-year-old kid that has known him since first grade.

We live in Trump country. Oldham County is very Trump. Even when they had done mock elections in school, I would say 90 percent of the student body voted Trump. There's also this feeling in Oldham County schools, that if you're a Democrat, you'd better keep your mouth shut, because you are going to be attacked for your beliefs. The day after the election, one of the teachers brought a few bags of candy. My daughter was a freshman that year. She asked the class, "Who supported Trump?" A teacher is not supposed to ask a class how they vote. It was not like a social studies class, anyway—it was health or something. The vast majority of the class said, "I supported Trump," and she said, "Here is a bag of candy for you." She said, "Oh, and you guys who supported Hillary, don't fret: I have something for you. Here's a bag of Dum Dums for you." Essentially, she was saying to them, "You're dumb and that's why you supported Hillary." All she essentially got was a slap on the hand for that. Nothing else happened to her. She's still at that school, still teaching.

One of the saddest days of my life was the day after the election. My husband, who is fifty years old, cried. He cried because he had lost faith in his country. That's not just his reality. That's a reality of a lot of people that are born and raised here and don't know any other country but this, like the DACA recipients. My husband contributes to this country on a daily basis. My father-in-law, my sister-in-law—they're all physicians. My father-in-law served in an underserved area for forty-seven years. When no physician wanted to go, it was Pakistani and Muslim physicians who were going and treating patients. For them, a Trump victory is a victory of bigotry and hate and exclusiveness and xenophobia and Islamophobia and transphobia and homophobia and all of those things.

Muslims were exhausted, because we were served on a platter during this election. Trump was calling us terrorists, and Hillary was not correcting him. At 5:00 a.m. when I woke up for the morning prayer, and I looked at my phone, I had *literally hundreds* of messages from young Muslim kids: "What are we going to do now?" There was this frenzy of, "We're going to get killed." That sort of debilitating fear is very hard to reconcile with or explain away. When I did start to return phone calls, my response to them was, "You are entitled to your grief, you are entitled to your feelings, you're entitled to your helplessness," because they needed to embrace all of those feelings and then come out of them and say, "We have work to do." They had to mourn.

Activism has to be inclusive. It cannot be, "I am an activist for Muslim rights only." If I'm going to claim to be an activist, then I have to be an activist for every single person's rights. In the past I was a lot more careful about what I used to say and how I used to say it, and now I feel like the gloves are off and that there is no easy way to call discrimination and bigotry out. Somebody's feelings are always going to get hurt and I have to stop worrying about people's feelings getting hurt when I'm calling out their discrimination or their bigotry or their hatred. I'm more vocal now, and I'm more in the forefront now, and I'm not afraid to take on a white supremacist, and I'm not afraid to go to a rally to oppose white supremacy. I'm not afraid to call a politician out in Frankfort and testify against the police and police brutality.

All three of the branches of government need incredible reform, and I truly, truly, truly believe that the reform is going to come from black and brown bodies, and I don't think it's going to come from within the establishment. One of my favorite things to say is, trust black women, follow black women. They know what they're talking about. They've lived it. They've died for it. They're getting killed for it. They're burying their children for it. They're burying their husbands for it.

What I would like to say to young people is: this is your time. Be the voice of the voiceless. Be unapologetically Muslim. Don't ever allow anybody to say that your faith is less than somebody else's, or that your hijab is up for questions. Your faith and your hijab and your existence are hands-off.

ATALYA LAWLER

Fumbling for the Light Switch

No Recompense

Where Do We Take Hurt People?

Fumbling for the Light Switch

ATALYA LAWLER

Growing up with the world on your shoulders gives you a bad back after a while. When I was younger, I was believed to have a special connection to God, and was destined to be a preacher with my own church. I received this recognition when I was six years old. I was at my aunt's house and she had pitbull puppies in the basement. I went down there to play with the puppies, but one of them wouldn't play with me, nor would he eat. All he did was sleep. Everybody started getting concerned and they were like, "T.T. should pray for him." I couldn't say no and I couldn't just walk away, so I sat there and prayed for the puppy until it was time for me to leave. When I came back the next day, my cousins and siblings swarmed me saying, "T.T., you did it! You healed the puppy!" I was confused. I went downstairs and saw that the puppy was eating and playing with the others. I was happy, but it didn't mean much to me. I just thought, "Oh, he was sick but now he's better." But everyone else in the family was convinced that my prayers had healed the puppy, and that this meant that I had a special connection with God.

Because of this I was thrown into the field of holiness and church every day, not being able to play with my friends after school, and having to go to Bible study every Wednesday. For years, I actually believed that this is what I was supposed to be, my

destiny, like I was born for that calling. I thought that I was going to become a preacher and have my own church. Everybody lifted me on this pedestal and had high expectations for me. I was really hard on myself even when I was little, and I was really stressed about having to "hear God's message." I was expected to deliver groundbreaking and hair raising messages from God. My cousins would tease me about being a preacher and exclude me from things because I was too "holy" to do anything with them. I would distance myself from them because I thought I was too pure to be around "spirits" like them, but I would also cry all the time because I was an outcast. I was miserable: I wanted to play sports, I wanted to get dirty and play in the rain, but I couldn't because I was "called" by God to serve the church, and people who are called couldn't act like the flesh we are ruled by. Anything I did was put under a microscope. If I got in trouble at school, everyone in my family came over to talk some sense into me. If I got a bad grade, the church congregation closed the service with a prayer for me and my mind. I had to get used to it because everyone had high expectations for me when I didn't even know what expectations were. I had a church bag, wore a dress every Sunday, had four or five different kid Bibles, wore white with almost anything because that was my Granny's favorite color, and I was put in the adult Bible classes where I had no clue about half of what they were talking about. Overall, though, I had a strong sense of belonging and stability in my church community and in my family.

Then my family experienced a disruption that no family should have to deal with. Imagine being awakened by a nice suit and a clipboard telling you to get some clothes together and leave your mommy for a while. I was confused and frustrated, but I did what I was told and got my shoes on midway down the hallway, hopping on one foot and juggling my stuff in my arms. The lady saw that I was struggling, gave me a sympathetic smile and said, "Here, hand me your bag. I can hold on to it till we get in the car." I gave it to her and we continued down the hallway. I saw my sister and brother leaving too but my sister was crying and my brother was really mad.

We got to the living room and my heart dropped because nothing hurts me more than seeing my mom cry and she was balling and pleading to the officers to reconsider the situation. That's when it dawned on me that they were trying to separate us again. All these emotions came flooding in me: anger, sadness, confusion. Especially confusion because I didn't understand why my mommy, the best mommy in the world, was crying to a policeman. I went to her and I started crying, which made her cry even harder, if that was possible. Next thing I knew I was being pulled off of her and taken to the car. I looked back and saw my brother hitting the police officer and them having to restrain him. I hated the fact that there was nothing I could do. I would repeat in my head over and over again, "My mommy is the best

mommy in the world." I was broken hearted because they were taking us away from her.

That's when I learned that life could be unpredictable. We were only separated for a few days, but it was confusing and upsetting to be taken from my mom and siblings and put with strangers instead. Once we were all back with Mom, we were relieved. Things were going great and we were all happy. Until one day I woke up and I went to turn on the light but it wouldn't come on, so I went to my mom's room in the back of the house and asked her why the lights aren't coming on and she said, "Don't worry about it. Go get ready for school." I didn't say another word and did as I was told. I got dressed, brushed my teeth and waited for my sister and brother to get ready so they could walk me to school.

At school we did our usual circle and share routine we did every morning. I would try to go last because it would take me a long time to think of something to say. After everyone else went, it was my turn, and the teacher asked, "What is new today for you?" All I could think of was, "Our lights got turned off today." The teacher just looked at me, shocked that I had said that, and the whole circle got quiet and just stared at me.

When circle was over, the teacher called me to her desk while everyone else was doing work. She asked me quietly, "Is your mommy having some trouble at home?" I just shook my head and she immediately took out a sticky note and wrote something on it. I asked, "What is that?" She ignored me and reached for the phone on her desk and whispered some stuff into it and looked back at me and told me to go to the principal's office. All I could think was

Wow, really? I didn't even do anything! I went down anyway, crying all the way because they were going to call my mom and tell her, "Your daughter got in trouble today." I felt my stomach drop every step I took towards the office.

I got there and the lady at the front desk asked, "Yes, what do you need, hun?" without tearing her eyes from the screen. I was sniffling and snotting everywhere and I tried to calm myself down before I answered her. "I...uh...I have...to go to...see the... principal." Her eyes stayed on the screen and she said, "Okay, hun, have a seat over there and she'll come and get ya." I sat down and cried even harder because I knew I was about to get in trouble. By the time she came and got me, I was bawling like I was getting a whoopin' right there. She gave me some tissues and asked if I wanted some candy. I snatched that candy out of her hand so fast I hardly got the wrapper off before I ate it. "Hungry, aren't ya?" she said. "So I heard your mom was having trouble with the lights?" I nodded my head because she wasn't wrong. "Okay, I'm going to get her some help. But I need your help. What's your mom's number so we can call her?" I started crying all over again and I said, "No no no no, don't do that!" She said, "You're not in trouble—we just want to help." Then I straightened up and gave her the number and she said, "You can go back to class." I asked her, "So I'm not in trouble, right?" "No, you're fine. Now we're going to get your mommy some help, okay?"

I went back to class and forgot about it. At the end of the day, my brother and I walked home and I went straight to my room and changed into play clothes. Then my mom said, "We going to the store, so put your shoes on and tell everybody get in the car." So I told everybody and hopped in the car. While we waited for my mom to get in the car, we play fought to pass the time. She finally came out of the house and was PISSED. She yelled for me to get out the car and I got out and she yanked me up and yelled in my face, "Why would you tell them that? I told you don't worry about it but you didn't listen. Do you want them to take y'all from me again?" She was crying and I was crying and then everybody else started crying. I was crying because the principal had said I wasn't in trouble and here I was getting in trouble. My mom was crying because she couldn't handle us getting taken away again, and everybody else was crying because they couldn't go through that again either. I apologized and she said it was okay but just think before I say stuff and if she says don't worry about it, don't worry about it.

That night we got burgers and fries from Rally's and sat around the kitchen table telling funny stories, then we played charades where we pretended to be people in the family; my sister would dance like my grandpa, with her foot tapping and fingers snapping. Then we acted out funny movies until, like dominos, each of us went to sleep: first my brothers, then my sisters, then my mom, and lastly me. The next day was my cousin's birthday party and we all went skating.

We had lots of good times like that back in those days, whether they be at our house, my granny's house, or my aunt's house. We were constantly cracking each other up, listening to music, dancing, playing with our dog, and getting to know each other and bonding. It felt like it would last forever.

But that was interrupted one day when my whole family was at my aunt's house. All the kids went to the store to get some snacks. We were joking on each other, loudly, the whole way. When we returned, the house was dark, dreadful, empty. It was quiet for the first time since we had been over there. I felt this weighing feeling. Then one of my cousins got a call telling her that my mom was in the hospital and that it was bad. I dropped to the ground, and my heart dropped in my chest. I cried so hard that I couldn't catch my breath. I didn't know what to do. All these questions went through my head like *Where is she? What if she didn't make it? I hope she's okay. How?* I thought this was punishment from God because I thought of myself as the righteous one and didn't give Him any credit for what He's done. So we all prayed and prayed and prayed some more because we were afraid. That was the first time my cousins and I actually got along and came together for something.

I eventually found out what had happened: my mom had been sitting in my aunt's living room when a stray bullet went through the window and hit her in the neck. I didn't see my mom for a while after we heard what had happened. I couldn't go to the hospital to visit her because she didn't want us to see her in her condition, so we just waited for her at the house. We all cried for three days.

Finally, I heard a car pull up outside our house. I ran to the window and saw my aunt get out of the driver's seat and go to the back door. My siblings and I waited patiently for the door to open, and once it did I felt like crying all over again. There she was. She had on her cheetah print pajamas one of us had gotten her for Mother's Day, and she had a sling around her neck, holding her arm up. I ran to her and gave her the biggest and strongest hug I could give, but everybody told me to stop. I was confused at first, but then I remembered the situation and immediately let go. I looked up at her face. She looked tired but happy to see us. I felt the familiar sense of family.

Before I was born, my mom and grandmother didn't get along very well. When Granny found out that my mom was pregnant with me, she had doubts, but everyone else knew that we were going to be the best of friends. On the day when I was introduced to the world, my mother immediately started crying when she first saw me. It wasn't out of joy—it was because I looked just like my grandmother, from the mole on the left side of her nose to her infamous ice-cold glare. And when my grandmother saw me, she instantly fell in love.

When I was in the third grade, I went to live with my granny for two years because my mom didn't have a stable place to live at the time. It I felt like I was living with my best friend and sometimes my parole officer. I was very isolated. I couldn't make a lot of noise and I couldn't run around or that would aggravate her. I was scared the first couple of days because her house was so old that it would creak and groan and of course I thought it was monsters. She also had nightlights that would flicker on and off. I would keep the TV on all night because it was the closest thing to company and it would distract me from thinking scary thoughts. I would sometimes stay up until 4:00 or 5:00 a.m. or even stay up until it was time to go to school.

I loved the bus ride to school because I could be a wild mess on the bus. I could be as loud and noisy as I wanted. I would cuss every word in the dictionary. I liked school because it was the only place where I had friends and was social. I was pretty popular, made excellent grades, and was in anything and everything after school. After school, Granny and I would get Indi's chicken and chill in the house with full stomachs.

Every Wednesday we would go to choir practice. The adult choir wore red robes with white tassels on the shoulders every Sunday, and I dreamed of wearing one of those every time I saw them. I went to school listening to gospel music on my small red MP3 player because Granny said that it would make my day go better and I would be blessed at school. The older kids thought I was weird because I would mouth the words to the songs. I wouldn't let anyone listen to my music, though, because I was embarrassed that I had to listen to gospel music.

I could call my friends on the phone, but I couldn't be long because Granny always needed to use the phone. Sometimes she would pick up the phone to listen to my conversations, so when I got my first cell phone I was more than happy. Granny would get a lot of toys for me because she knew I could get bored: a small china tea set with real glasses and tea pots, a sewing machine, an Easy Bake Oven. I felt grateful to have a granny who took care of me and loved me.

Atalya's grandmother

I had a lot of creative ideas, so I was rarely bored. I would be a detective trying to crack open the case of the century, or I would be a spy attempting to steal the Mona Lisa. There was nothing I couldn't be when it came to my imagination, but I had to do it quietly. Every night Granny would make me read the Bible before I went to bed because she didn't want me to lose my anointing from God, and if I yawned when I was reading she would say that it was the devil trying to stop me from reading. During the time I lived with her, Granny was strict, but she taught me how to be a young lady, and I appreciated that.

I still visited with my mom and had a good relationship with her. One day my sister Sha and I went to hang with my mom at her apartment. They had a pool in the apartment complex and my mom wanted to go to swimming almost every day. I loved the water so much that they called me a fish, so I went with no hesitation. My mom took a million and one pictures of the moment because it was so rare that we spent time like this. I acted silly and kept trying to dunk my sister, but she was too fast for me and always got away. My mom let me ride on her back when she went under the water like a submarine. She would rapidly drive up and out the water, and I would laugh so hard and choke on water at the same time.

Once we got out of the pool, we showered off the chlorine and put on our warm pajamas, picked out a movie, got ice cream, and tried to shake the water out of our ears. My mom braided my hair so it wouldn't be all crazy and nappy in the morning. When I woke up the next day, I heard gospel music blasting. I knew this meant I better grab the Fabuloso and broom

because I was going to be cleaning something. We would always dance as we cleaned the house; that was another way we bonded.

I was a good kid in school. I used to make great grades and was near the top of my class every year. But I had a lot on my shoulders; I couldn't screw up. If I did, the whole family would want an intervention session. I worked really hard to keep my grades together. I had great friends who I could depend on. I was well known and funny. I was part of the student council, and I was a lead stepper on the step team. I was involved in theater, and acting was my life. I acted in a lot of plays at school and was the Queen of Hearts in the play *Alice in Wonderland.*

Then, toward the end of fifth grade, something happened. I don't like to talk about it. Just trust me, it was bad.

It changed my view on everything. I hated everything, and I thought I was going to be consumed by all the hate I felt. I was scared at first because it all happened so fast; I would hide under the risers in choir and stay under there until the monitors had to come get me. I went through severe depression. I thought I was ugly and disgusting. I was so angry all the time, and if I wasn't angry, then I was sad, and if I wasn't sad, then I was scared. I thought this was just being a pre-teen, so I didn't tell anyone about what was going on with me. I would cause attention in the most ridiculous ways. I would sit in the middle of the floor in the main hallway until I was suspended, or I would call other students with bird noises like a parakeet, and that always got me sent out of the classroom. I was a menace to most of the teachers and I never kept the same classes for more than a week.

Finally, after getting in trouble one time, I told a teacher what had happened. She immediately sent me to counseling and from there it all went downhill. I thought I was being judged by everybody for going to counseling, but it was required in order for me to go back to school. My counselor was more than insulting because she thought that bringing God into my life would make me want to do the right thing; she failed to realize that I used to be God's right hand girl to everybody I met in church. The counselor would be so focused on me going to the Lord and confessing my sins that she didn't see that I was in turmoil about the whole situation.

I was always mad. 24/7. Like a never-ending wildfire burning for miles. No matter how many times I tried to douse and smother it with positive vibes, it still sizzled and crackled until it found a way to ignite again. Going to school was my wildfire's main fuel. That's where my fire grew. I made friends who had wildfires too and made a fool out of myself just to get their acceptance. I was in too many altercations to count. Every time I showed out was a cry for help because I was hurting, but teachers and police saw me as a "bad kid" who needed to be put away.

I first got put away in sixth grade, when I was put in the Ready For Life program, which was a secluded prison within the school. The room was small and it was right by the auditorium where I used to perform in plays. The Ready For Life program only taught me two subjects, reading and math. Two hours for each subject. After that we would go down to the cafeteria, grab our lunches, and get straight on a bus to take us home; we didn't even get to sit down and eat.

Atalya as the Queen of Hearts

There were only five students in the program, and I just sat back and watched them and saw their personalities instead of trying to make friends. They would talk about me and exclude me from things. I tried not to get into much trouble, but some days I got sent home earlier than others.

Every day I had to pass the door that went to the backstage area and it felt like it was taunting me. I was not allowed to be in anything after being sent to Ready For Life: no sports, no after school activities, nothing. I once was on that stage acting the part of the Queen of Hearts, yelling, "Off with their heads!" again and again. Now I *was* the Queen of Hearts—we both had a bad temper and we both made people scared of us—but without any power or authority. I had no one around to cut off heads for me, so I raised my own fists. Again and again.

I wasn't always acting out, though. No one at Ready for Life knew this, but I was volunteering at The Lord's Kitchen, a place that provided meals and groceries for people who were homeless or not financially stable. I would help there any way I could. When I first started going there with my granny, I would be so mad that my she made me come, but she said, "This will teach you to be humble and learn how to appreciate everything." I said, "Why do I have to be here? I don't like being around these people! They stink!" But after a while, I realized that a lot of people didn't have the things that I had. One Wednesday, a woman with three kids came in and I immediately noticed that they didn't have shoes. I stayed in the bathroom balling my eyes out because nobody, let alone a kid, deserves that. Ever since then, I have been really invested in going and helping people.

My grandmother and I would go to the Lord's Kitchen sometimes as early as 5:00 a.m. and leave around 2:00 p.m. or we would go from 3:00 p.m. to 9:00 p.m. We would be exhausted but that was a way me and my granny bonded. A typical day in the Lord's Kitchen starts with the chef preparing food. The people go to the main church right next door, listen to the Word, and when they leave they get a ticket with a number on it so they could use it to get some food. They come back in and get seated. They eat the food and then the fun part starts. The numbers get called and the first batch of people come through. Usually they are the slowest people going through the line, so they aren't very well liked

in there. Grouchy people occasionally come through and give you the meanest, ugliest looks. My favorite type of people to come through crack jokes, smile, and just bring life to the place. I never had a dull moment with them.

Sometimes it would be really busy and loud because so many people came out. And of course there could be drama, but it happened rarely. I would help give out groceries and small things around the kitchen. When we first started going, I would just hold the doors for people, but then I got to be one of the writers who would take down the name of the person and their address. We had to count how many people were in their household to determine how much they could take. Some people that came through for groceries didn't want to give me their info because I was too young and looked like I didn't know what I was doing so they just wouldn't come to me. This made me think that I wasn't good enough to get the job done, so I just stopped helping until my grandma told me to get up and help with something. Over time, I helped more without any nudging from my granny, and the people at the Lord's Kitchen saw me as helpful, respectful, and quiet. Police officers and teachers didn't see me like this.

My problems continued to escalate. In 6th grade, I was sent to Clark County Correctional Facility after getting into yet another fight. A police officer ripped me off the girl I was fighting, immediately put me in cuffs, and pushed me out the front door of my school. I made an attempt at going for the girl again and knocked the officer to floor. The officer was fuming, because he didn't like being beaten. So as we were leaving, he yanked me all around like a rag doll.

How To Beat The Brakes Off Somebody

1. Get into an argument.

2. Never back down.

3. Win the argument.

4. Meet up somewhere (not around rich people neighborhoods).

5. Argue some more when they arrive.

6. Square up.

7. Black out. It feels like being in a pitch black room, fumbling for the light switch.

8. Watch everything play out in front of you. Feel the blood and skin on your knuckles burn. See the terror and fear in everyone's eyes as you lose control and continue to punch.

9. Come out of your daze.

10. Let the police explain to you why you are in custody.

11. See your family looking disappointed.

12. Let them tell you how you almost killed her and how crazy you looked when the police pulled you off of her.

13. Think about it for a while and let it settle in.

14. Then don't feel anything and forget.

Authority Figures I've Known

I've spent a lot of my life in schools and interacting with law enforcement and the justice system. Here are some of the types of adults I've encountered:

I just want to help. These are the people who try to get in your mind and figure you out. You have to set a border for them, a baseline, a place for them to start the race. They usually want to have a cool vibe with you, but you instantly catch on to their submissive facade.

You can't beat me. These people usually wear a badge but some carry papers and grade books. I'm not too fond of these ones because they often see me as a threat.

Pish posh, I know what's best. These are the people who want things to go their way or no way. I bump heads with these ones, mostly because I'm just as stubborn as them and I like a challenge.

Bubbly and happy. These people who are happy and positive and outgoing. All the butterflies and sunshine spewing from them make me want to throw up.

The old school and traditional. They live in the past and try so desperately to bring it back. You typically see these people with a flip phone and a car so old and busted you would be surprised it still worked. They always try to spit some knowledge to you and let you know about when they were younger. It's interesting to hear their stories, but sometimes you just want to take a nap when it seems like the story will never end.

The Comedian. They love to crack jokes about anything from your shoes to your IQ. If you have a smart mouth they will target you the most. You can tell they don't like their job but it pays them well enough to continue their foolery.

I tried to swing at him a couple of times, but of course I missed. Once I got in the patrol car, I started kicking the window and cracked the glass and busted my knee in the process. I knew that was going to get me locked up longer but I didn't care.

Eventually we made it to Clark County Correctional Facility and I was ready to flip on anybody who tried to mess with me. They put me in their computer system and told me to sit down. That's when they took the cuffs off. I tried to run but they restrained me and put the cuffs back on. I sat there for what seemed like forever. No one talked to me except to tell me to stop kicking my chair. Eventually, they took me to a locker room and gave me a plastic tub holding a white jumpsuit, a white T-shirt, two pairs of socks, boxers, a toothbrush, and bedding. They let me go behind a curtain to change, but warned me, "If we find anything on you, that will be more time." They put me in a line in a hallway with the other new kids and told us, "Don't touch the walls, or we'll put you in solitary." They told us to go to the cafeteria, but I stayed on the wall. They took me to solitary for a couple of hours. Then two officers escorted me to the cafeteria for an inedible lunch. All of the girls in the cafeteria were looking at me like they had a problem with me. I didn't eat anything. They took me to my cell.

When a "freshy" first arrives at Clark, her cellmate will often give her the rundown. Over time, I gave this speech a few times myself. It goes a little something like this:

"First off, being in Clark isn't fun, so don't think you earn cool points for being in here. Morning routine is to wake up, make your bed, and make sure

you tuck your socks in your cover so you will have an extra pair. These kids steal your stuff and look at you in your face unapologetically. I learned that the first time I was here. I went in with a toothbrush, sandals, bedding, a pillow, and towel but came out three days later with the bedding, holey socks, and one sandal. The rent-a-cops who walk around in here like they run something will pop off at the mouth on you so keep your head down and mind your business. DO NOT MAKE PROMISES IN HERE. These girls are hurting and don't need another let down or that will be your life. Don't make permanent friends here because they will not be there to help you if you get jumped. If you trade, trade rationally. Don't trade your toothbrush for a bag of noodles, even if they offer you the sauce pack. Don't take off your sandals just anywhere. Your socks will be filthy by the time they touch the ground, just from the air alone. Don't even befriend a newbie cuz they're going to try to join a group of girls and will have to do something dumb to be accepted. Uncooked noodles with the flavor pack thrown in there will be like mama's homemade fried chicken to you. The first day you're not going to want to eat, so have something ready to trade. If you don't have anything to trade, steal and pray to the Lord that you don't get caught. Good luck and may God be with you."

Finally the school system and state had enough of the Anderson family and kicked us to the curb and we moved to Louisville. I thought this was going to be hell for me because I didn't know anyone, I didn't like anything, and I was closed off to everyone until I started to notice all the opportunities I had in front of me. I didn't want to disappoint my family again so I really worked hard to better myself and to do better for my family. I joined student council, I was in honors classes, and I was an ambassador for my school. Of course I had a few bumps in the road where my behavior wasn't the best, but I kept my head up and kept going.

It's 5:00 in the morning. My body is saying *Get up, no more sleeping*. I'm mad that I can't get more sleep and I'm freezing and hungry and still a little tired. I don't know why I wake up this early. It's now a routine. I sit on the bed for little bit and think about what to wear and I get it together. Then I take a shower, put on my clothes, and get my hair together. I look on my phone for the time when the TARC bus comes, I grab my coat before anyone else wakes up, and I'm out the door. I walk down the hill, pass the dog that always barks but never bites. I throw her a look—*Girl, you better move*—and she receives the message. I make my way up the hill. Cars come by but I pay them no mind. I sometimes go to the farthest TARC stop just so I can have a little more time to breathe and chill, then I wait for the bus with my music constantly playing and my fingers moving to the rhythm like a pianist.

The bus slowly approaches and I gather my things and grab my fare. The doors open and I step on. The bus driver immediately smiles and asks, "How are you doing today?" I return his smile. "I'm doing all right." We always talk to each other. One time I went to Subway and this same bus driver went in too because he was going to have to sit at Walmart for about twenty minutes before he left. I got a sandwich, but I didn't have enough money. The bus driver gave me three more dollars to pay for my sandwich. I thanked him and told him I would pay him back, but he said, "Don't worry about it. Just keep riding the bus and that's payment enough."

I proceed to the back of the bus and sit down. As we lurch forward, the hum and vibration of the bus soothes me. I look out the window and think, *What if aliens came and stopped the bus? Why is the sky blue? Who told that woman to wear leopard leggings with this fluffy pink scarf around her neck? Why am I so angry?*

All these questions simmer down when I focus on my music. I rub my fingers together and tap them as I listen. Sometimes I mouth the words and don't care who's watching. My favorite music is old school R&B like Bobby Brown, TLC, and Michael Jackson. I grew up on this music because my dad's a musician and he would play music all day long. Those songs bring a lot of good feelings because they make tough times seem like temporary storms and help me forget all my problems. They make me feel like I'm able to get through anything. My dad used to tell me, "Never forget how music made us. That bond is made with the strings of the older and simpler times." I didn't understand it until now.

When my dad and I were living together, he had a guest room that he made his music room and we would always sit in there making music together. He tried to teach me the drums, but nothing really stuck with me except the fact that they were fun to hit really hard. My favorite part of the drums were the hi-hats because the sound they made was so enchanting; when the two parts collided they made a sizzle sound and when they separated they made a holy *awww* sound. I would play the drums at my old church when the regular drummer was out. Keith, the piano player, was a huge help to me and he would tell me how to do it. I learned a few tricks but I didn't stay with it.

I just absorb my surroundings. We go through downtown and I wish this place was within walking distance of my house. I look up at the buildings and pretend that I work there. When I have extra time to get off the TARC, I get some Chinese food and walk around 4th Street. I feel free here. I don't have to explain myself and don't have to worry about anything.

It's Sunday, about 4:00 in the evening. I'm sitting in the enormous church with the eggshell cream paint peeling off the centuries-old walls. I'm slowly drifting from the pastor's booming voice, but I stay awake by focusing on the beautiful tall stained glass windows. As I analyze the art, the biblical stories I've heard about so much as a child gradually come to life. I am brought out of my mesmerized state by the angelic sound of the piano being played in the background of the pulpit. Pastor Kimbo comes to the pew looking exhausted and sweaty in his very expensive looking blackish-grey suit. Usually after the pastor is done speaking the piano plays to let us know it's about time to leave, but today Pastor Kimbo feels otherwise and has to say a few more words. Finally, the moment I (and I think everyone else) am waiting for comes. We all stand in unison like soldiers standing at attention. We shout our usual chant—"Jesus! Jesus! Jesus!"—and that concludes the service.

I stretch and gather my belongings, waiting for my grandmother/best friend to collect her ten-ton church bag full of her Bible and the notebooks she uses to take notes during the service. Once we gather everything, we say our goodbyes and head for the car. We settle inside the small black Kia and breathe a relieved sigh in sync. Then we giggle at the coincidence and slip back into a comfortable silence on the way to get a bite at Rally's. We both get chicken and fries. Once we pull up to the

The Congregation

These are the people who I have grown up with most of my life because I have spent so much time in church. None of them are perfect, but they're all part of my community:

Hi! Is my smile sweet enough for you? These brown-nosers are the best ones to get you basically anything you want. Without your acceptance, though, you won't get very far with them.

The old lady offering candy, waters, and hugs. Just the sweetest people you could meet.

The shushers. These people think a pin dropping is too loud. If you cough, you get shushed. If you breathe too hard, you get shushed. If you even agree with the preacher, You. Get. Shushed.

The I-don't-really-want-to-be-here's. These people mostly come along with friends or family not wanting to be rude and say no to their offer. They do a clap here and there but hardly ever stand for praise and worship.

The Holy Ghost catchers. These people are so dramatic in everything they do. They break off into more categories when they catch the holy ghost: the shoulder shakers, the laughers, and the stompers.

The offering hiders. These come in two types. The first one is the person who doesn't want to show how petty they are with their offering, and the other one is the person who pretends to not have the offering altogether.

second window, pay, and get the food, the aroma immediately fills the entire car. My granny says, "You better eat now because you can't bring it on the boat." I keep that in mind and we are accompanied by silence once again.

Cars and lights blend together as we zoom down to our location until we drive into a low parking area, under a huge bridge we were meet with fifty other cars. After what seems like hours, we find a space to park. It is a tight spot, but we make it work. My granny gets out and I follow after her. I stretch once again. As we walk in the semi-sandy ground, I can feel with every step the sand crunch beneath my feet and the anticipation building in the pit of my stomach. We approach a pretty lengthy line. As we wait, I observe the giant yellow, red, and black letters on the side of the Belle of Louisville. Lower down are big ropes tying the big riverboat to the shore, and in the back is a huge paddle wheel made of red planks of wood.

I avert my attention when I notice the line start to move and the anxiousness grows even more intense. We are next in line and my granny motions for me to move forward and I gladly skip ahead. I hand my ticket to a man who looks to be in his late fifties and we continue to the excitement inches away from us. A few more steps and we are on this amazing creation. I marvel at the glossy wooden floor boards. I look up to see this beautiful chandelier flickering and manipulating the light it reflects with a rainbow effect. It is so enchanting, but this is only the beginning. On both sides of the room there are approximately three chairs on each side. There are also about twelve windows on the wooden

dark brown walls. I waste no time at all to go on the upper deck. I feel like my five-year-old self again. Almost running up the stairs, I trip and bump my knee. I let out a little squeal but quickly cover it with a laugh when I notice a cute guy around my age with olive-toned skin and sandy brown hair is coming behind me. I nervously look down and let him pass by me up the stairs. I try to take the embarrassing moment off my mind with the excitement that was ready to burst.

I peek through the doors at the top of the stairs and instantly feel like I am in a different dimension. All of the anxiousness dissipates from me and is replaced by serene calmness. I look at the clear blue sky that feels so alive. As I go closer to the edge, I hold on to the slightly rusted metal bars and the faded, chipping red paint. The wind gently caresses my face like a comforting hug that reassures me that I'm going to be all right even though it can often be hard to believe. I look further into the distance and see the sun having a battle with the sky and the water. The sky seems to be desperately trying to claim the sun but gently gives up the fight and lets the sun slip away. The murky water openly takes in the sun and paves a shiny pathway in its glory. The water sparkles and shimmers on its surface like a dance. I spend the rest of the ride up there never wanting to go back to the real world. The dance of the sun and wind feels short-lived when we are back.

Slowly but reluctantly I turn to leave. I go back down the stairs to search for my granny, but to my surprise she is already waiting on me with a huge smile on her face like she knows something I don't. I

shrug it off but keep it in the back of my mind and we continued to the exit. We are off now and I look back, thinking I'm going to miss my other world that has more stories than I can comprehend. As I walk away I can hear the boards groan and the water splash, saying their goodbyes. We get in the car and our usual friend-silence comes. I look over at my grandmother and she still has that smile-that-holds-a-secret on her joyful face. It has been a good day. Maybe, just maybe, everything is going to be all right.

No Recompense

A MCELROY

Shelton has accomplished so much in his life to help teens and adults alike with the justice system. At the age of three he was put into foster care where he was thrown into institution after institution. He was sent to a juvenile facility at the age of eleven, which only made his situation worse. Now he helps people with similar experiences through The Bail Project and a lot of other good work. I was interested in interviewing him because we shared a lot of the same conflicts. He understood that there was a flaw in the juvenile system and wanted to fix it by telling his story.

—ATALYA

I went into foster care when I was three. I went into institutions all over the state of Kentucky. I think the theory behind it was that if they took kids from inner city neighborhoods and sent them somewhere rural, they might fare better, but it separated me from my community. People who resided in the community would have possibly become a foster parent, or an adoptive parent, and they weren't given that luxury. So I went farther rural, and really traveled throughout institutions from three to eighteen.

I was really hungry as a kid, my whole childhood. Really food insecure, really hungry all the time. Some of the earliest mischief I got into was breaking into houses, eating people's food. Break in, eat your Fudge Rounds, I drank your juice, and I was in paradise. I'd get your remote, and watch your TV, and get out of there before you get off of work or the kids got home from school. But I didn't take anything. I took food. I was just hungry, I was very hungry.

My first ever incarceration was Halloween related. I was going on twelve. I pulled out a BB-gun and pointed it at a young girl. I was in a really racially divided community, and she was a young white girl. It didn't have any BB's in it. I was at a home hanging out in front. Pulled the gun on the girl, said, "Give me your candy." Never took her candy. It was a hoax. I didn't think that she believed it was real. She went on trick-or-treating, and I was just laughing, being mischievous. Then the police showed up and arrested me. This was my first time going to a police station. When you watch TV and see these bigger stations, there's people in there and there's movement, and there's sound. This was a very small space. There was nobody there other than me and the two officers with me. They sat me down and called in my social worker, trying to figure out what to do with this kid who's essentially parent-less and who has had this incident of perceived wanton endangerment. They made a few phone calls and decided to send me to the juvenile detention center. When I heard them mention that, my heart sunk. You hear people talk about the wind getting knocked out of them? It felt more like a collapsing sensation. But it lasted. It didn't go away.

The community I was in didn't have a juvenile facility, they had a juvenile wing within the adult jail. This is in Nicholasville, Kentucky. I had actually watched this jail get built in this community. It was super big. This was at the very beginning of mass incarceration in the United States, and unbeknownst to me, they were gearing up to use their jail for economic infrastructure. When people are incarcerated for, say, immigration in Lexington or Louisville or any other community, they have the federal contracts for people to get transported to and housed in their jail. And they get paid a certain amount for everybody, so it was a business. They built this jail right across from the park that's in the black community, the park that I played in. Hearing the steel doors clanking shut behind me was worse than fingernails on a chalkboard.

They put me in some jail pajamas. They look like something you would see at a hospital, but not that thin material. This is more like blue-jean material, but it's a pull-over, and pull-up pants with spandex around the waist. I might have weighed sixty-five, seventy-five pounds; I was the smallest person in school. Super skinny, super short, super small. They didn't have any of these clothes to fit me, so I looked really awkward with this new garb on. Before putting on the garb, you have to take a shower. But even prior to that, you have to wash with this stuff that kills lice. Black people don't generally get hair lice because we've got a lot of oils in our hair naturally, but you

have to wash with this stuff, and you have to do it in the eyesight of a grown man who works there who you don't know. I washed with that stuff, and then I put these really thick pajamas on.

Then they give me a package lunch, more like a tray, and I go into this open pod. There's a few tables and a few people sitting out there. I'm eleven years old, and they're eighteen. The age disparity is huge. The area closes and everybody goes into their cells two at a time. I go into this cell with this seventeen year-old kid, Caucasian guy that I didn't know from anybody. I had been exposed to a lot of violence as a kid, but never had the fear that I had being in that jail as a very young person and not knowing what was going to happen. Is my social worker going to come get me? Am I here forever?

I was scared to talk to these guys, and they were purposely being frightening. They were mad that they were in there. We would be locked into these double-man cells from, say, 9:00 p.m. to 8:00 a.m. And then the double-man cells would open up, and you could go out into this open community area. I was so scared. I didn't play checkers, I didn't talk, I just looked up at the TV, and got a crick in my neck. I stayed there for about ten days, but it seemed like way longer than that. The social workers came and got me, and I was charged and convicted of wanton endangerment. In retrospect, I'd probably not charge an eleven or twelve-year-old with wanton endangerment. I think I did not have the aptitude to understand the perceived danger that I might have caused. So to be charged in that way, I think was an over-reach.

I get out of there, and I go to a boys and girls home. A lot less restrictive, nothing like the juvenile justice system. And I went to several of those. I got in trouble again and went in front of a judge for an Out of Control Petition that was being filed against me. I wasn't doing too good in the behavior area. An Out of Control Petition is something that schools and foster parents or mothers or dads can file if they feel like their child is out of control. I was intentionally not wanting to be at this foster home or in this community. My oldest brother had caused enough confusion that he had been sent away, so in my childish mind I was causing confusion to get sent away as well. I wanted to get back home to Louisville. The Out of Control Petition was taken out by the school, by my foster mother, my social worker, several people. The judge sentenced me to juvenile detention.

I ended up at a group home in Frankfort. There were twelve to maybe fourteen of us there. One of the most memorable things about the place was that it was violent by way of the staff. I never got into a fight with any of the other residents, but the staff were very cruel and violent. We'd be shooting basketball outside. "All right, y'all come in and get ready for cleaning detail." And if you took one extra shot, they would take you to this plot of land, give you a shovel, and have you dig mounds of dirt and flip it over. Your hands would be calloused, it would be 45 degrees outside and wet, and it didn't matter. They would keep you out there until you were in a complete state of exhaustion. They'd call you names. And they'd hit you, upside your head. Push you. Lot of verbal abuse. A lot of really grueling work as punishment. If you happened to not make your bed fast enough, it could be six in the morning, you were sent out to dig in a creek, flip rocks over. Just really grueling labor as way of punishment. And there was no recompense. There was nothing you could do. There was nobody you could complain to. It was from the very top down, all the way through the system. The reason I would know that is because some kids would come from other places and we would compete against them in basketball and they would have the same stories, and the same experience, sometimes worse. It was nothing to see a kid from the other group home or camp just get smacked upside his head. You just would think, "I'm glad I'm not him. I'm glad it's not me today." You walked on pins and needles. And nothing was going to change. It's like having a violent stepparent or a violent uncle in your own household. Who are you going to tell?

So I stayed there, and went to an alternative school. I don't know what their mission or purpose was; I think it was just, you stay in a place like that and when it came time to leave, you just wouldn't want to go back. I changed my behavior to a high degree when I left, but I don't know how associated it was with anything there. I probably just matured a little bit. What you do at eleven and twelve, you're probably not going to do at fourteen, fifteen.

I got out of there, and went to a couple of transitional places for youth, places where you're not there because you did something wrong, you're there because you don't have anywhere to go. Places where you could stay a maximum of sixty days while they tried to find you somewhere permanent. I was going to the public school in Scott County. I wouldn't tell people I was at a group home. I just kind of kept it vague so people wouldn't know too much about me. The last day of school, you know the sensation: everybody had plans, and we were going to see each other, and the pool was going to open. That energy. People were inviting me to stuff: "Hang out with us! Come shoot ball with us! Here's my number, here's my address, give me a call."

I went back to the group home for a couple of days on summer break, but it wasn't working. They would put us in a van and drive us to the library or whatever. I just walked off. For good. Just kept walking, and ended up bumping into some of the guys who I had befriended to a degree. I didn't know much about them, and I found out a lot. Smoked my first cigarette with those guys in the back of a pickup truck. Marijuana and alcohol came after that. I started sleeping in this guy's closet, and stayed in his closet that whole summer. Eventually his mom found me in the closet and told me to leave. I'd always sneak back in, sleep on his bed, switch up my location. I did that for a long time. I never went back to school, and I just lived from place to place like that.

I wish I could say that the juvenile system helps children. I wish I could say that. The problem is, it's built on a flawed idea. If a child is doing X, Y, or Z, it not because the child is criminal, deviant, a bad person. Because they start there, they harm children. There is no value added in having an experience in the juvenile system, because they start from the wrong premise. There's a way to do it, and people are thinking about this in different places. About how to support kids. What would have helped me as a child is somebody could have realized that I was food insecure. That I was not a burglar, or a future cat burglar, but I was a very hungry kid. And see, you can wrap something around me to support that, and could have pivoted me away from an institution. So, needs assessments instead of risk assessments. We have a system that starts off saying, "These kids are dangerous. They're super predators." You'd have to blow the whole thing up, you'd have to say, "I don't care what they've done. They're not the worst thing they've done. Let's unpack what caused that incident to happen. What happened? How do we help them?" Let's teach them how to ride a horse. Let's teach them how to grow something. Let's love on them.

Where Do We Take Hurt People?

YVETTE GENTRY

Yvette Gentry worked for the Louisville Metro Police Department for many years before retiring as Deputy Chief. After that, she was the mayor's Chief of Community Building, and now she leads Metro United Way's Black Male Achievement initiative and is the executive director of the Assisting Youth Foundation. She has firsthand experience with troubled youth through the eyes of a police officer. Interviewing Ms. Gentry was like interviewing myself. She expresses her strong belief that the justice system is broken and should focus on helping youths who are struggling.

—ATALYA

We think about the drug epidemic and how people are handling the opioid crisis now, and resources and things like that. But when the crack epidemic really hit the black community—well, every community, but really hit the black community hard—it was all about incarcerating. I don't feel bad at all for removing people who are dangerous from the community, like locking up drug-dealers, but I wish we'd had more alternatives to incarceration for longer periods of time. Because the more I was in law enforcement, the older I got, I realized that it's not a rehabilitative way to address those kinds of social issues. And I saw so many kids, especially those twelve- to fifteen-year-old kids whose parents were using drugs or not home, who were just trying to survive but couldn't legally hold a job. It's easy to lecture a child on what they shouldn't do, but when you can't provide them with the resources they need, then you really shouldn't. As I progressed in my career as a police officer, I always tried to balance that.

When I was in Park Hill as a Housing Authority officer, I saw all the stuff that was happening, and I saw the kids that were vulnerable. So I would try to help the grandparents who were raising kids. I would try to do outreach programs, and just try to help them with the resources. I felt so connected to giving them resources, because it's easy to say, "Don't steal," if I'm not starving. If a kid is starving, and they don't know when they're going to see their parent again, and they go to a store and steal, they're doing it because they're trying to survive. I understood that, but it took me a while to understand that. And I think that law enforcement, we're human. It takes us a while, sometimes, to see that even when we think we're helping, maybe we're not helping.

I think what really helped me be a better police officer—and I think it helps you no matter what your profession is—is to listen. I would always want to know the why. Like, I understand you have drugs in your pocket, but what's your home life like? What is your situation like? And the more I listened, the more I could start to pick at the root causes and then try to address those on the back-side. I felt like adults should know better, and they should make better decisions, but I saw some kids in some really sad situations that they didn't really have control over—I mean, you don't have a lot of control when you're thirteen or fourteen. It's not like you can just run out there and get a job and be emancipated and get your own place. That's not the reality. So you have to play the cards you're dealt. And when I saw enough young people dealing with that, I just couldn't help but try to do what I could do to make their lives easier. Even if it was just for one day.

One thing that I see a lot of in youth is their desperation, and that they've lost hope and faith in adults. I think that they have a lot of professional people that come preach to them, but they don't really understand—and don't seek to understand—what it means to be in survival mode. Dr. William Bell says, "What happens to the dream when the dreamer spends every day trying to survive?" I think that's the thing that adults don't think enough about. You tell kids, "Shoot high, have big dreams," and all that. That's great, but when you're in survival mode, you're not dreaming. You're just trying to get to the next minute. To see something six months from now, or a year from now, that's not real for so many kids. It's not that they don't think that they can do better,

it's just like, "I can't focus on the dream when I got to figure out what I'm going to eat at three o'clock." That's why I gravitate towards helping kids with the more immediate needs. I still have kids who call me and say, "Ms. Gentry, we don't have no food," or, "Ms. Gentry, I need Pampers for my baby." And I'm proud that they know that I will answer. I feel like I can do more with a twenty-dollar pack of Pampers than I can do with a program in some cases. Because I showed that I was legitimate when I gave you my number and said call me if you need anything. I answered. So that's what I try to do, I try to be honest with them, be trustworthy, and then meet the need that they ask for as much as I can.

I think the juvenile justice system is a broken system. If I'm already mad, and some guy tells me to sit and look at a wall, that doesn't help me get to the problem of why I'm mad. Do you even care why I'm upset? How do you respond to your friends when they're upset? You don't go cussing at your friends when they're upset. You don't go punishing your friends when they're upset—you rally around them and try to give them support. But for black kids, it's always, they're just mad. That's why I'm so happy to be at Metro United Way working on a campaign about that asset framing, about saying what's good about kids. I've been to Harvard, I've been all over the world, and some of the smartest people I know are justice involved kids. Who's telling their story?

I've seen eleven year olds, tiny kids, in juvenile detention for arguing with their grandparents or other people. Just very angry young people, for whom incarceration is not the answer. But we also are a system that lacks other resources. So where do you take them? Where do you put a child that's angry and acting out with the anger, but the reality is they're hurt? Where do we take hurt people? We always want to institutionalize hurt people, and that's the system in our country. And that's unfortunate.

The juvenile justice system was created when kids would still steal cars. You rarely saw a kid involved in a homicide, let alone a capital crime. In the first seven or eight years of my career, I never saw a kid charged with that. We just didn't see it. When I would lock up juveniles, it was almost always for stealing a car. It was never for killing people and setting them on fire and doing stuff like that. Then I started to see the role that mental health was playing. Kids born drug addicted. Started to see that kind of play out very differently, and the system has never changed to catch up with that.

The system is not set up to be rehabilitative. It doesn't really have the proper mental health supports in the jail. You're just sitting there, kind of biding your time. That's one thing if you steal a car and you're going to be there for three weeks. But it's another thing if you're going to be in there for two years. If you're going to have a child incarcerated for years, it has to be a totally different system. We have to look at that and figure out a way, if we're going to have kids in there, to work to make them better people, to address their mental health issues and such. Even if they serve a thirty-year sentence, if they're fifteen, they're coming back out. If you don't put anything into them, what are you going to do, turn a forty-five year old loose in the community without the resources? That's just not a system that's set up for kids to ever overcome what they need to overcome. So there's a

whole lot that needs to be changed about this system. Also in the juvenile system, there's no early release for good behavior. And I'm thinking that if the adults get that, surely a child should get that.

If I could change one thing about the juvenile system, I would make sure that the kids got to trial quicker. If a child gets arrested for a felony, and they're in jail, they could stay in jail for two years without even ever being convicted. You don't get those years back. Just imagine your ninth and tenth grade year being incarcerated for a crime. And your eleventh grade year they figure out, "Oh, you're innocent," and they let you go. You don't get those years back. Nobody gets their years back, but I think it's even more harsh on young people because those are your developmental years. And I think we overlook the fact that kids have the same constitutional rights as everybody else has, and we need to speed those up. If they're guilty, and they're going to be convicted, that's fine. Leaving them in there, pre-adjudicated, for years, is not appropriate, and our system has got to address that.

YENNIFER
COCA IZQUIERDO

This is the Coca-Cola That Will Make You Forget Us

Arnaldo Coca Minguez

Opposition and Transformation

This Is the Coca-Cola
That Will Make You Forget Us

YENNIFER COCA IZQUIERDO

I woke up to an eloquent symphony of sparrows in the almond tree outside my window on the first day of summer vacation. When I jumped up and ran into the living room, my mother received me with a series of prolonged kisses and hugs. The warm aroma of the cigarettes between her pale lips made me dizzy, while her kiss penetrated through my cheeks, leaving a bruise of affection behind. "How is the most beautiful girl in the world?" she asked and pulled me close to her chest, swinging herself back and forth in the wooden rocking chair. "I'm okay, Mama," I said, followed by a sudden cough. She inhaled the cigarette smoke one last time, then stood up and continued her routine.

Growing up as a child in communist Cuba, I was always instructed in the importance of patriotism and appreciating one's nationality. Every day I watched nationalistic programming on TV like Elpidio Valdés, one of my favorite cartoons about a patriot who rose with other *mambises* against the Spanish colonization and the Yankees' insurrection. Elpidio was based on Antonio Maceo, a Cuban leader who was known for his heroic role in the Cuban Revolution.

The television channels also showed random pictures of the Cuban countryside accompanied by nationalistic soundtracks like "*Hasta Siempre Comandante*," which mentions significant moments in the Cuban Revolution such as the Battle of Santa Clara, and glorifies Che as a Revolutionary commander. The song is popular among Cubans and everyone knows the lyrics. As I heard the tone every morning, the smooth melody and steady rhythm of the acoustic guitar swathed me into patriotic comfort, and I'd jump off the couch, proudly singing along as loud as possible while spinning around the living room. Dad would join me from the kitchen, and we would recite the words together.

> *Aquí se queda la clara,*
> *La entrañable transparencia,*
> *De tu querida presencia*
>   *Comandante Che Guevara.*

Here stands the leader from Santa Clara,
The endearing one with nothing to hide.
From your beloved presence,
   Commander Che Guevara.

To be honest, the programming itself was not that amusing. It's just what I was accustomed to watching every day. I was attached to its patriotic motives, even though I couldn't process the significance of such powerful statements of nationalism. I guess that's the purpose behind propaganda: people get used to regularly performing certain actions without realizing whether they actually agree with what they are doing until there is a climax, a moment in life when you finally notice that you need to put a stop to it.

I moved indecisively through the same seven channels, trying to find anything but politics to watch. To distract myself from the same routine, I put my favorite movie, *The Lion King*, in the DVD player. My mother smiled and shook her head at my complaints, amazed that I knew all of the scenes in the movie off the top of my head. Mom always laughed at how I burst into tears every time Mufasa died, yet, through the corner of my eye, I could see her staring miserably at the screen. I knew Mufasa's death hurt her as much as it hurt me. Perhaps she had a valid reason to conceal her emotions, but I was only a child.

"The coffee is ready." My dad was in the kitchen scraping off the roasted coffee powder at the bottom of the coffee pot. "Yenni, would you come take *el café* to your mom?"

"Papa, I want some strawberry yogurt."

"Nene, you know you are not old enough to get the yogurt at the rations market. You need to wait a few more years."

The rations markets are places set up by the government where you receive a certain quantity of food according to the number residents in your house. Since I was only six years old, I was only allowed to obtain milk rations. I had to wait until I was seven to receive yogurt. Mom mentioned how important it was for me to get the calcium from the milk, or all of my teeth would fall out, so I drank a full glass of cold milk as my dad chatted with my mom.

Los Olivos 2, our small suburban neighborhood, wasn't the best place in Sancti Spíritus. In fact, it was one of the most violent spots in the city. People sat on their front porches every evening to get drunk and conflicts flourished. There was always some kind of homicide, which of course was never portrayed in the news. My grandma asked us to move to her house in the upper side of town on several occasions, but my dad would kindly refuse her generous offer, saying, "We can't go, this is the place where my family is, where my *niña* was raised."

Our life in Los Olivos 2 was ordinary. We lived in an apartment that consisted of one small bathroom, two rooms, a kitchen which was connected to the living room, and a balcony overlooking a ventilation shaft surrounded by the rest of the compact apartment buildings. That area served as a playground for my friends and me every evening when our mothers would get together with their neighbors to watch telenovelas while our fathers rested to gather strength for the next work day. We would sit in a huge tractor tire filled with dirt and tell scary stories or just talk about our day.

The neighborhood was mostly known for having the only medical college and only sports academy in all of Sancti Spíritus. Many medical students from the Middle East who came to Cuba to get a college degree stayed in Los Olivos 2 and then returned to their native countries. It was the most diverse neighborhood in town.

Yennifer with her parents, Norma Izquierdo Gomez and Arnoldo Coca

The educational curriculum in Cuba is very rigorous. From elementary school until college you are not allowed to use a calculator in school, and middle schoolers usually take high school courses. But there's a notion that the free education system in Cuba places every student in college, which is not necessarily correct. In order to attend high school in Cuba, and later college, students must be at the top of their class and have a solid academic resume.

Most of the Middle Eastern students in my area paid my neighbors to cook and do laundry, since the food provided by the Medical Institute was not good. A young Palestinian girl used to come to my house to use the phone in order to access the internet. She'd bring me caramel chocolates since she knew they were my favorite, and sometimes she'd get together with my neighbors to cook her traditional foods. This was the first time in my life that I ate lamb. She was excited to try Cuban food as much as my neighbors were to try exotic Middle Eastern recipes. At first, I wondered why she covered her hair but didn't ask, scared I would seem disrespectful. Many of my neighbors also wondered and were judgmental at first. However, over time they realized that perhaps we share more in common than we think we do, even if it is something as simple as a chocolate bar or a recipe.

My mother Norma was a housewife. She quit her job right after she gave birth to my brother in order to take care of him and deal with the house's chores. After she gave birth to Pablo, she met my father, moved to the city, and bought a decent apartment in Los Olivos 2. Fourteen years later when she was 42 years old, I was born, and she continued her life as a housewife.

She always said providing her children with an education was far more important to her than having a job. But I often wonder if she really wanted that for her life: bearing a child, cooking three meals a day, cleaning, and doing laundry for every single person in the house. With her youthful spirit, she could have found a job at any school in the city, yet she set her dreams aside for us. My mother always wanted to work, but how could she find a profession if society encouraged her to remain at home washing dishes and taking care of the kids?

The cult of domesticity has been part of Cuban society for a long time, yet people fail to recognize its existence. When you have been living under the same principles your entire life it is difficult to emerge from such a conservative mindset. I remember getting my first doll when I was three years old. I would wake up every day, prepare her milk in my little kitchen set, sing her songs, and make sure she was always content in order to avoid pushing her stomach button, which would make her cry insanely. I was born in a country where instead of teaching little girls to stand up for what they believe in and be leaders, we toss them a baby doll, then expect them as adults to be self determined. But how can we be autonomous when all we have ever known is how to fulfill our maternal role?

Mom was such an adventurous woman then. She took kids on expeditions to the Escambray Mountains and to Tope de Collantes, two of Cuba's best known sierras. I would never criticize my courageous mother, who basically raised my brother by herself, for choosing not to follow her professional desires. I would never criticize her for being dragged into an abyss of societal expectations. She might not have a college degree, or even a high school diploma, but she does have the purest, most courageous soul in the entire universe, and she knows the definition of struggle, of loss. She knows what it is like to be betrayed by the people who promised her a stable future, yet she chooses to be the best version of herself on a daily basis.

My father had always lived in Sancti Spíritus and had always been self employed. At first, he sold bicycle parts and stereos. Eventually, he built one of the first rice mills in Sancti Spíritus. Every time someone mentioned our last name, Coca, everyone knew they were referring to the millers. It kind of became a family business and our identity.

My daily bike rides to the mill with my dad were undoubtedly the best part of my summer vacation. It was fascinating to wake up in the fresh Caribbean mornings, put on shorts, flip flops, and hop onto the backseat of his antique bike. I gripped my beloved father's torso tightly, never knowing what to expect next as we wandered around the isolated boulevards at 6:00 a.m. I lived for the thrill, the interest in new places and people yet to be discovered. These bike rides not only awakened my curious instincts, they were a way in which my dad and I could connect and talk about topics that we would not talk about at home, like politics, history, and religion. We knew our mother would feel uneasy if we chatted about controversial topics; she was raised most of her life in a conservative, communist household.

The early morning wind rolled through my hair making it flow like blossoms on a tree. I pressed my tiny feet onto the metallic sides of the bicycle as my dad's exhausted legs kept going. These rides allowed me see a part of Cuba I was not familiar with. My parents had always worked to ensure that I had everything I wanted, and I thought all kids my age were granted the same opportunities. Traveling around the city exposed me to the reality of the social classes in Cuba that are usually disregarded by many. I observed people's faces: some overwhelmed with despair, others robust with hard labor. Even though my dad thought some of the poor people we saw on the streets didn't want to work, I could not help but feel remorse for them. They would gather in Serafín Sánchez Park, wait for foreign visitors to come out of the main hotel, La Plaza, then supplicate for fifty cents or a dollar. I wondered how they could live in such circumstances when communism supposedly ensured financial equality for every citizen.

I was forced to believe my country was a utopia where socio-economic issues were nothing to worry about. "Socialismo o Muerte," my friends and I yelled at the top of our lungs every morning while standing in the school's plaza. But where were the Marxist ideals expressed in the Communist Manifesto? Even though the government attempted to enforce the utopian economic state where no social classes were present, it was not successful. Students were all required to wear uniforms, and schools prohibited the use of jewelry. Restrictions were supposed make us seem as equal as possible, but you could not help but see the imparity among us. The kid with the ripped socks and deteriorated backpack muttered

Yenni and Arnoldo in the rice mill

the national anthem right alongside Patricia with the red bow in her hair and expensive Lacoste tennis shoes who complained about the heat as the sun reflected on her gold necklace.

The streets of downtown Sancti Spíritus were extremely crowded. The merchants sold a variety of handmade artifacts and I often begged my dad to stop for chocolate ice cream as we were on the way to the mills. Dad pulled out three red pesos, Che's face poking out of the bill, leaving only a few quarters in my dad's pockets. The ice cream man had a polished head and affable manners. He knew me and would remember my order: chocolate ice cream with honey, and some kind of red coloring to replace the dessert syrup that was unavailable. "Dad, do you want some ice cream?" I would ask him every time, somehow aware that he was not able to buy two cones. "No, Nene. You can have it all. You need some meat on those bones," he said with a comforting smile. "Papa, you know this is too much for me," I said, trying to avoid the "you need to eat more" sermon. He would shake his head, but I shared my ice cream with him. His eyes were filled with love and joy.

My grandma's house in Colón was located one hour away by bike from my home in Los Olivos 2. It had multiple rooms and patios, and unquestionably was the biggest house around and, I would also argue, one of the most visited places on the entire avenue, almost like a sanctuary. People came just to sit around and talk. It was full of neighbors each afternoon who chattered with my grandma and drank cups of coffee, their kids running around playing with each other, chasing my grandmother's beloved cats.

In the back of the house, my uncle Chichi worked as a welder. He lived with my aunt and two cousins. All of his work and tools were out back in a chaotic zone overcrowded with wires, metallic chunks, disintegrated bike parts, bird cages, and a few livestock corrals that would be deserted during the holiday seasons when my uncles Chichi and Lazaro slaughtered the pigs.

In the front of the house where my grandmother and grandfather lived, my dad built a rice mill. Going there with Dad was always entertaining. As soon as we arrived at my grandma's house, he would put on his damaged and dusty working apparel and I would sit on my grandma's bed playing with dolls until I heard the sound of the mills turning on. Then I would run to the front of the house, sneaking through the front door hoping my grandma would not catch me so I could help my dad put the rice powder into sacks which later on would be processed by the mill. My grandma and mother were not fond of their six-year-old girl working in a mill with a shovel and covered in dust, yet my dad would let me work with him anyway because he knew how much I loved it.

Most of my dad's customers were farmers or people who owned livestock. The rice powder he processed had a lot of nutritional value and could fatten a pig by a few hundred pounds in less than ten months. We also received visitors from the countryside in wagons selling fresh milk and cheese. My dad would exchange the rice powder for their dairy items, since my grandma loved organic products.

My grandmother, Sara, is one of the most compassionate people I have ever known. She often brought food to her neighbors if they did not have any,

Yenni with her grandmother, Sara Minguez Carret

or gave them her bread quota. She wore a long tight apron on her waist, which in my eyes made her look like a medieval princess, and her voluminous silver hair hovered in the air like clouds on a summer morning.

Grandma believed lunch was the most important meal of the day and should not be missed no matter what. The entire family would come together to eat her delicious black beans. Even if someone from the family was working, they would get off work for a few minutes, have lunch, and then go back to their everyday activities. Every time we asked for her secret ingredient, she said they were made out of love, but I knew the secret was cilantro that she cultivated in a ceramic pot and took care of every day.

Her neighborhood is Tejar y Mambi. The name "Tejar" is derived from the tile factory located nearby, which was a job site for neighbors and family members. "Mambis" is the name given to patriotic farmers who fought alongside other combatants in the Cuban Revolution. Tejar y Mambi was a poor district. The main street was a straight dirt road lined with cardboard houses. Women rushed out of their doors sweeping carefully, ensuring their balconies were pristine while coughing at the commotion of dust. Despite the tropical music of Polo Montañez on the radio—maracas and tambours stirring the spirit of the occasion—their faces looked weary.

Tejar y Mambi was a typical Cuban barrio with a *panaderia* at the corner of the street, one small store, a polyclinic surrounded by food places, and a butcher shop on the balcony of a house. The butcher would place the meat on the rails of the balcony so all of my neighbors could see the day's meat when they walked by. I remember the house where I usually bought my candy, four pieces for one peso, which seemed like an excellent deal back then. The *panaderia* was a place of social interactions where the elderly met up every morning to chat and get out of the extreme temperatures of summer.

Once, when I was sent to the *panaderia* to get our daily ration of bread, I lined up alongside all of the elders and I heard a woman shouting, "This bread only gets worse."

"It is almost as if we were back in the Special Period all over again," a light voice responded.

When it was my turn, the woman distributing the bread took my *libreta*, the little notebook that keeps track of your food rations. She opened the page to the date and signed it with her scribbly handwriting. I gave her the few pennies my grandma had put at the bottom of the cloth bag, and placed the four small rounded pieces of bread into it. Outside, people were still talking about the Special Period. I had heard my grandmother and aunt mention the phrase before, but was never sure what it meant. Whatever it was, it must have been significant if you heard about it on the street corner.

As soon as I got home, I ran up to my grandma. "Abuela, what is the Special Period?"

"*Ay, mija,* don't you think today is not the day to talk about this? Why don't you go and take the bread to your aunt who is waiting to make some *torrejas.*"

"Grandma, everyone is talking about it, and you know I do not like to be left behind in conversations."

"You are a curious little girl." She calmly sat on the kitchen chair, so I sat on her lap as usual. Grandma moved a strand of her silver hair aside and positioned herself in a comfortable manner. I could see in her eyes that she was ready to open up and let all of these memories out.

"The Special Period was a time after Russia and Cuba broke their economic relations, devastating our island. We lost canned goods, chocolates, condensed milk, meat, and household supplies," she said. I wondered how could all of this have happened so fast in a country that had once had so many material goods. When Cuba and the Soviet Union kept good relations and Cuba traded sugar in exchange for inexpensive Russian products which overcrowded the stores, Cubans prospered for once. But after the relations among both nations dissolved, the island suffered a serious downturn. It was extremely difficult to find everyday products at the market, and hunger, poverty, and unemployment flourished.

"Did you know your cousin Yadira was born during that time?" Grandma said quietly. "It was really difficult for her parents, given the situation. There was no milk for the poor child in the stores. Your uncle Chichi had to work extra hard in order to provide for the little girl. People back then became magicians in order find ways to regulate their money. We had to fry mango chunks, when there were any, because plantains were too expensive to buy."

Out of all the things I could have said in that moment, the first words out of my mouth were, "Fried mango sounds disgusting."

"You'd be surprised how much the flavor resembles fried plantains. I will make some of those one of these days." she said.

El Período Especial is still considered one of the most devastating chapters of Cuban history. During the U.S. embargoes of the 1960's the economy collapsed and the Soviet Union was the only country that would sell petroleum to Cuba, and the nation's only ally. U.S. economic warfare weakened Cuba, but Soviet support made sure the country's economy would not crumble. But after the collapse of the Soviet Union in 1991, Cuba lost approximately 80% of its imports and exports. Gross domestic product plummeted. Agricultural and industrial systems were paralyzed. Domestic production of meat, milk, and eggs was hampered by the lack of imported animal feed. The disappearance of medicines from local pharmacies, together with food shortages, threatened the health and nutrition of all Cubans.

"It's ironic," my abuela said, "your cousin Yandira was born before the Special Periods, and she had the best childhood you could ever imagine: fine dresses, chocolates of all kinds, leather shoes. But her sister, who was born only five years after, had to go through all that struggle of the time. That poor girl. Our family was just not equipped to deal with this."

My family has always lived in Cuba. We have seen all of it. Long before the Cuban Revolution, my family was quite wealthy. They had numerous plantations, farms, and houses around the country. My grandma's father dedicated his entire life to securing a stable home for his present and future generations. After the Cuban Revolution triumphed in 1959, Fidel obtained power and made Cuba completely communist. He then passed a law known as the Agrarian Reform, which basically meant every person was to be dislocated from their houses, and the government took absolute control over their possessions. My family was left with the clothes they were wearing and 200 Cuban pesos provided by the government to buy a house in the city, although it was not even enough for a month of rent. They spent a few months wandering around the desolate Cuban towns until they found a decent house in a small barrio and were able to build their life once more.

I was recently looking through my computer and found a folder named "Grandma's scanned photographs" with some images of my grandma in her youth. One picture that I remembered as one of my grandma's most valuable possessions. The photograph was taken outside of a rustic ranch in the Escambray Mountains, a group of mountains and trenches at the outer side of the country. Twelve of my family members stand in front of the dilapidated cottage, wearing their best attire and staring numbly at the camera. The photograph was taken before 1959 in an estate called Saltadero de los Palmarito in Caracusey, Trinidad before the property was taken by the Castro government. The house belonged to my great grandfather, Camilo Minguez, who in the photo is wearing light pants, a long white shirt, and black boots and who is seated beside his wife, Isabel Carret, the woman with the silky dark hair and dotted dress who is embracing her grandchild.

Sara Minguez Carret's family in the Escambray Mountains before the revolution

Camilo immigrated from Spain with his father and settled in Guni Miranda, Santa Clara. When he was just nine years old, disease killed his siblings and his mother died of a heart attack. His father was killed in a battle between the Mambises and the Spanish colonizers. A nearby family took care of Camilo until he married Isabel, whom he met at a dance hosted by Isabel's godmother Margarita, who raised her. Isabel's parents were originally from France. They settled in the Valle de los Ingenios in the city of Trinidad, which had over fifty sugarcane mills in three valleys where 30,000 slaves worked on sugarcane plantations. Isabel's parents died when she was a young girl and left her a fortune.

Camilo had a farm where he made local cheese. He also had livestock, and cultivated the land. Camilo was really generous towards the employees on his farm and offered them horses so they could go visit their families during the holidays, and provided them accommodations when their families came to visit. He supplied them with food such as milk and yuca so they could get by.

Camilo was really jealous with his family, especially his young daughters. He was selective with their boyfriends and made sure they were from the middle or higher class. When my grandmother and her sisters would attend the festivities, my great-grandfather made sure they only danced with the gentlemen he selected who were from good socioeconomic positions. He did not let his daughters have boyfriends, yet they used to write secret letters to their crushes.

Next to Camilo and Isabel in the photo are their two youngest children, Eugenio Minguez and my grandmother Sara Minguez. Their personalities seem distinctly different. Eugenio looks like the reckless one. I imagine him running around the hen house, stealing all of the eggs, or sneaking out to go swim in *La Playa Ancon*. Grandma was the entire opposite. She was noble, and undoubtedly the closest to her mom, who encouraged her to read and be curious as a young girl. I can imagine Sara, sitting on the front porch every night on Isabel's lap, swinging a paper fan back and forth as Isabel narrated stories of her childhood; that is probably where Grandma got her passion for telling stories.

Next in the photo come my grandma's brothers and her three sisters, who are holding onto her nephew. Angela and Maria probably designed and sewed their own dresses, which seem to be made from the same material, but with slightly different details around the neck. The next two young women were family friends, who probably got together with all the girls in the house and went by wagons to shop in the center of town every weekend, or help with the planning of family celebrations such as Saint Blaise

Day, also known as the Blessing of the Throats, a Catholic feast day celebrated on February 3.

On that day, many Cubans came to Caracusey and an orchestra from Havana also came. During the celebration, everyone came to the house and danced all night long. Afterwards everyone went down the streets and walked around Caracusey holding candles, and then returned to the festivities. During that day, they also baptized little kids, and Camilo Minguez brought a circus, musicians, and poets to town.

The triumph of the Revolution of 1959 was an extremely difficult period for the entire family, but especially for my grandma's parents. Camilo could not bear losing everything he had ever owned. The stress was so overwhelming that he died two months afterwards of a heart attack. My great-grandmother fell into a state of depression and she never recovered. Fifty-eight years have passed, and my grandma cannot help but burst into tears every time she sees this photograph, not because of the money that was lost, but because she lost two of the people whom she loved the most. Grandma hugged me tightly. "I am sorry, Abuela." After ten minutes of conversation, those were the only words I was able to utter.

Arnaldo Coca Minguez

I've heard the story of our family losing their property to the Cuban government countless times, but I never really understood the reasons why, or the lasting implications, until my dad explained it to me. Taking the time to sit with him for an interview and talk about his past allowed me to see my dad as different person, to finally understand his roots and understand where he came from. I realized that even as a young boy he worked to ensure he wouldn't have to financially depend on his family, who did not have any money. Perhaps that's what motivated him to provide me with the best he could afford at the time. As a child I never really comprehended the reasons why he wanted to move to America or leave our family behind. Throughout his interview, he allowed me see the rationale behind his actions.

—YENNIFER

My mother and her family lived in the countryside, up in the mountains of Escambray. After the revolution, a large group of armed resistors, insurrectionists, anti-revolutionists holed up there. The fighting and resistance to Castro was so severe that the government had to remove all the farmers and peasants who had been living there, clear them out, so that they could better bring in troops in order to combat the resistance up in the mountains. My grandparents were landowners up in Escambray, and because of this relocation, for combating the insurrection, they were actually displaced.

They were forced off their land and sent to the city with very little in the way of resources. They had to leave their property behind, which included land, houses, as well as all their livestock, and essentially their means of livelihood. My grandfather arrived in the city with very little and he saw that everything that he lived for and worked for all his life had been confiscated and shortly after that, he died. My grandmother took the little bit of money that they had given her as compensation and she bought a little house in which she was to live with my mother.

Back then, it was very difficult to make any kind of claim against the government. The government had its priorities set, and there was very little that someone like my grandparents could do about being displaced. So nothing was ever done about it, and we

came along and we were born and raised under circumstances of poverty. As children, we grew up with the painful memory that my parents lost everything that would have contributed to their wellbeing. We set out to try to make the best of a bad situation. But we knew that there was very little with which to work. There were very few resources.

I grew up with my parents and three siblings in a barrio called Reparto Colón. My older sister's name is Esperanza. I'm the second, then Ana Esther and Armando. From the time I was very young, my parents always emphasized going to school because we're a studious family. My dad was never able to study in Cuba because back in his day it was difficult to take time to study. He had to work to help his family.

My childhood in Cuba was a happy one. I liked to play a lot and I grew up in secure surroundings despite the fact that we lived away from the city center in the barrios where people of limited resources live. The houses aren't as nice, but it was safe, just poor because of the economic conditions which, back then, were tough. Economic problems have been around practically my whole life.

My dad worked in a bar and he earned very little. My mom didn't work because we were four kids and she had to take care of us. And the truth is, I had a pretty tough childhood that was lacking many things like food and clothing. I have very sad memories of those days. My dad spent eight hours a day working and my mom spent her time tending to the household and taking care of us. The neighborhood wasn't bad because everybody in it was very close knit, and everybody got along together. With what little we had, we helped one another out. If somebody didn't have any food, a neighbor would split what he had and share a part of it.

When I got older, about twelve or thirteen, I began to be able to help my dad, who had started working with a friend delivering building supplies. When I got out of school, I would go with him to help him load the materials like brick and cement. I enjoyed helping him. My dad offered to pay me, but I wouldn't take it. I would leave it for the good of the household, for food and clothing. It was a matter of subsistence.

After I finished primary school, I undertook a three-year program of study in economic planning because it seemed that it would offer the most jobs, and these jobs would be in an office. After three years, I got a job at a company, and that's where I intended to establish myself. I started off there, working in accounting, which was not the job that I had been trained for, because you have to start off at the bottom. So there I was, doing accounting, rather than the thing I had trained for. I worked an eight hour day, I'd get off at about 5:30, then I'd go over and help my dad with his work. I spent a total of eight years working there, but the salary wasn't quite enough to provide me with much of a living. So I decided to leave and forge my own life independently. Even though I had studied practically my entire life, what I was making as a result of all this study wasn't going to get me through life. I just was not getting enough compensation or salary.

So I put my mind to trying to figure out what it was that I could do in order to help myself improve economically. I wound up buying a rice milling machine because there were a lot of farmers in the area who needed to have rice processed so that they could sell it or consume it for themselves. One of the most important things is to remove the outer husk, and the farmers didn't have any means to process the rice, so they'd come over with their unprocessed rice and I'd run it through my mill.

Our milling operation was very popular. The people that came to the mill were country folk, they were farmers. Some of the people were also city folk, of course they didn't have farms or they didn't grow products in the city, but sometimes on the weekend, they would come and they would be able to produce some crops and they would bring rice for me to process. They didn't necessarily pay me with money, but they would give me some of the processed rice and I would eat some of it and sell what was left over and make a little bit of money. I sold the rice that I had left over for a fairly modest price, because I wanted to be sure that people who didn't have much to eat would be able to afford it.

It wasn't easy. I had to buy the equipment and the parts, and I didn't have a lot of money. There were the electronic parts, as well as the motor, and those things were really quite expensive. I did have some money saved up, but it was not enough. It kind of pains me to say this, but I had to sell some household things in order to have enough money to buy the equipment.

I was working at this for several years, and the whole objective was to try to make some money, to move up ahead, and to make the business profitable so that I could afford the kind of life for me and my family that we needed. And after a bit we were beginning to make it. With the little bit that was left

over, we were able to improve our lives. I was able to barter with others, to get other kinds of food. We got beans for example, some meat. There was rationing back in those days. We would get a rationing book from the government that listed what the government proportioned to each family per month. It would contain basic foods in it, like rice, beans, grain, a little bit of milk. There was also an allotment of milk for families who happened to have children. But, the amount of food we got for a month would actually barely last a week.

We were able to save up and with our money and our savings. One thing we did was buy pigs so that we could raise pigs in order to slaughter them, and sell the meat—we didn't sell the meat for a high price, of course we had to sell it for a modest price, but between the rice business and raising pigs for meat, we were able to save up enough money to do improvements to the house itself. We would work from Monday to Sunday, every day of the week. I was able to make enough and save enough until I was able to finally come here to the United States to find a better life for myself, my family, and my daughter. Leaving Cuba was painful for my family because we were very tight knit. But at the same time, they were proud that this could happen. They understood that, by coming to the United States, I would have 100% of opportunities presented to me. Not only for myself, but for our entire family.

They didn't let me in right away. It was a very long and difficult process, and I had to prove a lot of different things. The program was for political asylum or political refugees and it was different for everybody. You answer all their questions, provide proof that they need to see, and if they're satisfied, the government of the United States will let you in. My brother and I were lucky in that we managed to satisfy everything that the U.S. government wanted to know, and so now here we are.

My brother and I came here to Kentucky and didn't know anyone or anything. A number of church organizations came to us and began to assist us with our relocation. They helped us economically, and they helped to integrate into a new society. After a number of years, I was able to apply for and get my daughter to come and join me here.

This is a very developed country, it's real different from Cuba which, of course, is lacking many, many resources and suffers developmental issues. I was taken by the economic and cultural circumstances here. I was on the airplane on the way to Miami, and when the plane landed and I got off, I looked around, and I saw all the big buildings, the beach, the whole city, the movement of the traffic, the cars, and all the people moving about. I felt quite a bit of stress because this was all new to me, I hadn't seen anything like this before. Here I was, finally out of Cuba, and there were going to be opportunities for me, and I knew that I was going to have to take advantage of these opportunities.

When I got to Kentucky, my brother was waiting for me and he brought me to where he was living. I spent a couple of months with him and then through Kentucky Refugee Ministries, I learned about the culture. They helped me learn English and I was able to kind of set off on my own, become independent and not have to live with my brother. So with the help of KRM, I was able to move out and rent a place

on my own. They helped us incorporate, get accustomed, and integrate into the society of this country.

The programs they had, they were pretty good. And they had people from all over the place. They had Cubans, people from Asia, they had people from Africa, people from all different countries, all different cultures. KRM gave us classes. Overall, it was a very nice thing.

The only job I've had here is at the JBS Swift Company, which is a meat packing company. It's the only job I've had and I've been there about eleven years. Things are going pretty well for me. I earn factory wages, but these wages are acceptable to me, they're totally adequate for me to make a living. The salary is adequate not only for me but for the support of my family. I'm a forklift operator, but I've done every kind of job that they have. Look, it's factory work, so it's hard work. But at the same time, I'm proud of what I do, because not having a lot of education, I make money and I make enough to take care of my family.

About 70% if the people that work there are Hispanic, and the majority of them are Cubans. By and large, the people that come directly from Cuba don't have the skills and they wind up doing factory or manual labor jobs. Some of them wind up advancing, learning what they need to improve their lot. Most Cubans, back in Cuba, spend the majority of their lives studying or trying to learn a profession. I find it painful because, as youths in Cuba, we spend our entire adolescence studying, and then when we get here and what we've learned back at home doesn't help up at all. In addition to the language problem, the diplomas and degrees that we get in Cuba aren't recognized here. They don't do us any good. In order to practice a profession that we might have pursued previously back home, we have to practically start all over again from the very beginning.

The language is the biggest obstacle for me here. Part of the problem is of course, I don't have any time to study. I spend all my time working. I work many hours and I come home and I'm tired, so I want to go to sleep. There are opportunities where I work for you to get ahead, or perhaps switch positions, but if you don't know the language, you just can't do it.

I'm the type of person that likes to focus on positive things. And for me, being positive, it means just trying to get ahead. In this country, you do have a chance to get ahead. Even if it's hard work or manual labor, if you put your mind to it and work hard, you can get ahead, and you also have the opportunity to pursue courses of study.

I brought my daughter here about three years ago so that she could have better opportunities, a better life, and so she could improve herself. We gave her private lessons in English so that when she came here, she would already know the language and be able to do better. Because of that she was able to start school normally. I'm very proud of her and I'm very proud to watch her as she makes her way in this country, as she makes progress day by day. I'm also very proud to know that the things I was not able to accomplish, my daughter is able to do them.

I know my daughter is in a country where she can pretty much do or become whatever she wants to. So long as she's intellectually up to it, this country will give her all kinds of support. She can finish high school, she can go to college at the university, she can pick whatever career path she wants. With that, I hope that she can advance and make a happy and satisfying life. And at the same time, turn around and use her skills and her knowledge to help everybody else in the community. The main thing I want is that she has a better life than me.

Kentucky is a nice state. It's peaceful, it's a quiet environment. I haven't seen any violence, maybe a little bit. I think that this is one of the best states in the United States to live in. I like it because the immigrant population seems to be growing, especially among Cubans. A lot of them have gotten ahead, made something of themselves. They have businesses, stores, restaurants. They've established the kinds of businesses that work well to help out the Hispanic community here. We're all a part of this, and we contribute to the development of the community. I'm proud of this. I'm proud of this state.

Kentucky has given me and my daughter the opportunity to get ahead. I'm very satisfied because I know that my daughter is getting ahead in life, in her studies, and me too, even at work. In the future, I'd like to get a different job. Something that isn't as difficult to do. I'd like to be able to improve myself intellectually also and just to live here with my daughter and whatever family she's going to have in the future. I'd like to travel to Cuba every now and again. I'd like to go to Cuba and visit my family that's there, but I'd always like to come back and live a normal life.

Yenni in her school uniform with her dad and the Cuban poet José Martí

Although my dad worked most of his life in the rice mill he built, it was not enough to support the entire family. When I was barely seven years old, without realizing the huge consequences it would have, my dad decided to move to the United States to find better financial opportunities. The day he left, I was sleeping in the bed Dad had gotten me when he realized I was too big to be sleeping in a toddler's bed. Dad gave me a profound kiss on my forehead. It was 4:00 a.m., so I thought he was going to work or to his daily trips to Havana as he usually did. "I love you, *mi niña*," he quietly said. I woke up for a second, observed his bleak face, and went back to sleep. What seemed to me like a visit to the street corner became a lifelong journey.

I woke up to the sound of morning birds, and my mom was standing in the kitchen, waiting for the water to boil. I found it unusual that my dad was not there. He stayed at home on Saturdays to have breakfast with us. Some Saturdays we even went to the *panaderia* together on his bike to pick up our ration of bread to eat with garlic, oil, and salt. I sat down on the couch for my favorite Saturday TV shows. "*Mi niña*, why don't you go and brush your teeth first?" Mom said from the kitchen. "Okay, Mom," I answered. I was surprised by how she did not comment on my dad's absence. I often wonder if she really was unaware of my dad's departure, or if she was too shocked to acknowledge that my dad was no longer there. Although her brain tried deceiving her, I believe my mom's heart attempted to warn her. She must have known something was not right.

The week before my dad left Cuba without telling us, there had been a huge celebration at my grandma's house where the entire family pretended to commemorate my cousin's quinceañera. In reality, the celebration was my dad's farewell party. All of my family members seemed to be aware of the situation except for Mom and me. If I had known Dad's plans, perhaps I could have stopped him from leaving and my mother would not have experienced so much pain.

That day at the party, my mother sat in a corner by the sink my grandma used to wash the clothes every Sunday morning. I saw her from afar, drowning in a cloud of cigarette smoke like she was trying to suffocate her preoccupations. Her rosy hands trembled like they did every morning when she covered the Soviet blender to prevent the banana smoothie from spilling. When she handed me the crystal cup, her hands would still be shivering.

Such a maternal instinct, I thought as she kissed my cheek unexpectedly and embraced me tightly, unleashing all of her tension into my narrow body. Mom remained still as Dad approached us with a declining smile.

In retrospect, I could have seen in his charcoal eyes the fear of loss, of facing the unknown, and leaving his loved ones behind. It takes a whole lot of courage to stand in front of the two people who you love the most and carry out a regular conversation, pretending everything is fine, when in reality you are melting inside.

"What are two of my favorite people doing here sitting all by themselves?" he said sweetly.

"Just talking to Yenni." I could sense from Mom's response that something was wrong; although she was an introvert, her quietness was a sign of concern.

Now I know that my father was dealing with his own demons at the time: preparing to move to a different nation and leave his family behind. But if he would have taken one minute of that conversation to tell us what was going on, perhaps my family would not have been separated. "I guess I will leave you all to it then," Dad replied, and walked into the crowd, my mom's cigarette smoke circulating behind him.

After my father left Cuba for America, my mother fell into a period of deep, major depression, and developed symptoms of post-traumatic stress disorder. Because of her medical condition, she was hospitalized for several months at the largest psychiatric facility in the province, which was always overcrowded.

The last time I saw my mother before she was hospitalized in the asylum was a Friday afternoon. The day had felt dull since I first opened my eyes in the morning. I started my daily school routine in the kitchen, where I ate a piece of crusty bread and grabbed a glass of cold milk from the chaotic fridge. I walked down to my bedroom, and took out my red uniform from the wooden closet whose nighttime shadow scared me as a child. I noticed the skirt was kind of wrinkled at the bottom so I tried to smooth it out. I collected the white socks I'd been wearing the entire week from the laundry bag and put my black orthopedic boots on. I walked down to my mom's room, knocked on the door, and found that she was still asleep in her green striped pajamas. Clothes, shoes, papers, and food had accumulated on the bedroom floor, and I struggled to climb into the bed to kiss her frigid forehead. She was exhausted and gave me one of those, "you better do good at school today" looks, and resumed her sleep. "I love you," I responded. I waited for a few seconds for a sign of affection, and with a feigned smile left home.

The day at school went as usual. I hung out with my friends, went to all my classes, and somehow lived through yet another history lesson proudly instructing us on the Cuban Revolution of 1959. Revolutions are supposed to be acts of change for one of the systems at play, the oppressor or the oppressed. One of them always maintains absolute power while the other fragments into submission. I was never able to comprehend why, if the entire purpose of a revolution was to achieve a "common good," so many things were wrecked afterwards: buildings torn down, death, poverty and political conflicts, family separations.

I guess humans persevere when it comes to doing what is best for them without realizing the damage they can bring to others. They try to justify their actions by making them fit into the "common good." But, after all, I was born in a communist society, where people mistake the common for the best.

For lunch, we usually went outside. My principal was one of those people who believed that mother nature had a solution for all your concerns, that a recreational event once a month would keep the students engaged in school, and that placing students at the front door each morning to collect the names of those who arrived late would help everyone be on time. Her office decorations revealed a dedication to Marxist principles common to all of my teachers. I do sometimes wonder if she actually thought communism would ever achieve the ideal as Marx saw it, or if she was one of those people who pretended to be a communist just to get by. After all, she was the school's principal, and she had to lead by example.

I sat under a tree by myself, devouring a round piece of bread, choking on a glass of thick yogurt and watched the disruptive kids running into each other, playing around like a marathon of wild puppies. Meanwhile, affectionate mothers passed lunch sacks to their kids through the school's gate. Inconsiderate kids, afraid of being mocked afterwards, ripped the bag out of their mothers' hands as fast as possible, avoiding being seen by others. I stared at them, jealous, wondering if my mom was doing all right.

I thought of the last time she cooked chicken and rice, her specialty. We went to the *organopónico*—an urban vegetable garden—and she asked me to pick up some carrots. As a kid I was always fond of small things, so I plucked the smallest ones and she made fun of me all the way home. She said she would not send me to pick vegetables ever again because I was still a baby. She knew it irritated me to be called a baby, so I just kissed her cheek to show her I was growing up.

I eagerly awaited the end of the school day so I could go check in on her. When I came home, my mom was sitting in her bedroom floor with a bottle of Clonazepam, *un alivio al dolor* she used to call it, a relief from the ache. Her legs were exposed, pale and defenseless, like a frozen turkey. I moved closer to her and asked if she was okay. Her extremities were tense, as if her body conspired to stop working at any given moment. Words seemed to be fixed in her mouth. She looked so frail. "Get out of my room," she said rigidly. Nine years have passed, and I still remember the emptiness in her voice, the way her defeated eyes consumed the tiny section of warmth left in my hollow heart. I do not blame her. I never would. Sometimes humans are presented with situations they are not equipped to deal with. I wish I had understood that back then. I did as she demanded. Even though I was aggravated, I could not help but be concerned about her.

My room was the only place in the house where I felt comfortable. I locked the door, crawled into bed and played with my Barbies. Even though I played with them daily, it was like I couldn't recognize the doll I was holding in my own hands, how lifeless and stiff it seemed. A few minutes later, I heard bangs, doors being slammed, and all the cooking utensils

The boulevard in Sancti Spíritus

being smashed into the kitchen floor like a dark symphony. I stared at the Barbie doll in my hands, and grasped it as firmly as possible, deflating her plastic body. I moved as if toward the door, but fear overpowered me, so I sat in a corner and cried.

When an ambulance pulled up in front of my house, I ran to the living room where my mom sobbed uncontrollably. I hugged her, told her that everything was going be okay, that it was not the end of the world, and not the conclusion to her story. Two old white men blocked the path toward her while an odious lady repeatedly said, "Child, you have to get

out of the way." My mom was so delusional she kept saying, "Yenni, help me, help me, they are gonna kill me!" as they took her to the ambulance. I got out the door and sprinted towards my angel with all the energy I had left. I wanted to hold her in my arms, tell her that I loved her, but it was too late.

All eyes were on me, and I began to feel uneasy. Individuals came out to their balconies and glanced at me, trying to conceal their curiosity. For a second I was lost in space. I didn't know whether to run, or scream, or cry. I wanted to program my brain to delete everything that happened in that instant,

As a kid, I would wrap a torn bed sheet around my narrow body and pretend I was a princess in my secret garden. My friends would come over and we'd sit under the trees, smashing the driest almonds with a brick to eat the nut. Neighborhood kids began to sneak up at night to steal the almonds and tear the branches, so my parents built an iron fence around it to protect their dearest daughter's playground, to make sure she was kept in a safe place. I crafted a little utopian world inside that fence, a world where I was a gorgeous princess, daughter of the king and queen, who lived in a place where affliction, depression, economic issues, and family separations were not real. Outside that fence, I know that the ache is what makes us human, vulnerable, what makes us feel, but sometimes I still wish to run and hide behind the almond trees.

Outside, the turbulent wind dried my tears into anger towards myself for not preventing this from happening, for not stopping them from taking her. Perhaps if I had cried louder, they would have felt sorry and let me stay with her. I turned back and I saw my brother Pablo walking towards me, his long polished black hair resting on his wide shoulders, and his narrow, furrowed brow looking for answers. When he saw that I was crying, and that all the doors at the house were open, he ran as fast as possible until he reached me.

"What is wrong, Yenni? Where is Mami? Why are you crying ? Talk to me," he said, overwhelming me with questions I did not know how to answer.

"*Se la llevaron*," I sobbed.

They took her.

to erase all the memories of my mother, father, my grandparents, my brother, school, communism, loss, financial problems. I wanted a normal life for once, to run free and play in the backyard with other kids without constantly worrying about circumstances that were out of my control.

But I remained still, leaning on the fence that protected the almond trees my father had planted in our garden when I was five years old. He had said they would make nice, refreshing shade when the Caribbean sun invaded our shelter in the afternoon.

After my father's departure and Mom's hospital-ization, I stayed at Grandma's house for about six months. I spent all day wondering where my parents were. Since Mom was not mentally stable, my aunts attempted to obtain my guardianship. My mother may have been in a mental facility, or "*loca*"—a word folks used to mutter when referring to her—but she refused to give up custody. It was comforting to know that although my mamma was mentally unstable, her affection towards me was strong enough to defeat all of her sorrowful emotions.

The realization that both of my parents had left me without explanation or even a simple "goodbye" obliterated me emotionally. When I asked my family members what had happened to them, I was completely ignored like I was some kind of an alien who was incapable of processing the somber moments of human nature. I was so overwhelmed by all the commotion, the ongoing mystery, that I started to believe my parents had passed away. I started showing signs of distress by acting angrily towards my family. My aunt decided that I needed psychological help, just like my mom. Apparently all of your problems back then could be solved at the psychiatric clinic.

The thing about emotions is that they *are* uncontrollable. A bunch of narcotics and counseling can ease the pain for a while, but then you are back in a constant loop of turbulent feelings, unable to escape your own mind. As much as you pretend to be "fine" in order to avoid the weekly appointments or your family's objection, you know the pain resides inside you. It has raised the foundation for a home, and has come to stay.

My family thought about moving me to an elementary school across the street from my grand-mother's house, but I could not bear the thought of leaving everything else I loved, so I came all the way from Colón to Los Olivos 2 to attend school. The bus station was located right in front of the house, and every morning, Aunt Esperanza and I would take the workers' bus which traveled around the entire city picking up laborers, and would leave me twenty minutes away from school.

Every night I would crawl into my grand-mother's arms and she would read to me from *Oros Viejos*, or *Old Gold*, a classic Cuban story book. Our favorite tale was about Dan-Auta, a West African story about a little boy whose parents had died. The last instruction they gave to their daughter Sarra was that her brother, Dan-Auta, should do absolutely anything he pleased so that he would never ever cry. As a result, Dan-Auta constantly put Sarra in haz-ardous situations, yet she always found a way out, and Dan-Auta was kept safe and never cried: when Dan-Auta was playing with a stick and poked out the prince's eye, all of the king's men were looking for him, so Sarra and Dan-Auta found protection by climbing into a tree. In the tree, Dan-Auta wanted to pee on the head of the king, who was standing down below, and Sarra had to let him. Before they could be caught, they were saved by a hawk who dropped Dan-Auta and Sarra in a town which was haunted by a giant dodo who Dan-Auta managed to kill, and he was compensated with a fortune. The story of Dan-Auta shows Sarra's commitment to her little brother, and to her parents' promises at any cost.

My aunt Esperanza used to say I was just like Dan-Auta, since my family, especially Grandma, always spoiled me after my dad came to the United States. I laughed, reminding them that I wasn't as reckless as Dan-Auta, but that I could get away with anything without any consequences. To my family, pleasing me was a way of smoothing out the drastic transitions of the moment: my father leaving, and my mother being hospitalized for a mental disorder.

During the weekends I would visit my aunt Ana, whose house was located just two blocks away from my grandmother's and was one of my favorite places. She had a two-story house with three bedrooms and a back patio. She also had a goat named Beba in her front lawn. I liked climbing onto the roof where my uncle Lazaro's grape vines intertwined onto one another, making space for a pergola. He had a hen house with several chickens, and three corrals for his five pigs. During the weekends at 7:00 p.m., he would put a huge bucket onto the washing sink, and I took the bread that had gone bad during the day and massage it into the water, making a liquid mixture. I would take a few cups of rice powder and add it into the bucket, making the substance thicker and "rich in proteins," as he used to say. We would carefully climb up the dilapidated wooden ladder resting on the patio wall. I would get into the pigs' corrals and empty the previous day's food with a broom while my uncle dispersed the food. He would smile at me with a tremendous sense of joy as he watched me working with farm animals, my little black work boots heavy with wet food accumulating on the soles.

I played with my cousins Danay and Dayana on the roof for most of the evening. The grape vines' heavenly presence sheltered us from the night. We would snatch grapes and give the tiny ones to the chickens who wandered around as we observed the industrial neighborhood, which had an eerie presence. What I loved the most about these moments was creating narratives out of anything catching our attention. If we saw a person rushing down the street, we would instantly assume she was running away from a crime. Or if we saw a shadow by the industrial region, it was definitely an evil spirit trying to take over human existence.

Sometimes we would not even talk at all and would just stare at the dark night sky. My eyes would go blank, connecting the dots of stars to create constellations. As I observed the sky, millions of questions journeyed through my head as quick as a glimpse of light. How can the explosion of one star create all of existence? How come every time we look at the stars we draw some kind of silhouette with our eyes, even though we know constellations aren't real? Most importantly, I was fascinated by the comfort we humans find in the night sky and by the people thousands of years ago who were trying to make it through, just like me.

I wondered if Dad was also looking at the same sky that I found so alluring, and I was convinced that wherever Mom was, she was certainly enjoying it. Nightfall was her favorite time of the day; she never missed it. Every evening we would sit on a wide rock in front of the apartment buildings and we'd talk and laugh at simple things. There was no need for long talk; her companionship was all I could ever ask for.

Mom was hospitalized in Camilo Cienfuegos Hospital for approximately six months. I stayed at

my grandma's house during that period of time. My brother Pablo would check up on me every weekend to make sure I was doing all right. We have always been close and did not want our mother's hospitalization to separate us. Meanwhile, he would spend most of his weekdays with my mother, making sure she was eating properly, taking her medications on time, and obtaining fair treatment at the hospital.

A few months after Dad's departure, Mom was more stable, and she got out of the psychiatric institution. She still had to go to the hospital for monthly check ups, and continued to take anti-depressants. Though there was some conflict in my family about

returning home, everyone agreed I should be with my mother during the weekdays and at my grandma's during the weekends.

I will never forget the day I came back home for the first time. Rain was pouring down, the streets were covered in water, the Yayabo River overflowed, and travel was not recommended. But my family had made an agreement that I would return back home on that exact day. So I got in a horse-drawn wagon with Aunt Esperanza, who struggled to carry the umbrellas while holding the bags of clothing and food we were taking home. We travelled through the main streets in Sancti Spíritus city: Serafín Sánchez,

Ignacio Agramonte, Máximo Gómez, Céspedes—all martyrs of the Cuban Revolution. The rainstorm intensified the closer we got to Los Olivos 2.

In Cuba, we have a tradition in which everyone showers in the open when it rains for the first time in May, to avoid bad luck for the entire year. I looked forward to this moment, and I hoped the rain would be as intense as possible. As soon as the first drops of water touch the ground, all the kids immediately run out the doors to the main plaza. Young women and mothers bring their hair care products, and wash their hair in the rain water, since it is thought to have healing powers. When the rain got heavy, my friends and I would get into my neighbor's garden, which had become a swamp, and play in the mud. As soon as the rain stopped, we would all go inside with hearts full of joy since we were guaranteed good luck for the rest of the year.

I knew it was going to be difficult to come back home again and expect everything to be just fine after all that had happened with Mom. I guess it frightened me to think that she would not be the same person she was before, or that my dad's departure had turned her into someone she was not.

I hardly recognized anything when I got home. I had been out of the house for so long that I'd forgotten where I'd put my favorite toys, or the mug I used to drink yogurt from every morning. My little rocking chair did not feel mine any longer. My dresses were covered in a light layer of dust from being in the closet. It was as though the time I'd spent away had made me outgrow the possessions that had once been important to me. I was a stranger in my own house, but I knew it was only a matter of time before

I felt at home again. That is one of the factors that make us humans: we are capable of adapting to new environments, despite the difficulties we might face.

My mother walked out of the restroom, seeming disoriented. Her luminous blonde hair had become outgrown with dark roots. Her complexion looked pale, and she was slimmer than she had been six months before. Her nails were short; if she had seen them she would have gone that exact same day to the manicurist's house. She couldn't stand not having nail polish on her fingers. She saw me and instantly gave me a genuine hug, embraced me into a ravine of parental emotions. She pulled me nearer her chest, her steady heartbeat pulsing through my narrow torso, releasing a hurricane of mixed feelings. Mom remained motionless. It must have been her anti-anxiety medications that kept her numb. Her distance hurt me at first, but I knew she loved and cared for me. My aunt's eyes showed disappointment at Mom's demeanor, but I sensed a glimpse of warmth in her heart, hidden beyond the sedatives. I had a mother who needed me, and I would not give up on her.

My brother coming home helped my mom's condition improve. He was basically the head of the house, and with Dad's financial assistance he sustained us economically. He made sure my mother was in a stable state of mind by managing her medications, and taking her to the psychiatrist's appointments. He also made my transition back into the house much easier. He woke up every morning at 6:00 a.m., ironed my school uniform, prepared my school lunch and snacks, made sure I was prepared for daily quizzes, and took me to school. At the beginning of every school year, he covered all of my school books with paper. Once a month, he would get off work early to take me to parent-teacher conferences, and discussed my grades with my teachers. We divided the household chores: Mom would cook, my brother did the laundry and cleaned the house, and I did the dishes every once in a while.

Every day after I was done with my school work, we would play hide and seek outside or go buy ice cream at the house on the corner of the street, and Mom would often join us. On Sunday nights, Pablo would bike all the way to my grandma's house in Tejar y Mambi and pick me up so I could arrive at school on time on Monday. Given that he was only twenty-two years old, my brother had a lot of responsibilities. I guess he understood how difficult it was to be raised by one parent. His father left him when he was only two years old, and currently shuns him because of his sexual preference. I would not have made it through those years without his unconditional love and protection. He stayed by my side every step of the way, and was one of the few people who never let my mother down. I am who I am today because he never gave up on me.

Every night I would join my mother on the couch and watch telenovelas while resting in her lap. *La Escrava Isaura* was her favorite one. It told a story of a Brazilian plantation owner who fell in love with one of his slaves, but she refused him. Some people attempted to set her free, but were unsuccessful. Once in a while my dad would pop up in conversation, but we usually overlapped it with a different topic. It took time for us to have a regular talk about what happened when my dad left, but I knew she was improving, slowly becoming herself once more.

My dad left for the U.S. when I was seven, looking for better financial opportunities. Although he tried to spend most of the holidays in Cuba with me, traveling can be expensive. But he visited the island every December. A month before he arrived, my family was painting the house, and making preparations for his comfort, even though they knew he was not carried away by luxuries. My favorite part was the family dinner the day after he arrived. My mom, brother, cousins, and all the family would get together at Grandma's house for an enormous meal on the patio under the night sky. Those were some of the happiest moments of my life. No problems were present. It was a step towards my family's reconciliation.

In mid April, the wind blew a refreshing aura into spring time. Flowers bloomed and the almond trees flourished once more: nature giving birth to a new self. It had been a year since I last saw my dad in person, and I had been counting the days until he arrived from the United States. I woke up early that Saturday morning and put on my best clothing. By midday I was riding in my uncle's antique Chevrolet to José Martí Airport in Havana, five hours away. The flight was supposed to arrive at 9:00 p.m., but we got there at 5:00 p.m. My aunt used to say an early bird always catches the worm. I spent a few hours sitting on a bench outside of the airport. I knew that if I set foot in the place, tears would run down my eyes. It had been one year since I last saw my father, and I did not want to relive my memories of his departure.

At 8:45, we approached the door where all the U.S. arrivals exited. As soon as I got close enough to the ropes for a clear view, I began jumping, trying to see my father who said he'd be wearing white jeans, a black shirt, and a big white sombrero. Minutes passed by. It was 9:40, and I still couldn't find him. It was like constantly opening your refrigerator door, snooping around for food, even though you know there is none left because your big brother probably ate it all.

Then he was out. I gave him a huge hug, and could not help but cry.

Looking back, I recall how much I detested crying when I was a child. I was a firm believer that crying was a sign of physical and emotional weakness. My dad used to tell me that when life throws you a problem, you have to work your way around it because crying won't solve anything. His advice was not necessarily wrong, but as a little girl I always felt like I was deprived of the right to cry without being judged or called out for it. I could feel tears brimming inside of me like a glass of water that was too full. I knew a minor move would trigger all of those emotions. I was startled when my dad also began to cry. That was the first time I'd seen him so vulnerable.

The next day, Grandma made breakfast for the family. I got up and rushed downstairs where the whole family awaited. All eyes in the room were looking at me when they were supposed to be looking at my dad, who was visiting from a foreign country. Beginning to feel uneasy, I asked what the commotion was about.

"Nene, we got great news," my dad suddenly responded.

"What is going on?" I repeated once again.

"Your interview is finally here. I got a call from the U.S. Embassy and already made an appointment.

It is in two days. Now you can finally come to live with me in America," he happily said.

"Wow, Papa, I guess that is amazing, but why didn't you tell me before?"

"I wanted to tell you in person."

I was surprised by the news that I was going to the United States. My family had tried to convince me my that my future would be in America for my entire life, but I had never actually imagined myself in a different country. The possibility of leaving Cuba just seemed too surreal. I guess I'd imagined such a world out there, but never visualized myself being a part of it. Of course I desired to travel and finally see with my own eyes "the land of opportunity" all Cuban-American immigrants constantly talked about. But I was scared to leave my mother after her long depression. My family was already preparing my mom for the news, though the immigration appointments and paperwork had made it evident. When my brother and I told her I was leaving in July, she reacted unexpectedly. Her face saddened, yet she seemed mostly calm. She had been preparing herself for this moment her entire life, knowing someday or another she would confront it, and she had to remain strong during the process.

"I want the best future for you, *mi niña*," she said, "even if it means I have to let you go."

I had two days before my meeting at the U.S. Embassy in Havana, and I spent them with my family rehearsing what to say, and the proper way to answer the interview questions. I practiced in both Spanish and English. Although I did not know the language, my grandma was convinced that if I knew some English the interviewer would see how ready

I was to come to America. "Jao arr yew?" my cousin asked with a thick Cuban accent. "I ahm oh kay," I replied. "Why do you want to come to the U.S.?" she continued. I always thought this question was kind of obvious; my dad lived in the U.S., and I wanted to be with him. My family and I continued rehearsing those two questions for two days. My tongue struggled with the "th" sound of the "with" as I practiced saying, "I want to be with my dad."

The American Embassy was located in one of Havana's best neighborhoods. It was a large building located in one of the main parks and surrounded by a high fence. An extremely strong security system protected the place from crowds who dreamt of leaving the country. Dad and I got there at 5:00 a.m. for our 9:00 a.m. appointment, and the line of people was already a block long. I thought it was impossible to attend to the more than 500 individuals who were outside of the building in just one day.

My dad and I sat in the car for a while and decided to eat the sandwiches our aunt had prepared for us the night before. I tried being optimistic and thinking that being there gave them hope, or served as a reminder that they could get out of the country one day. Inside, at 9:30, a woman with a paper in her hands called my name. She directed us inside where we checked in and waited for two more hours in a really quiet room filled with fancy people.

When we were called, my dad nervously stood up, picked up all the paperwork, and went to show my identification. My dad had spent over five years on the process of bringing me here, preparing all the paperwork and the documents necessary for my departure. Once I got to the embassy they knew my entire case, yet there was no way of knowing if I would be able to go. It was totally up to them.

The man asked me one single question in English.

"Why do you wanna go to the United States ?" he said.

"I want to be with my dad." In that moment, it did not sound rehearsed at all. The man could see I truly meant what I said, despite my thick accent.

"Congratulations, you're now allowed to travel to the U.S.," he said. The look on my dad's face was priceless.

It was April, and my dad decided we would wait until I was on summer break to take me to the U.S. so I would be able to adapt better once I got here. During those three remaining months I went to every place in Cuba I had always wanted to go visit.

Departure day was undoubtedly the most difficult moment. I had to leave my entire past behind and settle for a new future, one that I never thought I would be able to have. I remember going to my mother's house at 7:00 in the morning. She was waiting for me in the balcony of our apartment next to my brother, who was coming with me to the airport. Mom refused to go because she knew it would be even harder to say goodbye. She did not seem herself; she was nervously shaking her hands and tears rolled down her gorgeous charcoal eyes. I got out of the Chevrolet, ran up to her, and gave her a kiss on her cheek. The last words she told me before I left were, "Take care, *mi niña*. I love you." "I love you too, Mama," I replied.

I immediately ran up to the car, adjusted myself into the seat, and did not dare to look back, scared I would not be able to leave.

During the ride, I was already feeling the sensation of loss, even with my dad and brother, whom I loved very much, right next to me. My half-brother Pablo was fourteen years older than me, though I often ignore the word "half" because I could not possibly love a person in this world as much as I love him. We have always had a good relationship. Unlike many other older and younger siblings relations, he treats me like I am his daughter. I guess this is a result of all the time he spent taking care of me after my father came to the United States.

Once we arrived at the airport, Dad re-checked our flight and the correct gate while Pablo and I went into a little cafe where we ordered pizza and cokes. Pablo told me about all of the wonderful things I would discover once I got to America, like the internet, malls, and supermarkets. Our order finally arrived, and as I drank the coke, he made fun of me with a typical Cuban phrase, "*Te estás tomando la Coca-Cola del olvido.*" This translates literally as, "You are drinking the Coca-Cola of forgetting." But it means, "You are drinking the Coca-Cola that will make you forget us."

I told him it was impossible to forget about how much I loved him after all the time he spent annoying me. He kissed me on the forehead and told me to be safe. That's all I remember. I was too focused on observing him as much as possible, absorbing every part of him because I knew it would be a long time before I saw him again.

I woke up on a Friday morning with my eyes glued together, avoiding the sunlight that slipped through my window. The beginning of summer marked an official end to a stressful junior year; school assignments and the pressure of getting into college no longer overwhelmed me. It was finally summer vacation, and I was free from responsibilities. I jumped out of bed still in disbelief, stumbling, and holding tightly onto the stairs' handrails as I reached the kitchen where I grabbed a bottle of strawberry yogurt, which is still my favorite. I sat on the sofa and looked out the living room window of my house. I like to say "my house" because it gives me a sense of comfort, but as my dad says, nothing in this country will never really be ours. All that we ever had was left back in Cuba. He is not as content as he was before he moved here, and now realizes how difficult life in this country is. Although his life has changed tremendously in this nation, he's still thankful he is able to financially sustain our family.

Cars moved through my neighborhood on the crowded avenue outside. Back in Cuba, you'd never see so many cars in the street at once. In the United States, it seems like everyone's preoccupied with paying bills and improving their financial status. If you're an immigrant like my father—working twelve to fourteen hour shifts to pay the bills and sustain a family—you hope to save enough extra money to go home to Cuba every once in a while.

The homogeneous townhouse apartments are hard to tell apart. Given their small shape, wooden walls, and ability to catch on fire, my dad calls the houses "little matchboxes." All the neighbors hang distinct ornaments on the outsides their matchboxes to give them a sense of individuality, a taste of their own culture. The Iroquois neighborhood is really diverse, with immigrants from so many different countries. It is impossible to believe half the world could be present in such a small section of this city. We live across the street from the Iroquois Manor Shopping Center, which is just a large parking lot teeming with people from hundreds of cultures. We have Vietnamese and Chinese restaurants, Asian groceries, a Cuban store and jeweler, an African coffee shop, and a Middle Eastern cafe. The neighborhood reminds me of Cuba, where people gather around food with their families, laugh, communicate. There is so much humanity squeezed in such a small area here. It makes me feel at home. I have made friends with people from all over the world, and have slowly found myself blending into a cultural melting pot where I integrate my customs with theirs.

It's been three years since Dad brought me to the United States, where he hoped I would be able to create a future for myself. I had already experienced the loss of a parent at a young age, and I knew the emotional and psychological impact of family separation. But I was unaware of how life in a foreign country would not only be difficult for me, but also for my mother who stayed behind.

Eventually, I'll be economically stable enough to give her the lifestyle she deserves. I will be sure to repay her for all the effort she put in into raising me by herself. In America, I have the opportunity to succeed, and speak up for myself, something I did not have before. This puts a lot of pressure on me because I know my father has given up on his happiness to make sure I create a stable future for myself and for them. I know that someday when my dad is not around, it will be my job to provide for my own family.

I am a rising senior at Iroquois High School, which has opened many doors for me. I participate in school clubs that have helped me understand the world. I work with newcomers to help them with their English skills. As a Hispanic immigrant in this country, I am aware of the hardships we immigrants must face as minorities in this nation. To know that I can help my own people succeed in this new nation has made me realize that we are more than just immigrants; we are individuals with dreams, aspirations, and motivation to excel, and become better versions of ourselves. I want to go to college, and have a career I am passionate about. I want to advocate for change in my community. Perhaps in the future I'll write another book.

Finishing my strawberry yogurt, I went up to my bedroom, reached down to the wooden bookshelf where I kept collections of the artifacts I hold most dear: a copy of *The Alchemist, The Journals of Sylvia Plath, The Art of War,* a teddy bear my dad had brought me from here, and a yellow envelope I brought with me from Cuba where I keep photographs from my childhood. I scanned each photo, but one of them stood out to me the most. It had been a while since I last paid attention to this image, and I'd never thought about its significance and what it actually meant to me. Grandma always used to say photographs have a way of expressing what's beyond words. They retain so much history in every little pixel, but those are only visible when the human heart is willing to reconcile with the past, and where they came from.

I sat up in my bed to get a clearer view, and my eyes adjusted to the picture across a ravine of my recollections: Caribbean mornings on Dad's antique bike, days at the mill, storytime in my grandmother's lap, honoring the apostles of the revolution in my red and blue school uniform.

The photo was taken in my colonial hometown of Sancti Spíritus. The historic Rubén Martínez Villena Library, and the Iglesia Parroquial Mayor, where I was baptized, could be seen in the luminous background. I focused on the four people who were the center of attention. I gazed at their genuine resemblance, analyzed every detail, my heart expanding through my chest, feelings of anguish at losing these faded memories, lost like a favorite childhood toy.

Dad is standing right on the corner embracing me like a precious possession. Although his dark eyes might seem worn out from all the work at the mill and early morning shifts, I sense that he felt whole, as if at that moment his family was all that mattered. I was only one year old. I had my tiny arms wrapped around my dad's neck, relying on his shoulders for support. My body is inclined towards my father, slightly disregarding my mother who is standing by my side, her arm around my legs.

Mom smiles gently at the camera. Her posture is firm, secure, determined, not like the day at my grandma's party when she would be seated in a corner, defeated, as my father left without saying goodbye, or later when she'd sit on her bedroom floor with bottles of pills. She seemed happy that day, content with her life, and the individuals who were part of it.

Next to her is my brother, a teenage boy in black, standing still. His face shines with contentment. Pablo's always had a positive outlook on life; even though he was forced to deal with circumstances that were out of his control at a young age, he did an excellent job at keeping what was left of our family together. He knew he was all I had, and that we had to remain strong.

My confused facial expression reflects my unawareness of the moment. I was probably paying attention to everything around me except what was actually important: being there with my family. I couldn't have known that six years later, I'd long to be back in those moments of calm, the only times when I felt whole and part of something greater than myself, when I was part of a family, a stable home.

I find comfort in telling myself that I took the chance of coming to an unknown nation, driven by the motivation of giving my mother the best I could afford at the time. Sometimes I wonder what would have happened if I had stayed. Perhaps I would not be any closer to becoming a doctor or providing my mother with a daily ration of bread, but at least I would be with her.

I've slowly become more accepting of my past, my history, my roots. I carry them proudly on my back, since comprehending each one of them makes me the person I am today. Now I realize that the love of a mother is sacred, and that my dad has always stepped up and taken the toughest decisions: he was doing what he thought was best at the time. My family is precious, and they have always been there for me. And I know that love requires sacrifices, and those sacrifices often have consequences.

CASA DE LA
TROVA

24

Opposition and Transformation

HERGUES FRANDIN DIAZ

Talking to Hergues was one of the most enriching and thrilling conversations I have ever had. I was captivated by his accounts of his life in Cuba—from being a political prisoner, to accusations of sabotage, to collaborative opposition—and by the courage he demonstrated when standing up against the communist Cuban government.

He was a radio-electronic engineer in aviation and a university physics instructor in Cuba. Like many other Cuban professionals in America who have difficulty finding professions commensurate with their skill level, Hergues currently works a factory job.

Despite all of the difficulties Hergues had to face at first, he's adapted to this country and created a life for his family. He maintains a positive attitude at all times, taking advantage of every opportunity in order to prosper. Most importantly, he is grateful to be in a nation that provides him with the freedom to defend his ideas and speak without censorship.

—YENNIFER

I was born in Songo-La Maya, a municipality in the province of Santiago de Cuba. This is an agricultural town, despite the fact that in more recent times we have seen crops diminish. In the same way, two sugar factories, which were really the economic engine of the country and particularly of the municipality, were dismantled, affecting thousands of people who worked in these mills, although agriculture was also based on other crops such as the production of food, vegetables, and coffee.

I lived with my wife and our children in a typical Cuban neighborhood, with a plaza, an amphitheater, a church, neighborhood stores, and educational centers: a primary school, a secondary school, a pre-university. Places that provided employment were the textile factory and, lately, a tobacco factory. My parents, Dora Diaz Martinez and Francisco Frandin Cribe didn't have many resources. My grandfather was named Pablo Frandin Hurtado, known as Santa Bárbara because he had a store where he sold religious articles. Many people went there to buy religious items—a saint, a Virgin Mary, small devotional cards—but when the Castro Revolution triumphed in '59, all those small private businesses were expropriated. And then the store that my grandfather had was taken by the government and

turned into a butcher shop; when it passed into the hands of the government, the family's standard of living worsened a bit.

When I was born in 1971, the rhetoric of the regime was very strong. This is a totalitarian regime that controls all the structures of society and even what happens within the family. They controlled everything. It was normal in Cuba for a child to recognize Fidel Castro before they could recognize their own parents. The educational system is totally permeated with this hierarchical policy, everything that is taught indoctrinates, and there is always an emphasis on the supposed goodness of the government. You grow up with the rhetoric of "the pioneers for communism," the figures of Che Guevara and Fidel Castro, and it was as if every person in the country thought and believed exactly what the government said.

Now you are growing. You are no longer a child, you are maturing, and you begin to judge the information by yourself. You form your own opinions. And you begin to realize that things are not exactly as they have told you. I was raised in my family with these values.

I entered a military academy and became a cadet. Later I managed to become a radio-electronic engineer in aviation. Little by little, I began to ask myself questions about the things that had been said to me, the things that always appeared in black and white and that in this case did not fit, that is to say that the function of the military is to protect the people, but in Cuba they deviate from their main objective, which is to serve the nation, and not to defend a despotic, dictatorial regime and violator of human rights.

I have an uncle, José Antonio Frandin, who lives here in the United States. He became a political prisoner in '92 when he was in the Armed Forces. It hurts me to remember how they talked about there being no political prisoners in Cuba. The government denied the existence of political prisoners when one of them was of our own family. And this isn't any uncle, but the guy with whom I would go to the stadium, on bicycle rides to look for food for the animals, for the small goats and other things like that. I wanted to find out if I could visit him in prison, but they hid him from us. They would move him from one prison to another. We would plan a visit, according to the rules, and we would arrive with the things we had worked hard to gather and prepare: sugar, bread, some condiments so that he could make his meals there taste better. At the door of the prison, they would send us home, completely frustrated and disappointed that Uncle José Antonio was no longer in that prison.

I think it was when all these contradictions within me began to emerge with such force. I lived through that process, and obviously all those things were changing me. They were changing the way I saw things. I began to completely doubt all the things the government was selling me. I moved forward with my studies, I worked in the military airport of the city of Holguin for five years. But already my thinking was completely different.

It also happens that around the year 2000, my brother, Darwis Frandin Díaz, was expelled from his job as chemical engineer in the oil factory in Santiago de Cuba. He was accused of sabotage. Listen to why: my brother, as an engineer, comes to the plant with great hopes of getting ahead and also making a contribution to society. And in the production process at the plant, he wanted to improve the quality of the edible oil. His suggestions were not really valued, and he was not heard. But he insisted on improving the quality of the product and presented a project to improve it and ended up being expelled by the management, accused of sabotage.

With luck, my brother did not go to prison thanks to two Doctors of Science from the Universidad de Oriente in Santiago de Cuba who defended him. I remember that one of them said, "I am a Doctor of Chemistry, and if the proposal made by Darwin Frandin is bad, I will give up my Doctor of Science degree." Obviously, this completely destroyed the argument of the security agents. These can be colonel or lieutenant colonel or whatever, but if you do not have a graduate degree in chemistry, with what reasons can you prove that what a chemist does is wrong? Then he was released, but, since it's Cuba, he lost his job in the oil factory. They sent him to the Salvador Rosales Sugar Mill and put him to work peeling oranges to make juice for the workers to drink on their breaks.

He said he was not going to do that. He goes to Haiti, stays there for two years, gets a job and manages to get involved in a project to improve water quality in Port-au-Prince, the capital of Haiti. Things went pretty well there. He lives here now, but after two years, he returned to Cuba because because he had the possibility of leaving Cuba via the visa lottery program for the United States.

At that time I was still in the Armed Forces. Two officers in counterintelligence summon me to a meeting after leaving work one day. One of them tells me they know my brother is coming to Cuba in the next few days and they tell me that I have to stay in the military base for as long as my brother is in Cuba. That is to say, for thirty days I have to be in the military base because my brother did not share the ideas of the system and they did not want me to see him. Obviously, my position was that I was going to put the family above everything else: he is my blood brother, the son of my mom and dad, physically we look similar, he has eyes that are a little lighter than mine, but when people see us, they can't tell us apart. It was unacceptable to me not to see him. So I defied the order. I got together with my brother. I spent time with my brother.

When I returned to the military unit, they told me: "From now on, you are no longer a coordinate engineer and you are at the disposition of the regiment. Turn all your belongings in. You have ten days to deliver all your documentation and technical equipment. I was stripped of my rank as first lieutenant and they sent me to perform forced labor in agriculture for five months. It was forced because it was totally against my will. I was picking yuca, weeding, cleaning fields, everything that has to do with agriculture. I did not receive any payment for that activity. Nor did I have any benefit at all from the time I spent in the Armed Forces as such.

After that, I arrived at my house, feeling totally lost, without work, expelled from the army, unemployed. My wife, my little girl and I had only one income, which was her salary. I learned about this project at the municipal universities, and I went to see if I could enter. I managed to get placed in the Municipal University of Songo-La Maya. They gave me the position of computer technician in the computer lab, and after a Master's in Educational Information, I was asked if I would like to be a professor of physics at the Universidad de Oriente, to which I answered of course. For me it was an achievement, I accepted, and I joined the Universidad de Oriente as a professor of physics in the Department of Applied Physics of the Higher Polytechnic Institute Julio Antonio Mella (ISPJAM).

However, I always had my bond with people that could not be broken. To tell the truth, my way of seeing things was not the same as that of the system. I became interested in a project with the Municipalities of the Opposition (MDO), which, within the legal framework allowed by the constitution of the Republic of Cuba, channeled various concerns that many people had of any race, whatever their creed or political inclination, to resolve their problems. For example, there was an agricultural cooperative in the municipality that was the victim of large defaults for several months, and we filed a complaint with the government demanding that they get involved and pay salaries, comply with the agreements they made with these producers. They already had five or six months without a salary.

Being in opposition in Cuba is seen as a social deviation and there were consequences. The first consequence was my expulsion from the Universidad de Oriente. One day I arrived around nine in the morning to give a physics class to first-year computer engineering students. One of the heads of the department appears and says he needs to meet me, and he takes me to one of the department's laboratories. All the faculty is gathered there, and in front of all the professors, he says that from today I am no longer a professor of the department by order of the Rector of the Universidad de Oriente since I am the leader of the opposition in Songo La Maya.

Later I was arbitrarily detained several times walking in Santiago de Cuba. They constantly watched me in my house; all my movements were completely followed. Regardless of the values you have as a person, as a human being, you are seen as a social deviant, as if you were completely harmful to humanity.

Early one morning I was awakened abruptly at home by loud knocking at the door at 4:00 a.m., loud, heavy-handed, practically pounding the door down. And then twenty officers of the Regime Security services entered all the rooms of the house. They grabbed me roughly and took me through the house and sat me in a chair we had in the living room, and then they searched the entire house. They took a computer, a laptop, a camera, the cell phone that my wife had at that time, some CDs, movies, some cartoons that belonged to the children, a lot of literature, many books—some with religious topics, others about political science. One that I remember was a book that I read a lot, a contemplative book that I liked to consult, about the visit that Pope John Paul II made to Cuba in 1998.

I was arrested and they locked me in Santiago de Cuba for about 48 hours. At 1:00 in the morning they took me to interrogate, especially to try to stop me. All the questions were very hostile and, above all, there were many threats. *We're going to make you disappear. We're going to make your family disappear. At any time, you could be dead.*

I did not react to the threats. Nothing. At that time, you are determined, you are completely determined, and all those threats do not reach you, because everything follows the government's program, and you know their psychology. They try to weaken you, so the conditions in which they lock you up are completely horrible. There is a latrine and a dirty urinal, dirty with several days' excrement. The urine smells of ammonia, the smell of feces and cockroaches that run everywhere. Concrete bunk beds with a horrible crust, a layer of dirt from other prisoners who had been there before without mattresses or cushions. Walls dirty with body fluids of all kinds. Always the sound of the bars, the voices of prisoners who might be waiting for for a trial, or waiting to be transferred to a prison for having committed serious crimes like theft or rape. You are locked in there with them. And the food, you can imagine it. The conditions are totally hostile. It is designed to break your morale, your behavior.

A transformation occurs in a person when you have a lived experience and you believe that you are defending the truth. When you can show facts and what you say can not be refuted, and when you trust what you have read and what you have found and what you have lived, it makes you adopt a firm and unwavering position. And especially when you see the abuses, the censorship, when you see how the information is hidden, when you see them on the right and on the left, instead of weakening you it actually makes you feel stronger. And I had a lot of support from my family, and they were aware of the possible consequences, including what happened to my uncle José Antonio, and all the other Cubans who have experienced the dangers of the prison system, including illness and even death.

I could tell you about many of those occasions. The reason why I came here to the U.S. was really a consequence of the political work I did in Cuba. It was the refugee program that helped me come here. In Cuba, refugees are those who have been victims of abuse and persecution by the Cuban government due to their membership or activity in certain groups. This was my case. I was expelled from two employment centers. I received threats and defamation, property loss. My oldest daughter lost her college entrance. She was also a victim. These are some of the ways in which they mistreated us. I was attacked by a state policeman. It was really treacherous. I was in the house of a journalist working, and I heard someone say my name. I saw a figure and then it hit me right above my left eye and on my nose. My parents suffered losses. During the revolution, my grandfather lost everything. My brother was accused of many things. I was accused of many things in the University of Oriente. It was through all these arguments that I qualified for the refugee program and was able to come to the United States.

I came here with four of my children. I have five children, but the one who stayed is a child with another woman. The two oldest are from my first marriage and the two youngest are from my current marriage. We arrived in Louisville on November 16, 2016 shortly after 10:00 p.m. It was cold at night when we got here. In Louisville we were walking on the sidewalk and I could see my family and Wilmer, the representative of Catholic Charities. We arrived and could feel the cold outside, but when we arrived at the apartment where we lived it was hot. Inside the house you did not have to warm yourself. This could only happen in a country that is well organized. They all supported us. And little by little I got a job and started to get some independence. We could start living the life we wanted as a family. A better life for my children. They are like sponges, simply absorbing everything.

I arrived from Cuba understanding that I would be doing factory work. I had prepared myself. I knew that at first the immigrant's life would be difficult. I'm not the kind of immigrant who is a famous artist or athlete who has the means and can start a business and get ahead. I am the kind of immigrant who was the victim of a government that would never let me get ahead. I have to feed my family. I have to work. It does not matter what kind of work, as long as it is honorable.

We live with the idea that this is a country of possibilities. If you use talent and knowledge and have the support of those who believe in what you are trying to do, the opportunity is there. If you focus on what you want, you can do it. It can be incredible. I never felt discriminated against. I have been the opposite. In the short time that I have been here, I have been able to do much more than the 45 years I was in Cuba. The Constitution of the United States is very clear, and Martin Luther King fought for all these things. This is a free country. I have the ability to speak without censorship. I can formulate and defend my own ideas. I can be heard by an impartial tribunal. I know that this is a free country. I have to be responsible for my freedom. Therefore, I can not come here and impose my traditions or norms.

There is a culture here and it is your own nation. And I have to be respectful of the opportunity that this country has given me. In my country, I was denied these things, not necessarily by Cuban society but by the regime.

I would advise new immigrants to be positive and try to integrate. Try to see the best and most positive things in this country. With time you will see that we are all different but that we have something in common. The door is open so you can reach your goals. Respect the ideology, nationality, customs, culture of Americans, and you will not have any problem.

What has happened to me is, I think, the most transcendent part. In the short time that I have been here, I have been able to achieve many more things than my 45 years in Cuba. In Cuba, I had become a nobody. They depersonalize you. Here is the opposite. Here they appreciate the talent; they do not penalize you for it. In terms of my family, although we all have the language barrier, all my children are studying at school. My wife is working. We have been able to achieve autonomy. We do not need so much help.

Last summer, when we went to Kentucky Kingdom, my children told me they did not want to go home. It is very good for me to see my children so happy. To see them at the zoo. To see them on the Indiana bridge. Or at a dance where we were dancing our cute *casino*. And now my children are starting to plan another vacation. They are inviting American friends. They are opening. Now my children are correcting me. And I see that they are correcting me because they are learning. It has impacted me a lot and I feel great.

NARJIS ALSAADI

Dream big. Dream in color.

Mohammed Alsaadi

Dangerous Times

Dream big. Dream in color.

NARJIS ALSAADI

My father used to tell me a story about how I got my name. He'd smile and say, "Do you know why I named you Narjis? When I married your mom, my wish was to have a baby girl. I read a book once that talked about a beautiful flower called a Narcissus, which was also the name of a person in Greek mythology who was so beautiful that he fell in love with his own face when he saw his reflection in the water. After that, he died, but he turned into a pretty white flower that smells amazing." I asked him why my name was Narjis, not Narcissus. He said, "Because over time the name changed, especially in Iraq, and now the people know it as Narjis." It was his wish to have a daughter named Narjis and his wish came true. I think it's one of the most beautiful names in the world; it is very unique, so I feel very special and feel that my dad values me so much.

Until I was eleven years old, I lived in a house with my family and grandparents that looked like a palace in my eyes. Everything was perfect. Green grass grew around the house and the sweet, honey-like fragrance of rose, freesia, hyacinth, and jasmine was all over the garden. The backyard was full of lemon, orange, and palm trees, and tomatoes, lettuce, celery, and cucumber grew all around the ground. There were grape vines climbing on the wall.

Whenever we had an event or holiday, we gathered at my grandparents' house and my grandma and mom used to cook delicious chicken on charcoal with red rice and lentil soup. For dessert we would have a plate full of kanafeh, candies, and drinks such as juices and cocoa. My dad and grandfather and their friends sat in the garden and the kids played in the garage. Everything seemed perfect there.

My grandparents' house meant so much to me, and I can remember every corner of it and my innocent childhood. I used to walk around that garden all the time. Every morning my grandmother went to the backyard and picked vegetables for lunch or dinner. I used to go with her to pick up a tiny cucumber for the salad she prepared. I'd bring my pink bucket, and my grandmother would walk me through the process of watering the lettuce, guiding my hands and the bucket so I didn't water too much or too little. After that we would check the fruit trees to see if the fruit was ready to pick. My grandmother would begin preparing our lunch in the early morning because she liked to cook a lot of food for my uncles' families and mine. Sometimes my dad would tell her, "Don't cook too much, just enough for you two," but she refused. She has many grandchildren and she always wanted them to be close to her, so she cooked for everyone.

One afternoon I came back from school and found something marvelous in the garden: a cat with her fluffy brown fur under the green grass with five adorable tiny kittens lying next to her. They all looked newborn. I was anxious from what I saw because their eyes were closed and I thought they had died. I called my grandfather quickly and he came over with a smile on his face. He said the mother cat felt really comfortable in this area so she had given birth there and that her babies were okay.

My grandfather kept a huge bucket filled with water because sometimes there would be no water in the summer. I used to get up on that metal bucket next to the garden wall to watch the people on the street: people driving, some little boys playing soccer, and an old man watering his flowers in front of his door. I was so happy doing that every afternoon because sometimes when I asked my parents to go out, they wouldn't let me because they always worried about how unsafe it was.

Those are really innocent memories that make me smile when I remember them now. Even though I used to play by myself most of the time because I was an only child at that point, I wish to go back to those moments sometimes. I miss the traditions and the holidays like the Muslim holiday Eid, which we celebrate at the end of Ramadan. It is the second of two Muslim holidays celebrated worldwide each year. We break our fast by eating a large feast with family, friends, and relatives. Our fast lasts almost thirty days, but it depends on the moon; we have to see the moon after the sunset on the 29th day and check with our religious leaders to make sure that we break our fast correctly and never miss a day.

On the first day of Eid I woke up so excited. I cleaned the house with my mom and after that changed my clothes to the new ones that I bought. Starting in early morning, my mom, grandmother, and I started cooking the meat, rice, and fish. In the afternoon the relatives gathered at my grandparents' house and the street in front of my grandparents' house would be full of relatives' cars. My mom and aunts would bring the dishes to the living room and place them on the floor on a tablecloth full of colorful flowers, then put long rugs and pillows around it so we could sit. My grandma baked some fresh bread in the backyard in her wood-burning metal oven, which looked like a circular tall bucket that opened from the top and closed from the bottom.

We sacrificed animals such as sheep, cows, and sometimes chicken and divided them into three parts: one part given to poor people, one part given to family, and the third part to relatives and neighbors. My grandfather and my dad would always bring sheep for each Eid, but our meals mostly included Iraqi biryani, which is fried chicken with spices and tomato sauce and is so delicious. My grandma used to squeeze the fresh tomato, take the juice out of it, and then add lemon juice. She also squeezed lemons, oranges, grapes, and apples to make a fresh juice. One tradition during Eid is that, after this amazing meal, the adults in the house give money to the children as a gift. Every year my uncle gave money to me before the meal. He is an amazing person, really nice and funny. He wanted to see us happy.

My childhood was full of street games. There was a small area in front of our house where my grandfather planted grass, so it looked like a tiny park. I used to sit with my friends there. Because my neighborhood was unsafe and because I was the only kid in my family, my parents didn't let me go out, but they let me play there with my friends because Mom could see me from the kitchen. My mom bought me a lot of teacups because I loved to play with them with my friends at the park. My friend Aya would say, "Narjis, pour me some tea," and I would say, "Of course, Miss" and put some juice in the teacups. Our games were simple but they were so much fun. We focused and exercised when we played. There was not a lot of technology. My friends and I had no idea what a laptop or the internet was. Everything was simple.

Iraq has positive and negative sides. The positive side of Iraq is the rich culture that it has, the people with warm hearts, and the respected traditions. I don't want to focus on the negative images of Iraq, but it is the reality of Iraq that wars and conflicts have hurt many families and caused them to leave the country. It was hard on people when I was growing up there. My family worried about me going out because of how unsafe life was in the neighborhood. They worried that someone would kidnap me or kill me. It was so dangerous that nobody could even walk in the neighborhood. It's the hardest thing in the world when you feel that if you go out you might never come back home, that death is all around you. Sometimes I think Iraq will become an empty country because everyone will either get killed or run away.

When I was eleven years old, I had to leave my home country because my family was in danger. It was a scary moment. I didn't understand anything at the beginning. One day, I heard my mom and my dad talking about a threat. I went to my mom and I said, "Mom, what's going on?" She replied, "Nothing, honey. Just don't go to school today." When I asked why, she said, "Today it feels unsafe." I knew that every day was dangerous in Iraq, so I was not really surprised that I was kept home from school.

It all started when my dad got an anonymous threat. He worked as a party planner and he rented instruments as well. It was a small store, a long wide hallway with an open area with flutes, guitars, ouds, and other instruments hanging on the wall. My dad's dream was to have this store and have his own art, but it was dangerous to open a business such as this. Early one morning he found a piece of paper on the front door of his store that said, "You should leave your job." These anonymous people believed that his work was evil, that it was against God's will to rent musical instruments or plan parties. Nobody knew these people or what group they were with. I never saw them but always heard about them. Some of the families around the neighborhood said there were several of them in the area, holding guns and covering their faces. Their thoughts were all about "Everything is against God," like working or letting people succeed. They wanted to take everything for themselves, to control people and take their properties. They don't understand what art is or joy is. Iraq has a rich, and unique culture and art and literature has always thrived there.

We knew they were dangerous people and if we didn't do something they would kill us. They had killed many people, including some of our neighbors. Children were kidnapped every day and money taken from their parents, and bombs were put in public places such as restaurants, parks, and malls. The country was out of control. I felt scared the minute my dad said we would move because I was always afraid that those unknown people would come and kill us. I was so young at that time but I still understood that my family and I were in danger.

When I asked my dad who they were, he said, "Honey, nobody knows who they are." Maybe they were ISIS, but in 2011 nobody knew who they were yet. There were different issues in Iraq. People disagreed with each other, like Sunni and Shia issues; others wanted to control the country. I was really young so I didn't really understand. What I understood was that it was dangerous and people were killed and a there was a lot of fear.

We didn't leave secretly, but we left quickly because my dad was so scared that we would be killed at any minute. We didn't get the chance to say goodbye to our friends or relatives, except my grandparents, who we saw at the last minute. My grandparents are very important people in my life and I thought about how I much I was going to miss them. Until that time, I'd seen them every day since I was a newborn baby. I was sad and nervous but excited at the same time because I knew I was going to a new place, with new people and a new school. I had never been out of the country and I wanted to try new things.

The only thing that I worried about was how I was going to leave my grandparents, my relatives, and my friends. But it wasn't a choice; we had to leave to save my family and my life. Leaving the country in a short time period wasn't that easy, especially for my dad, because he had to close up his business and get prepared to travel as soon as possible.

My parents' main goal was just to save us. That's all they were thinking about. They didn't even care about our house or our possessions in Iraq. We packed our bags and left our house just at it was. We didn't change anything or take any extra belongings because my dad thought we might be able to come back. He didn't even think about selling our house. My grandfather told him we should sell the stuff in our house, but my dad said he didn't know what was going to happen so he didn't want to sell it. I left my room full of dolls and toys, the awards I got in grade school, and the pictures of me from when I was a newborn baby until age of eleven.

Since we left Iraq I have seen my house only once, when my uncle FaceTimed us and showed us the house. It was exactly that same as we left it. Nothing had moved. The three sofas around the living room, a big TV chained to the wall, shelves hanging on the left and right side of the TV, pictures of my brother Mojtba and me, and two big yellow bears that were a gift from my dad on my fourth birthday. The only difference was the large piece of gray cloth that covered the furniture and long piece of plastic that covered the rugs, and the dust covering all of it. It was heartbreaking. My grandparents had closed it off when we left, and nobody had been in the house since.

We left at sunrise. The air was fresh and cold. There was sunshine without heat. My mom had prepared cheese sandwiches and my dad had set all the bags at the front of the door and told us everything was ready; it was time to leave. I walked slowly, hoping to not reach the front door because I didn't want to leave my whole life behind.

My eyes were full of tears, my hands were cold, and my fingers were gathered together when I saw my grandparents outside our front door. My grandma wore her black coat and black hijab. She looked at me and my siblings with eyes full of tears and I could see that she was worried she would not see us again. I thought about how nice my grandma was and about her warm lap and the kisses she used to give my little brother and me on the forehead. She hugged us.

I went closer to my grandmother and she told me, "Sweetie, you will be alright." She put her hand on my shoulder. At that minute I wanted to cry so hard, but my grandmother was so upset already. That was the hardest and most stressful moment that I faced when I left Iraq.

I believe that there are different types of stress. That morning, I felt stress in scary way. My hands were cold. I felt like I was going to lose everything. I wanted to say something but I couldn't, I was shaking, and I couldn't walk. This is the kind of stress you get when you are scared. When I looked at my dad, I saw worry in his eyes too, worry for his wife and his children. My uncle came with us, and we were in hurry to get out of Baghdad. I went by bus from Iraq to Turkey, which was uncomfortable because it was not that safe at that time.

It took about nine hours to get to Turkey. Other than a couple of stops at restaurants and cafes, I stayed in my seat for all those hours, looking out the window. There were no houses, no people, just cars—it looked like desert so it was very boring. My parents

had normal conversations with other people on the bus. My youngest brother Zen slept on my mom's lap, and my brother Mojtba and I slept for most of the trip, too.

After we made it to Turkey, the United Nations Refugee Agency told us that we had been accepted into the United States but that it would take a long time to complete the paperwork. The idea of moving to the United States was something so strange and hard to believe. I had never thought I'd ever go to the United States. To me, the United States represented a good education, a career, and safety. My goals and dreams were going to come true.

When I stepped out from the airplane at the Istanbul airport, I saw a new different world. The women wore hijabs, but in a different style that I had never seen before. They spoke a language that I didn't understand. It sounded like rainfall. The airport was huge and full of people and bags. A bell rang every ten to fifteen minutes, and the ground looked like glass—I could see my body when I walked on it. There were many restaurants. When I looked at the menu, there was nothing I could understand; even the pictures were unfamiliar to me, like a white soup with rice in it and eggplant filled with meat and garlic. I didn't know what to eat. I found tea and donuts, but their donuts were not sweet and their tea was light-colored with no sugar.

Outside the airport many taxis waited to take us to a bus stop, from which we traveled to the city of Amasya, where we had friends and it was cheap to live. On the trip to Amasya, we saw the real Turkey, its people and their farms and the environment. In Turkey, people love to plant their own tomatoes, eggplants, and peppers and they eat healthy all the time. Amasya was a really beautiful city, and we enjoyed our time there. The Yeşil River runs through Amasya, and the neighborhoods are surrounded by grassland. The river is so long it seems endless, and the water is clear and blue.

We lived in Turkey for two and a half years while we waited on papers and interviews to go to the United States. While we were in Turkey as refugees, it was hard for us. Refugees can't live in Turkey forever, and don't have the right to work or go to college while they wait to go to other countries. Our opportunities were limited; however, we did have the ability to go to school.

When I arrived in Amasya, my dad registered me for middle school. I didn't speak the language and had no idea what was going on. I entered the front office with my dad and the first thing I saw on the wall was a huge picture of Mustafa Kemal Ataturk, the founder of the Turkish republic, its first president, and a towering figure of the 20th century.

I worried that no one would welcome me, but the opposite happened. The teacher knew that I didn't speak Turkish, so he called someone to translate through the phone. I held the phone and someone spoke to me in Arabic, "You can have a seat and we'll get your books and your schedule. By the end of the day you will have an idea of your classes. You have six periods and here are your books. If you need anything, come to this teacher. He will guide you to all of your classes." His name was Coach Mehmet, and his job was to help the new students. He walked me to my six classes and was an amazing person.

In my classes, the girls sat on one side and the boys on the other. The math teacher welcomed me to class and introduced herself. I didn't understand what she said but I got the sense that she was welcoming me. She started class and I understood some of the math she was teaching. After the bell rang, I stayed seated and four girls and two boys came up to me. I understood that they wanted to welcome me and they used their phones as translators to let me understand what they were saying. They said, "Hello! We are here if you need any help." They were good people and I really felt happy. They always tried to talk to me, even when I hadn't learned Turkish yet. They tried to help me understand, using signs and pictures. I learned Turkish from my friends at school, from dictionaries, and from Turkish children's books. I will never forget how nice they were to me. I really miss them, because they were some of the best people in my life.

Amasya is known for the many festivals they hold throughout the year. One of the festivals I enjoyed the most was the book festival where booksellers got together in the center of Amasya and put up tables from one end of the road to the other. It started in the morning and lasted until evening. There were many different kinds of books, written in many languages. When I went to the festival with my family, one of the tables caught my attention because it was stacked with Arabic dictionaries written in boldface type. I was as happy as a kid in a toy store. It was nice seeing something in my language. I asked the bookseller, "*Bo nakadar?*" How much is this? It was a tiny booklet, so I could take it everywhere I went. After we finished looking at that table, we walked around

TECRÜBELİ
GARSON
ARANIYOR...

Amasya, Turkey

Yeşil River in Amasya, Turkey

looking at everything. It was the end of the winter, and the air was fresh and cold and it hit our faces when we walked alongside the river.

The river surrounds Amasya just like the Ohio River surrounds Louisville. When I went there I would feel the fresh air enter my lungs, and I could breathe better. Sometimes I saw people standing beside the river and it looked like they might be remembering some old times, or like they were talking to the river and telling it what they were feeling inside. I know I had that emotion when I looked at the water.

We lived in Amasya for two and a half years while we waited on papers and interviews to go to the United States. In that time, I learned Turkish traditions and culture. I liked their clothes, their food, and even their schools, and I started being just like them. I adjusted to life in Turkey easily because I'd left Iraq when I was so young. This made me feel that Turkey was my home when it comes to culture. I still wear my hijab in the Turkish style.

In 2012 my dad, mom, little brothers, and I went to the UN in Istanbul three times to finish our interviews at the UN. The trips from Amasya to Istanbul were so long that we had to take a special

Istanbul

bus designed for long trips. It had soft seats and a tiny table that folded into halves, and there were soft drinks, water, snacks, towels, and sleeping masks. It felt like an airplane. Our trips took seven or eight hours. Those were rough days, especially for my little brothers, who got really tired of having to sit still for so long. The interviews were long too, and I would sit in the lobby of the office building with my little brothers, waiting for my parents to finish. I had no idea what was going on because they didn't interview people under eighteen.

The moment when we finished the last interview, they called my dad and said that after two years we were finally done with the process. That was one of the best things ever. My dad was so happy. I was happy, too, and went with my mom to go get new clothes, because hey, we were finally going to the United States.

We went to the Sea of Marmara in Istanbul. It was our first time there. It was a really nice view, like artwork, the blue clear sky with dark blue water and boats all over the sea flying the Turkish flag. There were many buildings and a mosque and houses with red roofs that looked tiny because they were across the sea. My mom dressed my little brothers in the same clothes, khaki shorts and navy blue T-shirts so

National Museum of Iraq

they looked like twins, even though one was eight years old and the other was six. I was wearing a long blue dress with white polka dots and a Columbia-blue hijab. We left my home country because we wanted to make our lives safe. My dad told us that if we wanted to make something happen, we had to work hard to achieve it. When we dream big, we don't only dream, we dream in color.

In Iraq, dreams might not come true. It feels hopeless. But in the U.S., you have the keys to achieve your dreams: a good education and a safe place to live. I will never, ever forget the moment when we learned we would be coming to America.

When we arrived at the airport in New York, we didn't know what to do. Some workers asked us if we needed help, but we didn't understand anything. It was funny because they really want to help us, but we didn't know how to ask for their help. After a while of waiting in the lobby, a worker from Catholic Charities called us and told us to take the airplane to Kentucky.

Finally we arrived at the Louisville airport and saw my uncle and his family waiting for us. It was a busy night at my uncle's house. We spent three days at his house searching for a place to live. After that I walked around my uncle's house to his backyard, and it was so quiet. It was around 10:00 a.m. and I didn't see anybody around. I went back and asked my uncle, "What's wrong? Where are the people?" He laughed and said there everyone was at their jobs or in school. "Narjis, you will be soon just like them; you won't have time for fun anymore," he said.

In my family, we relate to each other emotionally, take care of each other, and love each other. We discuss everything and understand each other to solve any problem we have. The relationship between us is lovely. We never have any problems that make us mad at each other or sad. My dad and my mom set rules for my siblings and me. This is what makes our house strong and great.

One time, we had a conversation at our first Ramadan dinner in the United States about different issues my family and I might face. My dad said that Ramdan might be little different in the United States because everything seemed informal to us in the beginning. We talked about how our traditions might change. He said, "You might change here in the U.S., because nothing is like Iraq. Our people are not here, the food is different, many of our mosque traditions are not here. This different environment might change you and make you forget your culture." He wanted us to do just one thing: keep our tradition and follow it just like in Iraq, because it's valuable. We all agreed, even my little brothers. And we are still the same here. We still pray, do Ramadan, Eid, and other holidays with my family, and sometimes with friends and relatives who are here. Of course, there is something empty here, something missing, but my parents do what they can to make it feel a little bit like Iraq.

I like to listen to my dad when he tells stories about Baghdad when he was young. Recently my father was sitting in the kitchen and my mom was doing the dishes, and he said the sound of the dishes hitting the sink reminded him of one of the oldest markets in Baghdad. "I miss the al-Safafeer Market." He told us that in that market you could hear the beating of hammers against metal all day long. It was so loud that it was even hard to talk to one another there. In that street everything was shining; dozens of shops sold souvenirs made from copper, like pots and statues. There were also many silver items for sale. My dad used to go there to find some good items for the house. Iraqis love handmade items.

My grandparents and their neighbors had really valuable things like pots, candle holders, and vases. Every object in my grandparents' house had meaning. There was artwork hanging in the living room, like a painting of two ladies wearing traditional Iraqi clothes with buckets of water on their heads, and a river behind them. Also, there were ceramic vases— white with blue dots—that my grandmother used to take care of and clean. She'd fill them with flowers from the garden. They were very rare and so beautiful. This is what I can remember from my grandparents' house; after these years and after the death of my grandmother, I have no idea if they are still there.

One of the hardest moments while I was writing this chapter was when I heard my grandmother had died. My plan was to finish this chapter and then send her the book, but she left me too soon. She died in Iraq, and I couldn't go to the ceremony or see her one last time. She called me a couple of weeks before going to the hospital and said, "Take care of yourself.

My wish is just to see you." It seemed like she knew that she would die soon. I hoped that I could make her dream happen. Then she hung up.

I feel something is really different inside me. I don't laugh like before. I still cannot believe that she left and I didn't see her. I had always thought that I would go back and visit her and find her sitting on the brown sofa in the garden in front of the door. She was the only one who would ask how I was doing all the time. If I got sad, she would know what was wrong with me from my voice even though she was in Iraq and I was here. It's really hard that I can't hear her voice anymore. She was a second mother to me and the only reason I wanted to go back to Iraq.

Early every morning I would go around the my grandparents' house, watering the backyard plants. Then I would go to my grandparents' chickens and I would see my grandmother sitting on the floor cooking, cutting fresh vegetables, cleaning fish, and frying it. She loved cooking in early morning and prepared it for her family. I would sit in the kitchen with her and she would tell me stories. She would put some of whatever she cooked in my toy pots and let me taste it. She would take me with her the store and buy me clothes. She would give me money and I would go to the store next to us and buy some cookies.

I really miss her smile and wish I could have gone back to hug her and listen to her stories one more time. In my culture, we remember those who have passed by saying *Allahyarhamha*, "God have mercy on her," and we read a short part of the Quran, the Kitab Al-Fada'il, that asks God to give mercy to her and asks God to show us the correct way.

I miss my country and my culture so much. Here in Louisville there are mosques and stores that make us feel the Arab culture. My family and I always shop at the Arabic store on New Cut Road, which looks like an old house. Out front, it has a huge sign listing the stuff available inside, such as meat, fish, bread, and vegetables, and inside there is a drawing of a piece of bread on the wall in the area where we buy bread and halal meat. Inside, the floors are gray and the walls are yellowish and scratched from wear and the light-blue tablecloths are clean. A table displays all the different kinds of Iraqi food this store carries, like red rice with chicken, beans, grape leaves, and Iraqi meatballs. The store smells of freshly baked bread, which makes me want to sit down and eat. I see the large bread oven heated from the top and the bottom by fire. Iraqi bread is totally different from American bread. Ours is made with white flour and is thin, circular, and fluffy. There are stacks of this bread for sale.

A tall blue counter holds most of the food, and there are three freezers filled with frozen chicken, fish, and Iraqi bread. On the other side there are cans of beans and meat, hot sauces, and rice, and on another table there are kebabs with garlic, lemon, spices, and grilled falafel—fried chickpea patties served with *amba* and salad in pita bread.

Of course, there are hot tea pots on the other side of the table. Iraqi people love tea, and we drink it after almost every meal. We drink tea even in hot weather. Last time I visited, men were drinking tea and talking. Two men in their forties looked at me with question marks on their faces when they saw me typing on my phone and looking at every object

in the store as if I was exploring a brand new place. They asked if they could help me with something, and I explained that I was writing about the Arabic community, including this Arabic store. He smiled and told me he really liked the idea, and to keep going and good luck.

I felt like I was in my home country for a while as I listened to the people around me talking and as I inhaled the smell of the fresh bread. It reminded me of entering my grandmother's kitchen each morning. At the end of the counter were traditional Arabic things such as hijabs, tea pots painted with blue symbols, hookah, and prayer rugs in multiple colors. They looked so nice! Iraqi flags of all sizes hung in

the door. The most beautiful thing in the place was not for sale: a big map on the wall with all the cities in Iraq colored in different colors. Baghdad was colored with green and when I looked at it I immediately thought of my grandparents' house and I felt heartbroken because I miss all of those things and I feel I will not see them again.

Shortly after arriving in the United States, we went to Dearborn, Michigan, to visit relatives there, which made me feel a little better because Michigan has a huge Iraqi community. My uncle took us there in his jeep, driving for four or five hours. It was a sunny afternoon. My uncle told me that Michigan is similar to Iraq because Iraqi people go there to

Al Yasmine Food Mart

buy Iraqi clothes, food and jewelry because there are so many Iraqi people who have opened businesses there. We all were sleepy, so there was no talking in the car. Then we stopped at a Subway and my uncle got us six tuna sandwiches with six cokes and we all got out and sat at picnic tables. My uncle said, "So how do you feel about the American food?" My dad said, "It's not that bad." He likes homemade food; he doesn't like fast food much. My brother Mojtba and I, however, said, "It's amazing!" And to this day when I go to Subway I ask for a tuna sandwich with olives, tomato, pickles, and lettuce.

After that, we got into the car and my dad asked if it was easy to find a job here. My uncle said, "If you speak English, it will be easy for you to find a job."

When we finally arrived in Dearborn, the first thing that amazed us was that the traffic officer was wearing a hijab, and all the way to my mom's relatives' house there were stores and restaurants with Arabic names. My dad and mom smiled, and my uncle said, "Yes, Michigan is full of Arabic people and they have opened a lot of businesses. You feel like you are in Iraq." I was so happy to hear that.

We arrived at my mom's uncle's house and they welcomed us and prepared a big meal of Iraqi dishes. There was *quzi,* which is very slow cooked lamb, roasted nuts, and raisins served over rice. There was *kibbeh,* which is onions and finely ground lean beef, lamb, goat, or camel meat with cinnamon, nutmeg, clove, allspice, and other Middle Eastern spices. And of course there was *masgouf,* which is a large fish cooked with tomato sauce and spices inside it, and salads, drinks, and bread. So it was a table full of all Iraqi food that we hadn't eaten for a long time because in Turkey there were no Iraqi restaurants and they didn't have all of the things we needed to cook our Iraqi food. We ate a lot, and it was so good. After that we went out and saw people all around talking in Arabic, and all the stores' signs in Arabic. I felt like I was in Iraq. I hadn't heard people talking in Arabic since Turkey. The feeling of stopping anywhere and asking people questions in our language was really good.

Some people dislike talking about what happened in the past and the conditions in Iraq. One time after lunch, my dad was in conversation with my mom's relatives about Iraq, and they refused to keep talking about it. They just stopped talking about what happened in Iraq in the 2000s. I had so many questions in my head when I saw that. After a while I asked my dad, "What's wrong? Why did they stop talking about Iraq?" I was so interested to hear about life before in Iraq, because I never really knew about it or what people went through. My dad said, "I don't want to remember those things in the past and get you thinking about it. You are my only daughter. I don't want to keep those black memories with you."

My dad kept saying, "People cannot even talk about the past because so many people died. Many saw their families killed in front of them. They lost their people in front of their own eyes. They couldn't even go out. Your mother couldn't go visit her family for almost seven months because it was so dangerous to go. I couldn't drive, and I couldn't let her go by herself. We lost our people. They killed our families in front of us." I didn't ask about it anymore because I felt that same way my dad did: it is so hard on people when we mention the past because it hurts them when they remember those things.

Mohammed Alsaadi

My father is one of the most important people in my life. He left his job and his whole life to bring us to the United States to save and educate us. He made me who I am today and always supported me. He didn't finish his studies because of all the distractions in his life and his dream now is for Mojtba, Zen, and me to finish our education and be what we want to be. He never forces us to do something we don't want. He always has our back. I decided to interview him because he has had experiences that nobody would know about otherwise. I want people to know that life doesn't have to stop despite the obstacles that you face. He lived most of his life in Iraq, and I think it was really hard for him to leave and start over in America. I wanted to hear him talk about his views about America, especially Louisville.

—NARJIS

When I was young, your age, I had many dreams. Some of them were to go to college and help my community, and to have a safe life. When I visit my children's schools here in the U.S., I feel really thankful—they offer kids everything: safety, education, etc.—and I remember my childhood memories. My childhood in Baghdad was very beautiful. It was a simple life. The schools were really active, a good environment for learning, so the kids were great students, almost like here. Our school was clean and offered healthy meals every day. They had anything that students needed to push them to learn, and there was electricity in the classrooms. But now there are classes that don't have electricity during school, and most of the year in Iraq is very hot. We didn't know violence or any bad thing that hurt others. Back in those days, you could go outside, hang out with friends. It was safe, not like now. Now it's hard to go anywhere because there are kidnappings and violence around the neighborhoods. People feel that there is no life anymore and no way to build a good future.

When I was in school I focused on soccer. Soccer was so important in my life. I played in a club for three years in middle school. In high school I started traveling to other cities to play. It was fun. But I never traveled outside of the country. I dreamed of being a soccer coach. This was my career plan when I was your age. But the violence increased, so I couldn't play any more because it was dangerous to go out. We felt like all our dreams were gone.

After high school I took courses on art and music because I was interested in that. Then I started a small store renting musical instruments, and I planned parties, events, and weddings. I decorated almost everything for them; I organized everything, including food. I'd worked in restaurants for seven years and had learned to make some popular salads and many other Iraqi dishes. A wedding should be a big event. One of our traditions in Iraq is that if someone wants to marry but he doesn't have enough money, we help him with everything.

In Iraq we have a really rich culture. One of the things I most loved was the "book street" in Baghdad. This street was just for books; people sold books on the street or in stores. It was open only on Fridays. It had any book you wanted: Arabic, English, French, musical books, education books. It's an amazing place.

We had music clubs too. Some people went to the cafe to smoke a hookah, spend a nice day, eat and listen to Baghdad's music. We had great singers and musicians like Munir Bashir and Mohammed al-Qubanchi. Some of them are still alive, but all of that was in the old days. Now it is not safe and most of this stuff is gone because of war and violence. I like to remember these memories, but I don't like to remember the bad memories.

In Iraq now everything is hard. The kids don't have the opportunity to study well or have a good life with their families because the parents are worried that their children might get hurt on the way to school. They are scared of what they hear from the news, that many people die or get hurt. The kids can't even go outside to play. The reason I moved to Turkey was because it had an open border for refugees and it was the closest place for me to go and save my family's lives.

Turkey is a beautiful country. Full of grass and rivers. That was a big difference between Iraq and Turkey. Both have different kinds of food, different cultures, different traditions. Like in Iraq, when we have guests, our tradition is that we have to give them something like sweets or drinks, and when we visit someone we need to take a gift for them, but in Turkey, they don't do this. Also, not all of our food is healthy but in Turkey most of their food is healthy. When all the family members meet to eat a meal—mother, father, grandparents, grandchildren, cousins—we all sit on the ground. We don't really use tables to eat.

Jobs are similar in Turkey and Iraq, but in Turkey they don't pay people by the hour, they pay them monthly. When we moved to Turkey I couldn't keep doing my job as a wedding planner because I didn't know how they did it there, and I didn't speak Turkish. Plus, I have health problems that kind of stop me from doing work: I have high blood sugar and blood pressure and am disabled and overweight.

We stayed two and a half years in Turkey waiting for papers to finish so it's legal to come to the U.S. We flew to New York then Kentucky. There is a big difference between Louisville and Iraq. Being here in America has taught me many things.

Jobs are a big thing. We should be on time. We should follow the rules. I think this is the most important thing in this country. Also we should go to sleep early to go to our work and school. The other thing is the tax system, which makes the people keep going and makes the country have strong bonds. In Iraq we didn't have taxes or any system like this. Also, here they have the food stamp program. This is a great thing which makes it so that nobody is hungry; in Iraq we have many poor people who go to sleep with no food. Here they have a great education system for students, but in Iraq the education wasn't that good. I give the education in America a ten out of ten. In America they have health insurance to take care of the people; in Iraq we don't really have health insurance. Here they have great traffic rules and everyone follows the rules. All these things are what makes America great. People have rights here. All of these are differences between here and Iraq. Even when I was young in Iraq, America was still better about their education, jobs, products, etc.

Here they have holidays like Thanksgiving and New Year's, but in Iraq we have two Eids for Muslims. We have Ramadan, which is thirty days of fasting from about 4:30 a.m. to 9:15 p.m. each day. Fasting makes you healthy, and it makes you feel what it is like to be poor, because some poor people don't eat for days.

The hardest thing I have faced here is the language; I cannot speak English. It is the only obstacle I have, and I am trying to learn. We lived at Colonial Oaks for a while, then we moved to Douglas Park. Everything is going great. My kids do well in school. I wish for you to go to college and achieve your dreams because that was my purpose in bringing you here. Everything is great here. They care about humans, they have rights and rules. It's a safe place and I am thankful that I am here to save my family and my children have a good future.

My mom is young, in her thirties, and whenever we go out people ask, "Are you sisters?" because she looks my age. This makes me happy, because she is more than my mom—she is my best friend. One time we went shopping and I found a long-sleeved navy shirt that I really liked, so I said, "Mom, can I have this shirt?" She replied, "Yes, sweetie, why not!" After a while I said, "Can we buy the same shirt for you, Mom?" She laughed and asked why, and I said, "Because I really want to look alike." She laughed and said, "Okay, as you wish," and we got those shirts.

My mom is the one who directs me the right way. She is everything in my life. She always tells me to do the things that I love because she says, "When you don't love something, you will never succeed in it." She taught me to try my best to treat people equally and respectfully all the time, to never give up when things get hard, and to always be honest with myself. My mother is strong. I don't ever see her weak or unable to do something in front of me. She is the strong woman who married at the age of eighteen and had three children by the age of twenty-eight and worked hard to give us be the best she could. She encourages us to finish our education and be what we want to be. She always says, "My babies, I was unable to finish my studies and never reached my dream. Now my dream is for you all to achieve your goals in life."

One of the reasons that my family came to the United States was so that I could have a better education. This motivates me to work hard and get good grades. The most important thing in my life is school. I was a top student from the first grade to when I went to school in Turkey. I learned so fast there that

it was not a problem. However, when I came to the United States and entered school, I felt so stupid because I did not know any English. Everything was hard for me and I was alone. But I got past all that. I have not only learned English and raised my grades, but have also become active as a volunteer in my community.

I really like Kentucky, and Louisville is a quiet city with nice landscapes. There are trees and grass all over the city. The weather is different from where I used to live; Iraq was always hot and never snowed at all. But now I'm used to it. My lifestyle here is different from Iraq in every way. In Iraq I used to live in really big house with an upstairs and downstairs, three gardens, a backyard, and a big garage. But here we live in a house with only three rooms. I don't have a problem with it, though. As long as it's a safe place and I go to school safely, this is all I need.

I volunteer my free time and help the people who have recently arrived to the United States because I don't want to see them having a hard time like I did. I got involved at Americana World Community Center three years ago when my father went there for English classes. When I saw how the classes benefited him and our family, I decided to give back by volunteering my time. I also volunteer with first through seventh grade students to help them learn how to plant tomatoes, garlic, and grapes in Americana's garden. I love to go to Iroquois Library, where there are many clubs for refugees. I volunteer in the English as a Second Language program. I teach basic English for refugees and also translate for Arabic speakers. This experience has helped me to meet new people every time I go there, and taught me about new cultures, new countries, and much more.

Ever since I was a young girl in Iraq, my dream has been to be a pharmacist. When I went with my mom and I saw the people working in pharmacy and filling prescriptions, I was so excited to do the same thing. I am working so hard in school to reach this goal.

Here I am in Kentucky, living safely with my family and going to Spalding University, working to achieve my dreams and my goals in the United States. I still remember the Iraqi traditions, and I try my best to help my brothers remember those traditions too. Iraq is where all my family lives, and I'm always afraid that I might lose one of them because of all the conditions there. Iraq is rich in so many ways but poor in terms of personal safety. I see Iraq as a huge picture but without colors. And I believe the saying, "When we dream big, we dream in color."

Dangerous Times

ANSAM RASHID

Sometimes I hate being the only girl in my home and really wish I had a sister. I explained this to my mother once and she said, "Narjis, you have a great best friend, Ansam, and she is a sister to you."

The first time I met Ansam was in the school cafeteria during my freshman year. I was interested in talking to her, so one of the teachers introduced us. She told me her story. She lived in Iraq longer than I did, and she has traveled many places. I wanted to hear about Iraq from a young person so I would have a clear view of it from someone my age. She is the youngest kid in her family, and grew up in a really Iraqi environment. She knows more about Iraq and the traditions there than I do. I have learned about Iraqi traditions, language, and clothing from her. Ansam also had the same kinds of struggles that I did when she came to United States. She is very, very sweet and has a warm heart. Whenever I have a problem, she is the first one to be with me. She is not only a best friend to me, but she is a sister. And she is my sister forever.

—NARJIS

My childhood in Baghdad was wonderful. I had a lot of friends in Iraq. In the evenings we'd go outside in the street and all of the children would come in the front in my home and we'd play *tuki*. We'd draw squares on the ground, number them, then throw something like a rock or a marble and jump for it, sometimes with our eyes closed. If you cross the line you fail. It was my favorite. But I couldn't go outside every day; sometimes we were scared because it was unsafe.

When I was in fifth grade I came home and saw my mom crying. I asked her, "What's happening? What's going on?" and she said, "Your father was kidnapped." It was really hard. For four days, we just waited. We didn't know anything about him and it was really hard. They came back and said they wanted money.

My dad was working in the army, helping the American people, so we went and talked with them. The American army helped my dad get back to our home. My dad was in a lot of pain when he came back.

On the same day that he came back, the bad people came to our home again and took my brother.

The same day. They just came to our home and took him. My dad couldn't do anything because he was really, really in pain. They took all of my family in one room except my brother and my grandma and they just closed the room, and we didn't know anything about my brother and my grandma. It was really hard. We just cried. We couldn't do anything. We prayed.

My grandma told them, "Don't do that. If you want to take him, just kill me."

The bad man respected my grandma because she was so old and she didn't work a job, she just wanted to save my brother. One of the men kissed her head and said, "No, we just wanted to talk to him. We won't do anything to him." But they were lying. They put him in the car. And after that there were about three hours when we didn't know anything. I guess my grandma scared them, though, because the bullies just told my brother to go back to our home. When he came back, my grandma fell down, she was so scared. That was a really, really bad day.

It was 2007 and it was after Saddam, a really dangerous time. You couldn't go outside. We were scared to be in our home and we didn't know who the bad people were and who the good people were when we went outside. Some Islamic people don't wear the hijab, but some of the bad people killed girls if they didn't wear the hijab. So in our country, when we went shopping, we'd think, "Maybe there will be a bomb and some people will kill us." We were just thinking about all of that.

I was thirteen. About one month after they kidnapped my dad and brother, they came again and said, "Don't stay in your home. Go to another home, go to other country, we don't care. If you're still here, we will kill all of your family." We didn't do anything bad. My dad was just in the army and he worked with the Americans. They said, "If we see your children, your wife, or anyone else in your family, we will kill them or we will take them. So, you have to move from here." My dad said, "Okay, I have to move."

There were a lot of Iraqi people who went to Syria because it was safe, and the U.N. was there. We went there because it was so close, and because they speak really good Arabic. We went there and told our story, what happened with my dad. We had an American friend who helped us to come here.

When we went to Syria, my dad found a job making shoes. We stayed there seven years. I went to school in the sixth grade. I was in school for just two years, then I stayed home.

Syria was really, really nice because if you went outside, you didn't think it was dangerous. But I missed my home. It was just me and my dad, brother, and sister, that's it. But in Iraq, I have a really big family. I missed doing a lot of things with them, like Eid and Ramadan; I couldn't go back and see them, even if somebody in my family were dying. I couldn't

see my childhood friends or talk with them again. But I lived my life. It was really normal. My dad had work and all of my family was home.

I went to school in sixth grade. It was not really good because the teachers were the same as in Iraq: they didn't respect you. Everything was my fault because I wasn't a citizen. Some of the people were nice to us, some of them not. One girl came to me and she said, "Iraq is trash." I was really mad. I know it's dangerous, I know all of that stuff, but I love my country. I can't hear anyone talk bad about my country. I just left. I didn't say anything, I went to my teacher and I told him what was going on and he said, "It's okay, it's not a big problem." I cried and went back home and told my dad. He said, "Don't mind that stuff. It's okay."

Also, the teachers in Syria hit a lot. Maybe this is why I hate English, because of my English teacher. I was doing my homework and I was talking with my friends and he said, "Okay, Ansam, read this." I told him I couldn't read it because he hadn't taught me how to read English. He said, "I don't care. You have to read it." I said, "No, I can't." He said, "Okay, come to me." I came to him and he put my hand up and hit it with a stick really hard. I cried and told him I just wanted to go home. He said, "No, you can't leave."

I went back home and told my dad all of that, and he said, "Okay, we have to go to the police and tell them what's going on." We went and the teacher just said, "Okay, I'm sorry for that." That's it. After that, I really hated school. My math teacher did it too but on my feet instead, really hard. I couldn't walk. My dad said, "Okay. Don't go to school." That's why I left my school. It was a really big problem.

Narjis and Ansam

We went back to Iraq because it became dangerous in Syria too. But we didn't go back to our home;
we went to a different state in Iraq. We went to Najaf
and stayed with my uncle. After one year, they called
us and said, "You can come to America. We just have
to talk with you, interview your family." We went
there and did all of that and then after six months
they called us and told us to go to the hospital for
a check up, and when we finished that, one month
later, they gave us a visa and we came here.

When I came to school in the U.S. I didn't know
any English and I came home and just cried. I told
my mom I didn't want to go to school because I
couldn't understand anything and if I wanted to talk,
I couldn't. It was really hard for me. She said, "No,

you can do it, you can learn. School is your life." I just
kept going, and worked hard, and then I took some
more school. I had my phone to learn how to speak
English, and Ms. Sanchez helped me a lot too. So it
was really hard in the beginning, but when I learned
how to speak English it got better.

I hope to go back to Iraq. That's my home. I just
want to see my grandma again. Her name is Raja.
She likes to play on the phone, and she's just like my
friend. I never ever feel that she's old. I would just
like to hug her.

AUTUMN WILSON

My Wyandotte is not on the TV news

Jennifer Nunn

Toni Lynette Cristy

Robert Wilson

My Wyandotte Is Not on the TV news

AUTUMN WILSON

When I was growing up, my best friend was my grandpa. There were times when we would spend every day for a couple of weeks together. My grandparents' house was my favorite place to be. They'd take me fishing and camping, we'd build things together, do arts and crafts, and go to the store to waste his money on unnecessary things that I looked at as luxuries.

My grandparents were characters for sure. Grandpa was a tall and very slim man with long, thin, cotton-like gray hair that he'd wear in a small bun at the nape of his neck. He wore cargo shorts without shoes or socks or a shirt like it was his uniform. His outfit would always be completed by a silver watch and his big, silver, round "grandpa glasses." He had a few tattoos spread out all over his body which somehow told his stories but made no sense to me. When I think of them now they're just a blur, but I remember one tattoo that said *Dad* and one written in Chinese, which I'm sure he didn't even understand. I assumed they were last minute decisions with no thought in them because the quality looked so bad to me. He was never disappointed with them, though. That was just his character: he looked at the bright side of dark things, like a really bad tattoo.

My grandma was very different than he was,

almost out of his league. She would wear makeup and jewelry and always had her hair dyed chestnut brown. Physically they were not compatible but they were in every other aspect. When I was at the house they were always laughing and looked genuinely happy together.

My grandparents' house was my favorite place. I was with them every weekday, and most weekends while my mom was at work and my dad was away at what at I thought was work. At this point of my life my father was in jail doing a couple of years. I was young and didn't understand what jail was. Their house felt more like my home than my own house did, and still feels more like home than any house I've lived in up to this point.

When I think about my childhood, that house comes to my mind. Their place in Jeffersonville was originally a small house until my grandpa built it into what it is today. Each nail and coat of paint held his personality and love that we felt every day we were in the home. My favorite place to make memories was the den area located behind big glass double doors off of the kitchen. It looked like a living room with a makeshift office to the left. In the office is a desk where my grandpa would spend hours doing paperwork or watching TV. The office had a copy machine and we'd put our faces on the printer to take our pictures and hang them on the walls in my bedroom and in his office. I'd spin around in his worn down office chair even though I knew it would make me feel sick. I loved it. My bedroom was pink and purple and filled with handmade dressers, shelves, and my bunk bed. Across the hall was a spare room we called the "Chestnut Room" because of the type of wood he used when building it. At the very end of the hall was the "big room" with its own porch, bathroom with a bathtub that was more like a hot tub, and a huge walk-in closet.

One of my favorite memories there was when we'd get an arts and crafts box delivered about every month and my grandpa and I would sit in the den and complete the workbooks together. Each box would have different themes and learning activities and the workbooks or crafts would correspond with them. I specifically remember one box that had theme of time. It came with a yellow clock with blue bold numbers and red hands. There are two clocks in my childhood that are stuck in my memory, and that toy clock is one of them. Grandpa would turn the red hands to a time and I'd tell him what time it was. I heard the pride in his voice when he'd say, "You're as smart as a tack." Anything I learned would make me "as smart as a tack," even if all I did was learn how to blow bubbles with bubble gum. Learning that the "fast hand" makes a sixty second trip around the clock and the difference between the "baby hand" and "big hand" made me as smart as a tack. He said this so much it could've been my own name.

When I played house, I'd use the clock to teach my "kids" time as well: breakfast would be at 8:00,

lunch came around 1:00. When it was bedtime for my dolls, in real time we'd go pick up my grandpa from work. My grandma and I would hop in the black and red Thunderbird and drive to get him at the Colgate factory where he worked as a technician. I knew we were close when the moon-sized Colgate clock appeared closer and closer until I was looking up to it through the heavily tinted window. The clock was prettiest at night when the bright red hands were beaming, turning our faces and everything around us red as we looked up at the twelve lines representing each number.

Sometimes we'd drive to the clock for a look, and I would sit in the passenger's seat of my grandfather's van to watch the long hand tick as I counted each sixty seconds. I would watch and wait for the question I knew was coming, preparing myself to recite the answer, growing anxious, worrying I'd forget how to calculate. When my grandfather finally asked, "What time is it?" a smile grew on his face when I uttered the correct time, down to the exact minute.

"You're as smart as a tack."

My grandpa started to get sick one day. It started off with him just sleeping on the couch for a few days. That wasn't like him in the slightest. My grandpa was adventurous and active and that part of him was drained as he absorbed his illness. I was thinking that maybe it was just the flu or a really bad cold until he ended up in the hospital. Being young, I was oblivious to what was really going on. My mind could only believe that if you're sick, you'll get better, but this time it was not the case. I still wasn't aware of this fact during the hospital visits and phone calls.

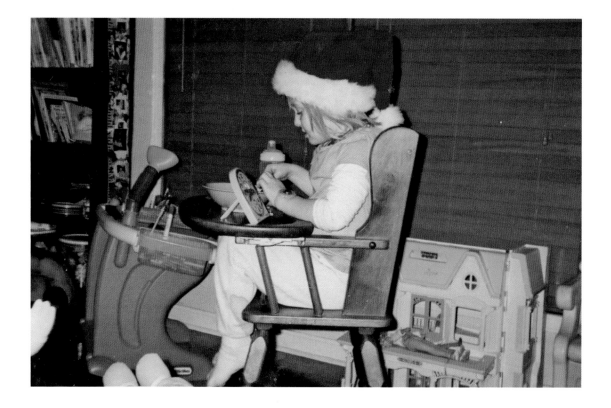

One day my grandma drove us to Clark Memorial Hospital, and my excitement to see him grew as we got further down 10th street. I can still remember feeling uncomfortable being in the hospital because of how dull it was. Everyone was expected to be quiet. Everything was clean and white, and there was no warmth or color, which I wasn't used to in comparison to the home I'd grown up in. Going past each room and knowing there was pain and illness behind each silent door made me even more comfortable. Walking into my grandpa's room was no different. He was hurting and sick and silent like everyone else.

My visits to him were very scattered and normally short, so when I did see him, he was happy. I could see that. I could tell he wanted to be happy when he tried to get up and smile even though his illness wouldn't let him. His smile would quickly turn to a frown accompanied by a squint of pain. That visit consisted of small talk mainly between my grandma and him. I still enjoyed being there with him, even if there wasn't much to say.

A few days later, my grandma told me he would be coming home. I immediately assumed that meant he was better. I thought that the house would begin to feel warm again until I saw the hospital bed rolling

Autumn and her Grandpa, Les Merkley

into the Chestnut Room: the same white blankets from the hospital and the same bed that was more like a machine. I knew he wasn't comfortable as the doctors changed the room into a jungle of wires, bags, lights, and buttons. The medicine, and most importantly the distance from the family, made him uncomfortable in his own home.

Even though he was just behind the Chestnut Room door, I rarely saw him. My grandma would assure me that he just needed rest and that we needed to keep quiet. I walked through the house with resistance, tiptoeing down the halls and avoiding every part of the floor that I knew would creak. I

silenced my laughs and giggles, worried that they would somehow reach through the house into the Chestnut Room. The uneasiness of the house didn't keep me away, though. The overall presence of my grandfather still made me feel at home. The love he had for the house and the family made up for everything else. I was just happy to have my grandpa home again.

Then one day my grandma said he wanted to see me. The idea made me nervous because I wasn't sure what to expect. I came up to the room where he was staying and remained silent like I thought I was supposed to.

Autumn with her dad, Robert Wilson, and her grandpa, Les Merkley, in Jeffersonville, IN

"Hey."

"Hi, Pawpaw."

We continued the small talk about if I was helping my grandma at home and what I'd been doing. My grandpa would always ask if I'm making sure grandma is doing okay while he was sick. I enjoyed letting him know everything at home was doing fine because I know that made him feel better. My grandma cut the visit short, which disappointed me. She told me to tell him I love him, which I did, and he said so too.

Over the next few days my parents were coming over more frequently. I'd be told to stay in my grand-

parents' room and was oblivious to what was going on and why they were showing up so much. I knew something wasn't right. One afternoon, I was laying on their bed watching the Disney Channel when my mother finally walked in to see me. Suspecting nothing, I greeted her with a smile that she returned, and then she sat on the bed with me.

I have a very nontraditional family that doesn't really have serious talks, so when I saw the serious look in my mother's eyes I began to become anxious. She asked if I remembered how Pawpaw was sick, to which I replied with a slow nod. She explained what his sickness meant and that he wasn't going to get better and what it meant to go to heaven, and then she told me it was Poppy's time to go to heaven. I didn't understand what my mom's statement meant, but my eyes still filled with tears. I was sad because what I did understand was that my grandpa wasn't coming back. Before he was gone all I had known was that he was sick and we were waiting for him to get better, and now he didn't have a chance to. After his passing, the house in Jeffersonville was different. His aura of love and happiness went with him and the house didn't feel the same. It was missing the one person who managed to keep us all in check.

My grandma was alone in a home she was used to being happy in. My family and I moved in with her to fill the house again and make it more of a home, but it didn't last long before she moved into a little house in a good neighborhood called Wyandotte and sometimes called Oakdale. I wasn't familiar with the area when I first saw it, but I was drawn to the park directly across the street. I started going over to her house to spend the night more often, and my mom, dad, sister, and two pets moved from Jeffersonville, Indiana, to the Louisville house with my Grandma.

We thought fitting all of us into a small two bedroom house was a great idea, but we quickly realized that was not the case. In that house, the "master bedroom" was the living room, which is where my sister and I stayed. We separated our twin size bunk beds into two and lined them against the walls along with our dressers, toys and TV. The living room barely had enough space to fit our furniture along the walls while still leaving a small walkway in the middle. My grandma and parents had their own rooms, which wasn't much of an upgrade from us considering they were much smaller. Living together and always getting along was something we had issues with. There was tension and uneasiness painted along each wall. After about six months my grandmother realized that being in a house together wasn't the best idea, and she moved out. I was disappointed that she was going but glad the tension wouldn't linger any longer. I love my grandma and loved spending time with her, but seeing how it affected her relationship with my parents made me realize it was the right time for her to move.

We lived in that house, directly across the street from the park, when I started middle school at Olmsted South. After school, my best friend and I would hang out at the park nearly every day. I grew an attachment to it, as if it were actually my own. I had my own favorite spots. When we felt like swinging, the left one was my swing. The ladder on the left side on the park was my favorite. The shortest drinking fountain had the coldest water and I knew which park bench was built in an awkward way that I didn't like. It was a place I fit into my daily life, and I felt I could claim it as my own.

My home in Wyandotte is where I begin and end every day with my family. It's where I work my hardest and rest the most. I learned how to swim, read, and ride a bike in my neighborhood. What brings comfort is relationships you have created with the community. Living in Wyandotte for about eight years now means that I've seen the good and the bad. Unfortunately, some outsiders only seem to

Wyandotte Park

recognize the bad things that happen there, like drugs and violence. It's a place that people say, "Oh, you live there?" in disbelief. It's no secret that there are some problems in my neighborhood. I'm always reminded to "stay out of trouble" as if that's all our community holds. I almost don't blame people, though. We all resort to the news to know what's going on, and my neighborhood finds itself in the news for crime all the time, but very rarely for positive reasons. Living in a place that's viewed so negatively often makes me feel embarrassed to talk about where I live, knowing I'm going to get that same look of disbelief and concern. I feel like I have to reassure them that my neighborhood isn't what they're thinking, which is something I wish I didn't have to do.

Lots of times kids my age love drama and use fighting as the first resolution to an issue. They do things like go into the park and cause trouble, usually for attention or to fit in, and for the thrill they get from their friends. Sometimes it's hard to blame kids who are left at home while parents work and need to find something to do when there aren't enough activities in the neighborhood for them. Sometimes it gets more serious, though.

 PHOTO BY AUTUMN WILSON

A couple of years ago my friend and I were walking down Taylor Boulevard past the basketball court. At that time, we'd walk around the neighborhood every day for hours without a destination or reason. We were going to the gas station just past the overpass on Taylor. Like usual, the basketball court was full with people playing basketball. We weren't expecting anything bad to happen while we were distracted by the nearly fifty people running and the basketballs flying around the court until we heard a fight begin to happen. We saw people spread to the outskirts of the court and begin to dissipate. Two men were arguing and yelling over the failed basketball game, then we saw one of the men reach into his shorts and pull out a gun.

So many thoughts flooded my mind. What if he's not the only one who's armed? What if instead of aiming for the air, he chooses my best friend, or even me? I remember everything about the moment except what his face looked like. He reached into his red basketball shorts overlaid by the white fitted tank top for the handgun. His slender, muscular arm reached in the air and shot. I know that my fear made the sound louder than it really was, but it was loud enough to catch the attention of a police officer passing by the park. We heard the loud sirens as two police cars drove through the grass by the court, and many of the players spread out and ran. We continued walking under the I-64 overpass and could no longer see what was going on at the park.

The whole time, Haley was on the phone with her dad. He had heard it all over the phone. I imagine he was worried, because she had removed the phone from her ear for a moment while we were watching what was going on. We explained to him what had happened, he reminded us to be careful, and then we continued like nothing even happened.

But we can't ignore the things that concern the community. People getting assaulted and property getting damaged or stolen from homes is scary. I've had to talk about needles in the street with my little sister and her friends a few too many times for my comfort.

My dad is protective of his family. He says, "If you can't rest your head in your own house without worrying about someone stealing something, then you aren't in a good neighborhood." When I've talked to him about it, my dad says that with drugs and shooting everywhere, keeping to yourself is in your best interest. He's helped the wrong people and ended up getting hurt. He has lived in the neighborhood longer than I have and he sees it "just getting worse and worse every week." I understand that if you constantly have your guard up, scared that something is going to happen, subconsciously thinking of the worst possible circumstances, you are going to want to protect yourself, your home, and family. I understand how that may also prevent you from seeing the good things in the community we have built. He sees things that could potentially harm the family, which changes his perspective of everyone in the neighborhood, and he's right, you never know when something bad could happen. But you also never know when something you think is bad may have the best outcome.

So yes, there's a stigma that Wyandotte is filled with nothing but crime and drugs. But that's only if you rely on the news for information before your own neighbors. I choose to interact with people which is maybe why I see things in my neighborhood that others don't.

I've seen the same mailman nearly every day since I was nine years old. I don't know too much about him, but he works on the coldest and hottest days of the year. He rarely misses a shift, and so I know he's very hard working and dedicated.

The lady who works the night shift at McDonald's lives a few streets down from me, and when she takes her kids to the park on weekends to get out of the house for a while, I know she is a hardworking mother who provides for her family and works to give them a good childhood.

When I go to the dollar store, I see the same kind workers I've grown up communicating with. I often wonder about them, who they are, and what they're personalities are like outside of the workplace. But I know they are genuine people that are here to help.

There's a group of older men who have created a senior baseball league in the park and play for fun. They practice together on Saturday mornings. I'm not really sure how "professional" it is or if they even play other teams, but it's sweet and is something I love to see in my neighborhood. I see the bond that they have brought into the community.

The Salvation Army Community Center has church service where kids and their families come to spend time with each other and God. They have an open gym for kids to keep them in a safe place instead of possible unsafe situations.

The community is a very family oriented place, despite the issues we may have. From the workers at the small drug store, to the Kroger on South 4th, just about everyone is genuine and big-hearted.

When people see me with my family and recognize us, it shows they too pay attention and notice their neighbors. They care about how my family is and what we're up to. I wouldn't say they're friends, but I wouldn't call them acquaintances either. So what do I call them? Well, I call these people my neighbors, and I call this realm of comfort and happiness my neighborhood.

I want to show other people the love within my community so that they can share the appreciation I have and even bring it into their own neighborhoods. This can not only make Wyandotte a better community, but make the South End and every part of Louisville better too. I'm writing about my neighbors for the same reason we write down notes or our shopping lists, because they are important and need to be remembered.

I wanted to know more about my neighbors, more about the people I'm creating a community with, so I started introducing myself. I began by walking around the neighborhood more and saying hi to people when I saw them sitting on the porch. It put a smile on their faces, which shows character. I enjoyed seeing my neighbors happy to see someone else in the neighborhood being friendly, and this led me to step two: meeting the people I was introducing myself to. I started looking for someone who could talk about the community I was becoming a part of. I knew I wanted someone who plays a strong role in the community, so I began searching for something online that would lead me to them.

I don't really find myself on social media too much. For my generation, social media tends to be an outlet for violence or drama, and I don't like that kind of negative energy, so I mostly stay away from it. However, there is a Facebook page called "The Oakdale Neighborhood Discussion" that is a safe place for the community to turn for help. If you have extra coats in your storage, you can find someone on the page who may need them. If someone needs clothes for the winter or help with food, the Facebook page is there. Social media can be such a great way to communicate to people and provide help for families and their homes.

I looked around for someone to talk to and ran across Jennifer Nunn. Jennifer works at the Center for Neighborhoods as their education and outreach associate. As a mother of four, Jennifer wants to make the neighborhood a better place for the children and started working on many programs for kids. Her family's involvement in numerous sports has translated into soccer programs for kids in the neighborhood.

What drove me to talk to her was to learn what was going on in the neighborhood and how other people are working on getting involved. I'm drawn to Jennifer because she is a role model with goals for the community. As I learned more about the issues Jennifer is passionate about, I became passionate too, and excited to meet more of my neighbors.

Jennifer often hosts neighborhood get-togethers at her house where everyone talks about what's going on personally or within the whole community. She hosted a donuts and coffee party, and I got to experience my community outside of social media.

Autumn, Robert, Amy, and Alaina

I was nervous to be social with my neighbors, but when I got there I realized there was no reason to be nervous. I was meeting people who I had a natural connection with. The environment Jennifer had created strengthened my appreciation for my neighbors. Jennifer had met so many people that she knew were good people and wanted to introduce us all. She knows the neighborhood has potential, it just needs someone to say, "We are worth it, we are capable, and we can do this."

Jennifer Nunn

When I started getting involved in the neighborhood, the first thing I noticed was that, if somebody had something important to say, there's not really any clear avenue to get the word around. Someone had already made a neighborhood watch group on Facebook, so I was like, "Why don't you make another one, just for regular stuff?" So we made another Facebook group, and sometimes I just write questions like *What are you guys good at? What are your hobbies? What are you guys doing for the holidays?* I ask a lot of questions. Sometimes people engage, and sometimes you have to push them. I remember asking one time, *What's something that you are good enough at that you could teach somebody else how to do it?* I don't think people see themselves in that kind of way, but that conversation really ended up taking off. I ended up using those "what people are interested in and what people are good at" responses to make some connections down the road.

The Facebook group is where I've made a lot of my connections to people in the neighborhood. I would like to see more people meet each other, because when we all know each other I think we feel better about being supportive. Like just recently, someone was having a really hard time finding winter clothes for her kids, and because we all know each other, we're helping her find the things she needs to make it through the winter.

There's a stigma that people put on us in the community, but even with those bad feelings that the community has about themselves, I think there's still a really deep pride that people have about living in the South End, and I love that. For a lot of people, we grew up in these neighborhoods, and our parents, and even our grandparents, and so it's our history, really.

I am the education and outreach associate at Center for Neighborhoods, and I assist with the Neighborhood Institute class. We just started another class in partnership with the Office for Safe and Healthy Neighborhoods. They do an Ambassador Institute training, and you can take the Gold Level training. We're offering one of the Gold Level training on community organizing, so I am assisting with that class. I create our newsletters, *Neighborhood News and Happenings*, that goes out once a week on Friday mornings. Most recently, we just had the Neighborhood Summit, so a lot of my time was devoted to that. I did all the organizing and planning for one of the mobile workshops, so I did a lot of work with the Portland Museum and the *Portland Anchor* to organize the History and Culture and Preservation Workshop. The organization as a whole has really grown recently.

I started at the Center for Neighborhoods when I got interested in getting to know the neighborhood and the community. I would sporadically go to neighborhood association meetings. I found a flyer somewhere for the Oakdale neighborhood planning meetings at Most Blessed Sacrament on Saturday mornings. I participated so we could write a plan for the neighborhood, and then eight months to a year later, I participated in the Neighborhood Institute, which is a twelve week class to help adults be more civically engaged in their communities.

The first part of the class is geared towards getting to know how the city government functions. You might get to know different departments in the city government, especially the ones that are important to neighborhoods. Then you learn a little bit about urban planning. Then you learn quite a bit about project planning, and then each person chooses a neighborhood project and is challenged to see it through. They recently starting giving a micro grant to some of the class participants. You have to apply for it, and they selected a couple of winners.

There's a broad range of projects. One lady just made a billboard, and some signage in a parking lot for an AMVETS post. There's a lady in the Parkland neighborhood, who just got a micro grant to buy solar Christmas lights to project them on the vacant houses on her block during the holidays. Ladies from the Taylor-Berry neighborhood are working on some public art, trying to get a mural in the neighborhood. I met a lady in my neighborhood, her name is Casey, and I could tell that she cared about a lot of the same things that I did, but she wasn't really involved in the neighborhood. So when the next Neighborhood Institute came around, I encouraged her to apply and she just graduated from the Neighborhood Institute. Her project is rain gardens in backyards and

in alleyways to reduce flooding in the area. There's somebody else in the South End whose project is getting a soccer pitch in the South End. We don't have any soccer organizations, and we also don't have any fields that are designated just for soccer.

My project went a little broader than the neighborhood; there's not any youth soccer in the South End either, so I wanted to get youth soccer started. For the past year we've been doing clinics either at Olmsted Middle School or at Americana Community Center. We've done one in the spring, one in the summer, and six weeks in the fall. We're talking about a recreational youth league for the upcoming spring. It's really geared towards South End neighborhoods.

The South End struggles with a misconception as a whole. Once you get inside of the Watterson, I think that the perceptions get a little bit worse. I think that people think that there's a lot of drugs and drug addiction, and that it's not necessarily a safe place to be. I'm from Louisville, Kentucky. I grew up in the South End in the Taylor-Berry neighborhood. I've lived in the Oakdale neighborhood for about seven years.

When I first moved into my house in Oakdale, I was really not aware of the neighborhood. I think there was some violence that happened maybe three or four years ago that really hurt the neighborhood and the way people feel about the neighborhood. There's a lot of people who don't feel safe. I don't know that I've really seen that ease up, but I don't think that the violence has sustained at the same kind of rate. I have not experienced violence in the neighborhood.

I realized that I could make a greater impact by focusing my energy on other things, so I planned a couple of neighborhood cleanups at the park. I did some work with Grace Church in the neighborhood for a while. Grace Church focuses all of their resources on the kids. We planned an Easter egg hunt at Wyandotte Park. We did a Thanksgiving dinner the same year, then we helped with one of their Christmas programs for kids. That year they had an angel tree kind of thing for around fifty kids and we connected with the families who really needed it. I've had more organic things too, like just inviting neighbors to come over and sit on the porch for a while: have some sweet tea, or a baked good or whatever. We recently had a stone soup party at my friend Casey's house where everybody brings an ingredient and you make a soup out of whatever is brought. It turned out pretty good.

Another time, some neighbors just got together and made wreaths. I invited some people who I met on social media who I knew were in the neighborhood and who I hadn't met yet. I've made some good friends through things like that, just like, "Hey, somebody come sit on the porch!" I made a peach dessert, and was like, "Come on guys. Come have some!" Four people showed up, so we just sat on the porch for a while.

I'm also working part time for the Green Heart Project, which is a partnership between the Nature Conservancy, the Institute for Healthy Air, Water and Soil, and the University of Louisville. They're studying the intervention of trees in a neighborhood as a medicine. They want to see, if we plant a whole bunch of trees in a neighborhood, does that reduce a person's risk for heart disease? It'll be conducted like a medical study, and I think in the next year or so, we'll be seeing the planting. We'll be bringing some really mature, like thirty foot trees into the neighborhood. I'm excited about what the results of that study can do for other neighborhoods too, because if it goes the way they think it will go, it will show that the trees in our neighborhood are as important as our roads or our sidewalks.

I don't think that what I'm doing is unique, so that's why I get excited to meet other neighbors. "What are you doing? What can we do together?" I know that I will keep trying to meet with neighbors. I'm sure that there are other people in the neighborhood, somebody that is just like me that I haven't met yet, who's doing the same kinds of things with a handful of different people.

My neighborhood started forming around the same time Churchill Downs, the famous racetrack, was being built. In 1890, Oakdale was a lot smaller, just a few houses and many still being developed by investors who built homes along what is now called Southern Parkway but was previously known as the Grand Boulevard. The middle-class neighborhood was semi-autonomous along with other neighborhoods like Highland Park and Beechmont and fought to remain this way, but after numerous legal battles that were taken to the Supreme Court, Oakdale and surrounding neighborhoods were included into the city of Louisville in 1922.

The current borderlines of the neighborhood is Taylor Boulevard, I-64, Southern Parkway, and Longfield Avenue. The Grand Boulevard was constructed to be an easy access in and out of the Wyandotte neighborhood. Many long term residents have reported seeing racehorses walking down their neighborhood roads and watching small horse races along the Grand Boulevard.

In 1935, construction on a park began that was named after the Native American Wyandotte tribe. As the neighborhood continued to add homes and stores, and as the park became its central point, the neighborhood became more commonly known as Wyandotte. Landscape architect Carl Berg created a plan for the park consisting of a splash pool, courts for sports, a shelter house, and even plans for the trees. In 1937 the Works Progress Administration finally built the community building and splash pool, which remained in the works until the 1950s along with the playground.

By 1964, Wyandotte Park included the playground on the Taylor Boulevard end, the community building, the sports courts, and the splash pool. As the Watterson Expressway was being constructed, it cut off a section of the park that included a volleyball court and part of the splash pool. The Wyandotte park construction led to the whole neighborhood being renamed Wyandotte in 1970.

To me, Wyandotte Park consists of the Community Center/Salvation Army, the baseball field in the middle, and the two park playgrounds. The community center is a great yet underestimated place in the neighborhood. It offers a church and a safe place for families, who depend on it as a place to keep their kids safe and out of trouble. It plays the role of a second home to many because if the kids aren't keeping themselves busy there, they could be finding negative things on the streets and maybe get hurt. When the community center is closed, the park plays the same role. The values that the center has instilled in the children, follows them to the playground which also acts as a place for children to go spend time and make friends.

There's a church in the community called Southside Baptist Church that has made its mission to help folks in the neighborhood who are experiencing hard times. Every Tuesday the church holds a drive that gives away boxes of food to people who may not be able to afford it. They give out quality food that I've seen help so many families out firsthand. The mothers who would distance themselves from the community now become a part of it when they see someone is there for them. They thank the church and their God for helping them, because that one box of food can really help a family in more ways than some may think.

Every night during football season proud families always come to watch the football team, the Colts, as they practice. Cars line up bumper to bumper along both sides of the street, leaving barely any room to drive in the middle. Kids come from all around to watch and play games, eat food, and make new friends, and people are always happy. Everyone comes to see their kids, family members, and friends have a fun game and a good time together.

Every year in early August or late June, Metro Parks hosts a celebration where they have free food, games, music, school supplies, and learning experiences for the kids in the Wyandotte neighborhood, although people all around the city come to the celebration. Money is an issue for many families, and Metro Parks comes to make sure every student has what they need to get the best education while still making the experience fun. Students can get a backpack full of supplies based on their grade. Every year they include food, face painting, and a fire truck where we can go in and see what the inside is like, and everyone's favorite, the dunking booth. Although the day is meant for kids, it's a place where the community makes sure every student can have educational opportunities equal to students in other parts of the city.

Money more specifically affects the community around the Christmas season. In general, things are more expensive during the giving season and some families aren't able to give to their kids like they want. Some years, the LMPD has hosted Christmas parties where they raised money and bought new toys for kids at Semple Elementary, which is located in the center of Wyandotte.

My neighborhood and my neighbors deserve to be thought of. They have great intentions for the neighborhood and the people in it. I'm writing about them because they've given me a sense of appreciation for everyone. We have made the neighborhood into a community of people with genuine goals and love for it.

Toni Lynette Cristy

Toni Lynette Cristy loves that the neighborhood is growing and has participated in many projects and has talked with Metro Council members about improving the business and aesthetic appeal of the community. She also brought something new to Wyandotte Park: yoga. Toni aspires to be a community leader, and with the things she has done thus far, I'm sure she will be.

While talking to Toni she revealed how humble and caring she is for people and for the community. She told me that her goal is for the city as a whole is to look like Southern Parkway, where there's flowers and trees, where people are happy and healthy. The two of us share a similar perspective about the crime in the neighborhood. We both recognize it and know it's an issue but still love the community for what it is.

—AUTUMN

I was only supposed to stay in Louisville for two days, but it's been two and a half years. I'm from Chicago, but I like to move around a lot. I can't just go visit a place, I have to live there. That's just my thing. I lived in Indianapolis, I lived in Fort Wayne, I lived in Tennessee, Texas, and Washington. Right before Kentucky, I lived in Lafayette, Indiana, near Purdue University. I wanted to go on a trip, so I rode my bike a little over 300 miles from Lafayette to Louisville. This is the longest I've ever lived in a place as an adult.

I've been in the South End the whole time. I like it here. I just feel like, this is what home is for me. My place now is on Southern Parkway.

I lived in Jacobs with my cousin and her family about a mile away from Wyandotte Park. I like the price of rent, especially as it compares to Chicago, and I made some really good friends here. The longer I stay, good things just keep happening.

I teach yoga about six days a week. I didn't have any real intentions of becoming a yoga teacher. I just loved yoga. I did it for five years before becoming a teacher. After I really got into the yoga community, I made some soul friends, and these connections keep happening. I was supposed to leave Louisville in April but then something else happened so I'm staying. Again.

NEIGHBORHOOD REVITALIZATION & THE CREATIVE FLOW

I work with Kentucky Yoga Initiative. We give free and low cost classes all around Louisville. Plus some in Paducah, Owensboro and Lexington. We have a bunch of different free classes. I teach at South Louisville Community Center, but there are classes at the Family Health Center on Broadway, Cyril Allgeier, and more. We also have classes at JCPS for the kids. We do classes at places like Kentucky Refugee Ministries, Gilda's Club, and Dismas Charities for the staff and residents. KYI is amazing, and I'm so lucky to be part of the organization.

I want to start my own yoga nonprofit, but it's going to be a mobile community yoga studio. I want to go to different retirement centers and places like the Boys and Girls Club, and tour, not just Louisville, but America, with my mobile community studio. I want to create communities, like what KYI has at the different community centers, as I go from state to state.

That's why I went to the Center for Neighborhoods' Neighborhood Institute. They gave me a lot of information on how to create communities as I travel and resources for different community projects. The structures for city government are pretty much the same from one city to the next. You're going to talk to waste management for this thing, you're going to talk to city council for this thing. I was in the program with people from different neighborhoods. I learned more about how culturally diverse we are over here in the South End as compared to anywhere else in Louisville.

But Louisville is super segregated, and that's why I like it in the South End. It's more like Chicago where there's a bunch of different cultures living in the same neighborhood. Even just on my block we have Jewish people and Muslim people. We have middle class people and poor people as opposed to the other neighborhoods which are so divided ethnically and socioeconomically.

I have a lot of gig jobs that take me all over the city. I really don't feel the same sense of neighborhood as I feel over here. I've been around my friends' houses in other parts of the city and I say, "Do you know your neighbors? What do you mean you've lived here this long and you don't know who they are? That doesn't make any sense." And it doesn't make any sense to me because there's so many joggers, people out there walking their dogs, but they're not talking to each other? And how did they get all this without talking to each other? Who have they been talking to?

I talk to everybody. In the morning, I see a lot of neighbors sitting on the porch. Everyone has something nice to say, or a good attitude. Nobody ignores me, which happens a lot in the Highlands. It just burns my biscuit. In the South End, everybody speaks when I'm walking down the street. These are my neighbors. They are kind.

The lady on 5th street, with the beautiful garden, I've talked to her a few times. I rented those Louvelo bikes when they came out. And the guy who I see a lot up and down Southern Parkway, he rode with me for a little while.

One of my neighbors is an arborist, which I think is really, really cool. I went to job corps to be an arborist. I think it's one of the coolest things.

Another neighbor is a massage therapist, but she also writes for the *LEO*. She was in the Neighborhood Institute with me and is starting a program promoting rain gardens to collect rain in the alleys since it floods so much in the neighborhood.

Another neighbor works at the Ford factory and has too many cats, but they are so cute!

I'm not a big fan of our president, but one of the things that became popular after he became president is the Coexist Movement. This movement of being aware of what other people's problems are, supporting them, and having them come over to support you. Not just focusing on what your problem is—*my problem is bigger than your problem*—but saying, "I have a problem, and you have a problem too. I think we could work together to solve our problems." I feel like that movement, that thought process, is happening more than it was happening before. Makes me feel like there's still hope for humanity.

I've had depression since I was a little kid. I went to therapy and learned nonviolent communication, which is not just not yelling at someone, but it's learning how to listen to someone as well. Empathy and sympathy and openness are skills. Some people are very innately empathetic, but they try to fix people instead of listening to them. A lot of people will come in trying to fix the South End, not realizing or celebrating the assets that we already have. I think the biggest skill is to learn to listen, and to be open to not doing anything about what you hear. Everybody has a story—you can't not have a story.

Growing up, I knew all my neighbors, not only in my grandparents' neighborhood, but mostly everywhere we went. If I took the same bus route, I saw the same people: this dude who was selling newspapers and stuff, the same people playing music on the streets and subway, lots of people. It's not like you see all these people every day, but when you see the regulars, you feel the sense of community. That's something I grew up with. I don't know if everybody in Chicago has a sense of community, but I lived in the north, south, east suburbs, north, south, east of the city itself, and it's something that people do there. Talking to their neighbors, walking down the street: these are not things everybody does anymore. But if you're sitting on your porch, why wouldn't you say hi to the people sitting on the porch next to you? It's something I grew up with, so I didn't know it wasn't something other people had.

That's one of the big reasons why I love Louisville so much, because I came to the South End, and I was able to feel that sense of community here. I don't think I've really been able to feel that in other cities.

I think that our cultural richness is our best virtue. If people come over here and see how we coexist, I think it will impact some of this redlining that's happening with different people buying houses in other neighborhoods. Because it works over here, that's why the prices are going up. I see a lot of houses. The for sale signs will be like ninety or a hundred thousand dollars, for a house in the South End, so I know it's coming up. I know that we still have work to do, but I want to acknowledge the work being done.

I want to be more of a community leader. I'm trying to work with my neighbors to get more restaurants and more small businesses over here to make the South End more attractive. I want to bring more attention to the small businesses that are already over here. I'd like to display our sense of community, that sense of "cool," we have over on the South End. There's no Heine Brothers over here. There's like three in every other neighborhood. There's none over here. Not that I don't like the coffee shops we do have, like Sister Bean and Sunergos, I'm just saying. Heine Brothers is a really big staple of Louisville, and they're not over here. I don't understand. Louisville itself is still growing, can't say enough good stuff about the businesses in the Highlands. Plus the West End is getting so much attention, like really good restaurants and places to shop and stuff. It doesn't have to be a choice when it comes to city promotion. There's enough business and attractions to share.

I'm also a community liaison for the Green Heart Project. It's a scientific study to see how planting more trees improves people's heart health. They are planting six thousand trees in the South End. They planted one thousands trees and other greenery in St. Matthews at a school, and it was incredibly successful. So they're doing it on a larger scale now in Jacobs, Wyandotte, Beechmont, Oakdale, and Hazelwood. Its sponsored by the UofL School of Medicine. The Nature Conservatory is working with them too.

Spring 2018 we started recruiting people in the neighborhood to be a part of the study. Green Heart Project will start planting soon, and it's going to be a five year thing. The plan is to reduce the amount of pollution that gets into the neighborhood by planting along the highway and major roadways.

I love the fact that more people are getting on board with making this sustainability thing a factor. Because it's not like climate change is a thing you can deny anymore. Promoting a cleaner environment is a movement, and more people are realizing the need for change. And even if there's nothing we can do about climate change, that doesn't mean that we can't live better, like recycling and planting: is this a bad thing? Are trees a bad thing? It doesn't make any sense. I'm glad that more people are thinking around that, rather than trying to keep filling landfills, keep cutting down trees, and not caring for our environment.

We are invisible in the South End! I've heard so many people say things like, "I don't go south of campus," like that's a thing: *South of Campus*, like *West of Ninth Street*. Everybody knows about that divide, but I don't think everybody realizes the South of Campus thing is happening. I think that people don't think that the South End has anything to offer, and we don't have as much as the other neighborhoods. I just don't think that they see us at all. I couldn't really explain the invisibility to you, because Iroquois Park is pretty big. It should bring more businesses over here. Nothing else needs to be over here but that park and we should get more attention. But that's not reality. I don't know. We're just invisible.

Yes, there is a high crime rate over here compared to other neighborhoods, but there are a lot of people who come outside and try to be with each other too. And I think that people can come over here and see that. Not just at Iroquois Park, or down Southern Parkway, but at Wyandotte too.

I don't see this neighborhood as a bad neighborhood compared to where I'm from, but my friend does. She goes all the way to St. Matthews to take her kids to the park instead of going to Wyandotte or even Iroquois Park. It wasn't an option for her. I had to convince her to consider it. She likes the splash pad at Wyandotte now. She keeps talking about seeing the Overlook at Iroquois Park. I love going to the Iroquois Amphitheater to watch movies and see concerts.

People see the stuff that's on the news instead of actually walking outside and being a part of the neighborhood. They see that "so and so got shot," or a car ran up the curb into the park. All anybody outside the neighborhood hears about that park is that some drunk drove up there and almost hit some kids. That's what on the news. Well, I was at that park a couple of weeks ago for the Taylor-Berry Neighborhood Association; we had really good hot dogs, stuffed mushrooms, and potato salad. My friends in the Taylor Berry Neighborhood Association were playing their guitars and stuff. So that's what happened to *me* at that park. People see our neighborhood as something bad, because all they see is what's on the news.

No news team came out to see us at the Taylor-Berry Neighborhood Association Party. Supreme Peace Yoga has free community yoga at the Beechmont Baptist Church: no news coverage about that. They're having the Buy Local Fair in the South

End this year, there's no newscasters coming out for that. It's not in the *LEO* last I checked.

I'm sure news outlets have proof that negativity gets ratings. But people love feel good stories too. To regularly put the good and the bad in the news would be a more accurate portrayal of life instead of showing people bad bad bad bad bad all the time.

People think that they're going to have this event in the hood, and somebody's going to start shooting. This has never happened at Wyandotte Park at any of the events I've been to. But a shooting could've happened years ago, so they just stopped going to events there since then. So if more people would report on "this good thing happening," if more people requested it, it would happen. I don't know what that would look like. Maybe more people being open to community instead of going into their houses and not coming out. I think they should take a chance on the South End and see what happens. I don't know what would motivate people to get out here. I'm working on it. I hope it's yoga.

NO PARKING
ANY
TIME

Robert Wilson

My dad is very social and can talk to anyone about nearly anything. He's funny and that attracts people to him. I knew work was important to my family, but I didn't know what it really meant to my dad, so I sat down with him and asked how he has worked, how it has impacted his life, and what it means to him. Dad is observant of people and their intentions. He's social and open, and yet very cautious because of experiences he's had in his life, beginning when he was just a kid.

—AUTUMN

We lived in Denver, Colorado, for two or three years when my dad was in the Air Force, then moved back to Louisville. My mom and my dad split up because he was a fool. They were both young, and they were both fools. When we moved back it was me and my mom and sister. We moved in with my grandmother, my aunt, and my grandpa, and my uncle in a three bedroom house in St. Matthews. Then Mom found another boyfriend. When I was seven or eight we lived in J-Town. My best friend lived a couple apartments over. There's a lot of good memories there. Being a kid at seven or eight years old, playing with toys, hide and seek, you know. Getting in a little mischief. We threw rocks at cars, knocked on doors and ran, and all that stuff that kids do. Nothing extravagant. It's common for boys of a certain age.

When I was around ten my little brother David was born and we moved to a house in Fern Creek. Fern Creek was a lot nicer neighborhood. We moved from an apartment to our first house. I had my own room. It was nice. Felt a little bit richer than living in an apartment, and there were more kids to play with. I had a good time there. First girl I kissed was there. Played football for Fern Creek, I played baseball at Fern Creek. Shot someone with a BB gun, all the kids ran wild back then and had a good time doing it.

My stepdad took care of us pretty much my whole life. He and mom were together pretty much my whole childhood. We went fishing together when I was younger. But as the years progressed his alcoholism progressed. My stepdad was a drinker, beer and whiskey. They owned a florist and there was a bar next door, so he drank all day. Fifteen years of drinking all day changes you. My stepdad didn't hit my mother, but he had a bad mouth on him. You can only mess with someone's mom so many times before you interact, and when I interacted, I hit him in his eye. That's when I got sent to Texas. Mom had three kids and my stepdad was pretty much the provider; she didn't really have another choice. I had to go. It was not a good thing, and I went from one headache to another headache.

I went to stay with my real dad in Texas, which was the first time I ever met him that I can remember. As a kid, when he was in the Air Force, he wasn't around a lot. So, being as young as I was, there was no memory. And through the fifteen years, never talking to him or seeing him, it was like moving in with a stranger. When I got to the airport, I was nervous. It was just a weird feeling because I didn't like him very much. There's no reason why he couldn't call. I tried to go with the flow or fit in, and he was an alcoholic and a druggie. He wasn't a dad. He was more of a friend. I guess it's hard to be a dad when you never was a dad.

Down in Texas, I didn't know anybody. The whole culture down there was different, and while I was down there, I went to two different high schools within two or three months. It was just a big headache. It wasn't like Kentucky. It was country, and when I was down there, they'd always ask me, "Did you ride horses to school?" It was way different. At fifteen, I was thinking about girls and trying to have fun, but down there, it was like I was an alien. I was different from anybody else. They thought I had an accent. The way I dressed was different from them, and it was just hard to fit in down there.

And then they'd rather have their alcohol or whatever they were doing instead of buying me sheets for my bed. I said, "No. That's just not how I'm growing up." I wanted to come home. Bad. I'd rather have been back home where we always had the roof on our head, Christmas, supper on the table. I was stuck between a rock and a hard place, and what do you do? Went from one hell-hole to another. I'd rather have been back home where I had my grandmas, and my sisters, my brothers, where I had a family, and down there I had nobody. But I was with my dad who's an alcoholic and druggie there. He was never really there, so I was ready to come back home.

Before I turned fifteen, I never did anything bad besides talking in school too much. I never snuck out. I always had decent grades. I always had a little job cutting grass. I worked summers with my uncle.

But when I came back to Louisville, Mom had another boyfriend and we moved out to my grandma's. She was out doing what she did and was never really around. I resented my mom for kicking me out, and sending me away for taking up for her. It was a whole different ball game after that. Everything changed. I had such resentment when I came back; I didn't listen to anybody. I was just doing what I wanted to do. Running the streets, coming in when I wanted to come in. I didn't have any discipline. I was hanging out with the wrong crowd, drinking, going to parties, trying to get with girls. Fighting. If my mom tried telling me to do something and if I didn't want to do it, I just wouldn't do it. I just rebelled real bad, and experimented with a little bit of marijuana. Just didn't care. I had older friends, and I guess I had, not a family, but I guess I started feeling close to people because, hell, they didn't have nothing else to do either. So we just hung out. Whatever you weren't supposed to do is what I thought was right to do.

I was a mad kid at fifteen, and I went to five different high schools in one year. I tried to get back into football. Then my mom was like, "You'll never be good enough for football." Low blows like that. It's easy to forgive, but hard to forget. And every time she did something like that, I'd just get worse, and didn't really care much.

I was living with my grandma in a trailer park in Newburg. She had two jobs, and was never there.

Moving from Saint Matthews and Lyndon where it's more middle class, to a Newburg trailer park was hard. Down there, you don't want to fall asleep with money in your pocket, because you might not have it when you wake up. No one cared about anybody but themselves. It was an experience.

I really didn't come home a lot. I was still dabbling, drinking a little bit. Passed out somewhere, and that's where I woke up. That's why I don't drink today, really. I don't need to do it anymore.

Around the age of seventeen, I got my own apartment with my best friend from Fern Creek, his girlfriend, her baby, their friend, and me. Her friend couldn't keep her end of her bills, so they broke their lease and left, which left me there by myself. Seventeen years old with an apartment by myself. It was a fast four or five months. Everybody started hanging out there, and we eventually got kicked out. We just partied, and destroyed stuff: the walls, carpet, and stuff we didn't care about that didn't belong to us. Now it makes me sick, because I have to pay for stuff, but back then we really didn't care. I was young, and I didn't have respect for people. I didn't really respect myself, let alone anybody else around me.

I tried to go back to school. I went to Seneca but dropped out. I really wanted to graduate. But it's hard to graduate and go to school when you ain't got a parent there to help. It's hard to do anything by yourself. I had no backbone. I wanted to graduate, and I thought I could do it myself. Then when I was seventeen, I got in some trouble and ended up doing a little bit of jail time. The only way to get out of jail was my GED. They had classes.

When I met your mom, we had a daughter who passed away. And then later we had you, and I had big plans, but I was still a punk. I tried to keep roofs over our head because we had a kid, but I did things the wrong way, and it caught up with me, and I had to go back. I broke probation and went back to jail when you were a kid. You were probably two.

I was just grabbing at life. I lived a fast life, until it caught up to me. It was rough there for a little bit. I did the best I could.

Then I said, "Enough is enough." I worked and did whatever I could to make a little bit of money. I worked in Ohio, New York, Alabama, and Tennessee building football stadiums. New York is nothing like what you're picturing. When someone says New York to me, it's the sky-scrapers, the downtown, and whatnot. But we weren't in that. We weren't in the city like that. We lived in hotels. You're with the same dude every day, and the experience was different from here. You're lonely. Go to work, go back to the hotel, throw something in the microwave, and go to sleep. I'd be gone for two, three months. Sometimes I might not even talk to my family on the phone for two days. That gets old quick. Then I'd come home for a day and they'd want us to go right back out.

After doing that for a little bit, I was like, "Man, I gotta get home. I have girls at home." The money was good: forty-two dollars an hour. But you have to pay for your own hotel. The checks look good, but what comes out of them ain't that good. But not being at home, that got me. I mean, I liked the job, the money was good, but to heck with that. I wasn't doing that.

Then I went out of town with a buddy. We tried to do our own little thing with electric and piping machines. We'd go out of town for a little bit, come back for a couple days, but the jobs weren't as long. And he had a family too, so he wanted to come home and see them. I wasn't there with my kids, and I didn't want to lose them to the system: that's not my plan, and I'm not letting that play out like that. I'm gonna try my damnedest not to let that happen. I'm hoping and praying they go to college.

I wish I had a better relationship with you and your sister. Wish I had more money to do stuff. Stuff costs so much money these days. And it's hard enough to try to think about how to get your daughters through college, or keep them from getting pregnant. It's a job in itselfa. In the neighborhood I live in, I see sixteen-years-olds out of school and pregnant, and that's not gonna happen on my watch.

I've got a sixteen-year-old who's too smart for her own good, and I've got a ten-year-old we call The Mouth of the South. Two totally different personalities. I got one who thinks she's tough, and one who thinks she knows it all. I'm doing something right, because I'm here today with you. I might be an a-hole sometimes, but it's paying off.

When I came to Iroquois High School as a sopho-more, which I thought was the worst school in the city, I was very upset. I thought it would be full of crime and negativity, and my first impressions didn't change my mind. There was a uniform that consisted of black or khaki pants and collared polos, some-thing I wasn't used to. There was yelling and arguing, which made me feel anxious and uncomfortable. My stubbornness led me to forget that the same things would happen at my previous school too. Now, I am a junior and Iroquois is my favorite school I've been in. The other schools I have gone to may have had some better qualities, but Iroquois blows them out of the water when it comes to the quality of the people and the teaching.

My family always has a lot going on and we keep very busy schedules, and before starting my sophomore year at Iroquois, it was even crazier. My sister and I were both in school across the bridge in Jeffersonville, my dad worked in Clarksville, Indiana, and my mom worked on Hurstbourne Lane in the east end of Jefferson County: all while we lived in Wyandotte. All of our different routines required a very specific schedule, and the four of us had to be up early every morning to get where we needed to be. First we took Dad to the very end of New Cut Road so he could catch a ride to work with one of his work friends, then we'd head across the river to get me to school, after which my mom left my sister with my grandma, who took her to school while Mom made it back to Hurstbourne to work: a nearly fifty mile trip, twice a day, five days a week.

For work, my parents currently buy, repair, and sell all types of things. For example, they will go to a pallet auction and buy a pallet they believe is worth money. This started when one day they bought a pallet that was filled with vacuum cleaners and other household items that they knew would be worth money. They also buy different things online to repair and resell. The pallets can range from any number of things, like phone cases, coffee, makeup, washers and dryers, anything, really. My parents bring home their new-found treasure and look through it as soon as they can. As my dad pulls out different things he mentally puts a price tag on it and moves on to the next thing. They sell their finds on the internet or in yard sales, and throw the rest in the garage until the next sale. Once they saw how much they enjoyed the process and the money they got in return, my dad left his job. It's not always easy and it doesn't always work out, but as a family, we're a team that makes it work.

My mom was still working at Bob Evans when they first started selling. When she began having her own issues with her employers, she left her job of many years and helped my dad make their side-job more full time. They enjoy it because it gives them the freedom to work all day without actually putting in work if they want, and to have more availability for the family.

At a young age, all I wanted to do was work. Everyone around me had manual and skilled jobs, which I admired. I loved the idea of working and making your own money and having real responsi-bility. The adults around me at a young age never told me to work as hard as them, but their habits were something I picked up on. They found contentment in work.

I learned that work was essential when my family was not working: being at work is hard but being out of work is even harder. When my dad worked at a granite and countertop cutting shop, he'd work long hours under hard conditions carrying granite. It was a job that could come and go, and it wasn't uncommon for my dad to be laid off for a couple of weeks at a time. Although he never admitted to that, I could sense that those two weeks were hard weeks for him. My dad was happier at work, and from those moments I knew the value of working and making your own money, which are persistent goals of mine.

The things we needed were always taken care of. With both of my parents' jobs there was enough money to stay in good shape financially with some to spare. On weekends when my dad would be off, we always had something to do. We would go to the mall, drive around downtown, visit my mom at work at Bob Evans—anything to keep out of the house. I wanted to work, though. I would ask my mom if school counted as a job simply for the satisfaction of saying that I worked.

Even before I was thirteen I looked into babysitting. I'd beg my mom to contact everyone she knew to see if I could babysit for them for a decent price my dad had formulated for me. I can still hear him saying, "It's easy. Twenty bucks per kid per hour they're out." Still, nobody would hire me. I started to look online for "jobs that hire at thirteen" or "teen jobs near me" and filled out countless applications in hopes of getting a job. A couple of years later, I heard Kentucky Kingdom was hiring minors for their summer season. At the very top of their website

I saw a large section that said, "Now hiring teens at fifteen!" My mouse quickly moved across the screen to begin the application process. After filling out the application I saw a red note at the bottom of the page stating that they were no longer accepting applications from minors.

My mom had worked at Bob Evans as a server for a long time, and when I finally turned sixteen and was ready to start a job, she had a job waiting for me. I went to talk to the general manager of the store and as soon as he saw me he started off by telling me the dress code and what my job would be and that I would begin the following week.

I had been to Bob Evans many times as a customer, but my first day was the first time I had the perspective of a server watching the other servers. I saw all of these women communicating and working together, building relationships with customers, but also being strong enough to respectfully deal with the snappy customers who disrespect them.

At work, I'm surrounded by strong women who I consider mother figures. For example, Michelle is someone I've known my whole life. She met my mom when they were about fifteen or sixteen, and they've stayed close ever since. I was always friends with her and her kids, who are around my age. I even lived in the same house with them for a while. I also work with Buffy, another mother figure who has been around nearly all my life. These women are what make me comfortable and proud to be at work at a job that is often not easy. I know being a server at a place with predominantly women can sometimes be difficult because it can often be based on looks, and special treatment between male customers and the server. It becomes a struggle for servers to decide whether or not they should feed into it for the sake of their jobs or not. Even in a place that's predominantly women there is still male superiority in some aspects. As servers, we are taught to please the customers because in the end that's what really matters, and we're also taught that if you're young and pretty, you'll get your money.

Before beginning to serve, I was told, "You're young and you're beautiful; that's where your money is." However it's hard to have to please the men who are attracted to the young and pretty girls because it can get to a point where it can be disrespectful. I respect the women I work with because I know they deal with people like that for the sake of their families and priorities.

I've worked at Bob Evans since July of 2017, and someone who has worked with me since the beginning was Kaile. She has worked the night shift with me almost every Friday, Saturday, and Sunday since I started. She was there for me when I was so busy I was nearly in tears, helping me with my tables. Kaile was there when my mom and dad didn't have jobs and things were rough at home. And she's there when it's slow in the restaurant and we have nothing to do but roll all the silverware until there is none left.

Something that's often the topic of conversation is her family. She's married with two girls, and she's subconsciously teaching me motherhood and its importance, because prior to her I was oblivious to what it's really like. Kaile had a lot of fun before becoming a mother. She wasn't afraid to live her life.

But once her life took a turn and she found out she was having her oldest, she recognized it was time to be responsible so she could be a good mother and have a family. By telling me her crazy stories of growing up and her stories of the hilarious thing her youngest said in the drive-thru, she's teaching me that it's okay to have fun before it's time to be serious. Her stories have taught me things I definitely do not want to do, and things that I someday want to experience.

Every weekend I'm excited to see Kaile and work yet another shift with her. On a good day, it's slow when I get there, giving us time to prepare ourselves for the rush we know we'll get. We'll play around for the next hour by putting salt in each other's drinks, making fun of each other, and talking about the week we've had since the previous Sunday. Then when the rush comes we work together while still staying in our own sections. I help her by traying this table's food while she gets drinks for that one. The rush is something we beg for when it is slow but during it, it pauses our fun and games and brings us close to being overwhelmed. The rush will slow down and we'll be able to talk again. I'll mention how Table 53 was so rude for no reason and she'll mention how annoying her party of seven was at Table 14. We'll wonder if this rush was worth it, money-wise, and do our rounds to see if any of our un-bussed tables have what we call "little pockets," or tips. She gets off early and leaves only when she knows I'm okay to be on my own for the rest of the night. She always makes sure I'm good with the rest of my side work before she goes, even when I tell her to go home to her babies.

The way I see it, women are the root of everything. They're the ones who create lives and raise people to be who they are. The people who have changed the world at any point in time were made by women. But, to this day, women are the ones who often get mistreated in homes, the work force, or the media. Everyone has a strong woman figure in their lives, a teacher, an employee, or another family member. Mine is my mother and I appreciate everything she does for me, back to before she even had me. I have a strong respect for my mother, other mothers, and women who are mother figures to motherless children. My mother has always provided for me. When my father wasn't present for a small part of my life, she had to work as much as she could to make sure I was okay, which meant that sometimes I didn't see her that often. I respect even the little things she does, like every text or phone call I get when I haven't talked to her for a while.

One misfortune women have is that they often don't get the credit they deserve. Whether they're mothers or not, women provide for people in remarkable ways. Women have a natural nurturing persona that will be there to help someone who's sick or connect to children as though they've known them forever. They can read a baby's mind when they're crying, they know how to cure people when they're not feeling well. All of the predominantly female careers are nurture-based jobs like teaching, health care, social and community work. I'm proud to say I'm surrounded by women, was raised by women, and that I too am a woman.

Over the past year, I have seen positive changes in the neighborhood where I grew into a young adult, began to recognize my community, and started to have my own beliefs, where I began to figure out who I am and where my place in the world is, and make my own decisions. I got a job and started to appreciate work and labor. I recognized what my family had been doing their whole lives and respected them even more for it. I began wondering about my community, about people, and I began noticing more about them.

I wanted to be more of a citizen of my neighborhood rather than just a resident, so I reached out to other citizens in Wyandotte. I wanted to give credit to the ones who deserve it—my neighbors and family. Writing about my neighborhood creates history for the future, and writing about my family creates an idea of who I am.

I found opportunities to meet people and talk to them about what we all had in common, which is the neighborhood, and what it meant to us, which varied from person to person. I documented what led me to my neighborhood and the impact it has had on me. From that I learned that each person in my community has their own ways of getting here, so I documented that too and started writing about my whole life and important people and events because they're important to remember.

I didn't know much about the neighborhood. I didn't know about the Center for Neighborhoods, the Facebook page, or the Green Heart Project. I see irony in that because their goal was to help the people, which included me, and I was oblivious to it. We're making the neighborhood into a community. I'd like to see the community improve even more.

We're making a safe place, a home to many, and an outlet for anyone who's looking for that sense of community. We have always welcomed people with open arms, but now when they come they feel welcomed as well. Maybe the media and other parts of Louisville can see what we've made of ourselves.

The past year of my personal life has been one full of growth in all aspects. I've found out who I am and learned things about myself that I never did before, like who I see myself being in the future. This year I have served people at home, at school, in my neighborhood, socially, and at work, and I've been genuinely happy to do so. I've thought more about my career than I ever have, and I know that I want to help people. I see myself continuing serving throughout my whole life: I love people and want the best for everyone.

HAFSA JAMA

A Radio out of Range

A Lot of Explaining

From Dadaab to Kentucky

A Radio out of Range

HAFSA JAMA

The photo album sits on my lap, heavy with the weight of the past. I run my fingers gracefully over the gray hardcover, admiring the piece of cardboard that carries dear photos of ours. On each page are three rows of photos. I go through it page by page, admiring the golden days. I am bombarded with joy, sorrow, a sentimental longing for the life that I once had in Kenya, and contentment for the one that I have now in the United States, but these photos prompt the nostalgia that I am trying to overcome. I beam when I see toddler photos of my brothers Keyse, Farhan, and Ahmed all wearing black shirts with white stripes and khaki pants, their miniature hands holding red lollipops. Mom had a thing back then for matching our clothes. We thought they were humiliating. I stare back at the little girl with chubby cheeks who looks at me with soft, youthful, brown eyes. She is wearing a flowy coral sundress, and her dark brown hair is in pigtails. I nearly burst into laughter. *Is that who I think it is? How young was I?* The picture becomes more vivid the longer that I look at it. Suddenly I am once again the young girl with the soft heart and electric soul, the girl drawing hopscotch squares on the ground with chalk stolen from school, the girl squelching mud through her fingers trying to sculpt an abstract figure. I can see

her grinning while jostling her friends for a spot on the slides. Children's giggles echo all around. *I remember this day.*

My friends and I were playing when the clouds above our puny heads started to let water fall down. As soon as the first droplet hit the ground, parents started calling out for their children—a reminder that play time was over. But the call of my mother's voice didn't stop me from dancing in the rain: anyone who says sunshine brings happiness has never danced in the rain.

My shoes were overwhelmed as water seeped in through the stitching. The trees were moving like professional dancers showcasing their talents, and, apart from stumbling here and there as my shoes stuck to the mushy ground, so was I. Mother nature had just announced her arrival in the best way and I was there to witness the glory.

Things deteriorated when my mother's voice called for me again. I stopped and so did my giggles, and every other sound. I could feel every single beat of my heart echo in my ears. I looked around for a pair of angry, flaming eyes but I didn't find any. I quickened my pace, holding my hands skywards to fend off the rain even though I was drenched.

The door stood shut. *Knock knock.* At the drop of a hat, my brothers' faces were planted on the window, their eyes reflecting the trouble I was in. *I can tell her that I got stuck in the slides, or I can go through the back door or run away while I still have a chance to do so.*

My heart raced like a runaway train going faster and faster as the door swung open. A quick glance at her eyes and I knew that I had hit her mark. "Get inside, now!" Mom growled. I dragged my drenched body inside, leaving wet footprints on the grey carpet. I was trembling like a feeble leaf on a stormy day and felt the cold spreading across my skin into the bones. *How much trouble am I in?* I was worried. I sank into our couch after I warmed up. There wasn't a soul outside. Everything seemed peaceful, yet I was stricken with dread. To my surprise, Mom didn't say anything else. With my back curved, head bowed, legs bent and drawn up to my torso, I watched as the wind whipped the frigid rain.

Grandma called out from her room, "Keyse, remove that red shirt! How many times have I told you, we don't wear red on stormy days?" Keyse, our third born, objected, "But it is my favorite." I drifted off to sleep with the rhythmic rise and fall of my chest soothing me. My mind went into free fall, swirling with the beautiful chaos of a new dream. The last thing I saw was the flickering of an old lamp that stood firmly on the wooden table.

A swarm of cars are parked nose to tail down both sides of the sleek tarmac road. The street is barely wide enough for two cars to pass in opposite directions. At intervals are street lamps with bowed

Baby Hafsa held by her mother, Ayan Ibrahim

supple necks as well as cable wires strung from posts that dangle in the breeze. Parallel to the parked cars stands the prominent International Mall where many people in Louisville's Somali community go to shop. My feet take steps across the concrete pavement, my dusty grey sneakers next to my aunt's brown sandals. Inside, we are greeted by melodious tunes jumbled with the distinct accent of the locals that drift through my ears as they amble past. There are a wide variety of shops that run in an unpredictable grid pattern. The stores sell traditional Somali clothing like *macawis*, a garment worn around the waist for men and the *dirac*, a long, light cotton dress for women. There is a cafe, a restaurant, a bookstore, and even a barber shop and a daycare. The grocery store sells products imported from the Middle East, like cow ghee and spices, canned goods, drinks, ziploc bags of frozen meat and sauces. Some stores even have antique accessories like ceramic vases, vintage jewelry, and incense burners arranged neatly on the counters.

This place is a treasure trove to my aunt. Her brown eyes light up as she enters, greeting the local merchants like old friends. I wander aimlessly across the cement floors from stores that have posters with tempting deals that make you spend more all the way to the board game cafe where men play dominoes and talk smack. "I can't believe this; we had them," one of them says. "Man, y'all are cheating or something." He throws his hands up and folds them against his chest. His opponent sits with a triumphant smirk on his face. "Losers weepers. Can we get some cups of tea here?" someone yells out. They continue with their game. This is not a place where

you hold your wallets tight and your kids tighter but a place of great amenability.

I come upon a cafe. It is as not as packed as I thought it would be. Inside are wooden oval coffee tables with splendidly proportioned legs. The fans are moving at a leisurely pace. Exhausted, I plop down into a chair in the corner of the room. I take a deep breath and suck in the aroma of the baked pastries that fill the air. Across from my table sits an old couple diligently bent over their meal. I let myself soak in the ambient music, lost deep in my thoughts.

Out of the corners of my eyes, I see an old man approaching. He wears a cream shirt and black tailored pants with brown sturdy brogues. The old man's gnarled skin breaks into a smile. "Welcome. What would you like, young lady?" he asks.

I thank him and tell him that I am just waiting for my aunt.

"First time here?" he asks.

"No, I come here quite often," I answer. Then I ask him what they serve.

"We have food from different cultural cuisines. This place is home to most people. Some of these dishes are only found in their native countries," he proudly announces. "We have *anjera* and *suuqar*."

That's my favorite. I fix my eyes upon the stranger who is filling my ears with interesting information. Hassan has lived in Louisville for fifteen years after migrating from Mogadishu, Somalia. He tells me that he wanted to create an environment where people interacted, stayed connected, and felt welcomed. "This is also a great way to stay in touch with the town news and gossip," he adds with a laugh.

Scarves for sale at the International Mall

From nowhere comes the sound of my phone playing a merry little tune. I stand, soaked in my sheepishness, and excuse myself from the table. I have to say goodbye to my new friend because my aunt is ready to leave. I'm not ready to leave, though—mainly because it reminds me of the cafe my mom used to own back in Nairobi.

Her mini cafe was located five minutes away from our home. She sold baked goods, tea, coffee, and snacks. The shop had plastic tables and chairs scattered all around according to Mom's preference. She would join them together when it got crowded. There was a red floral circular carpet that was placed at the center beneath the tables. Behind the tables was an aging wooden stand where mom placed her thermoses full of tea and sealed containers of baked goods. *Anjera*, a spongy flatbread that is served with soups and vegetables, was popular amongst the customers. There were *samosas*, which are fried dough filled with meats, spiced potatoes, and vegetables, and also *mandazi*, which is fluffy, light fried dough that is popular among the Swahili people.

The entire front of the cafe opened up to the street. Plates, ceramic and plastic cups, cutlery, and condiments were placed on the wooden shelves that were nailed to the walls. Beyond my mother's cafe were grocery stores, clothing stores, and butchers. There were also a couple of hawkers out there who roamed from street to street selling clothes, shoes, fruits, and special potions that would "cure any pain." Buy one get one free. Don't miss out!" they would bawl whenever they saw someone.

My whitened knuckles tighten around the wheel, my right foot steadily alternating between the brake and gas pedal. I focus on the pattern of the traffic lights, the smell of gas, the soft beat of the music, the chipped rear windshield of the black BMW in front of us, the oxygen flooding in and out of my lungs—anything to distract me from the voices inside my head. I constantly glance at my driving instructor, pleading for reassurance. *Am I doing the right thing? Am I tailgating the car in front? Am I in the right lane?* My inner dialogue simmers down as she places her hand on my shoulder and smiles her lips into a tight line. My tensed shoulders sink lower into my body and I ease the pressure that I was exerting on the steering wheel. My foot immediately pushes the gas pedal as soon as the green light appears. The black BMW is still in front, driving at the same pace that I am.

"Don't get too close," my mother warns from the back seat. "No. Focus. Don't get out of your lane!" I glance at my mother through the rearview mirror. Her remarks are not helping at all. Her chocolate brown eyes are wide and her eyebrows are raised half an inch, her face engulfed with a blanket of fear. Mine is, too. Truly, the apple doesn't fall far from the tree. I glance at her once again, questioningly. *What happened to the woman who would calm us down whenever we heard the murmurs of the soldiers down the streets? The woman who taught us to be strong? The woman who told us that we were going to be fine when we left without our father? No, focus,* I keep telling myself.

Abruptly, I start receiving past memories like signals from a radio out of range. I wish I had a box to lock out these wretched memories that feel like they were etched in my head with a sharp knife. But if wishes were horses, beggars would ride.

For seven years I lived in Nairobi, Kenya, in the Eastleigh neighborhood, which was mostly populated with refugees from different parts of Africa. They had all been looking for peace, security, and a place that could give them hope, and Kenya had extended its arms to them. My family settled there after we escaped a civil war that broke out in Somalia in 2006. It welcomed us with open arms and we gladly accepted it.

In March 2014, the Kenyan government executed an order called Operation Usalama Watch. Their plan was to relocate all Somali refugees and even the indigenous Somali Kenyans living in Nairobi to the Kakuma and Dadaab refugee camps or their country of origin, violating their human rights. A series of diabolic attacks fueled the Kenyan government to conduct such an amendment, and we Somalis had always been the scapegoats, labeled as the "terrorists," ready to be swept out of a land that for years had carried imprints of our souls.

Hardly had the announcement been made when thousands of *askaris*, government security forces, deployed in Eastleigh. We heard the *thud thud thud* of their boots stomping down the streets: the warning thunder of a coming storm. A wave of green uniforms swept through my neighborhood carrying away our people: children, students, the elderly, even parents who had children at home waiting to be fed. The *aksaris* raided homes. They tore up their identification cards and took them to a place they called Kasarani Stadium, where they would wait for days for the bus that would take them to crowded refugee camps where diseases spread like mighty flocks of sheep. The spontaneous repatriation invoked fear and disrupted our lives.

Refugees were advised to stay inside their homes until the situation settled down. We weren't even allowed to go to school. The Usalama Watch had been criticized, described as an "inhuman and total violation of refugees' rights" by United Nations officials. But when the government casually said, "The Usalama Watch is a way to enhance our national security. There are armed groups that hide behind the residents in urban areas to carry out attacks on our soil. To defend our lands, we have to carry out drastic measures." They went on and on about their plan while the legal documents that permitted us to stay became null and void. But we clung to the thought that there were people out there who knew the Usalama Watch was callous. Day after day, we huddled around televisions, eyes almost turning square, hoping for an announcement that would halt the destruction. Hoping that the light at the end of the tunnel would not be an oncoming train. The tele-vision displayed the ways our people suffered: elders cried, parents worried for their children, and people lost their jobs. We were bombarded with captious remarks from the interior cabinet secretary, every word becoming fuel added to the seething pit in my stomach: "I assure you that soon there will be no more refugee camps, we have rounded up thousands of refugees...." I didn't want to hear what he would say next.

Every day we heard that people we knew were taken away and dumped into a new place that they didn't know anything about. Families were broken up. People feared going outside their homes because there would be a dozen officers standing outside like attentive hawks, scanning the premises and ready to snatch their prey. This went on for months, causing hunger, unemployment, and people being kicked out of their homes. We could not go back to Somalia because of safety issues, and out here in Kenya they did not want us. Did we belong to oblivion?

When people had had enough, some of them decided to try their luck and go back to work. Most of them came back home safe and sound. They said they paid the police forces to let them go. I could not believe it: we had to buy our freedom.

Askaris started knocking on our doors to demand money or else they would take you to the camou-flage truck full of wailing people that was waiting outside. People would collect whatever money they had earned and pay them. Most had to borrow from their friends. As the *askaris* got used to the money, their demands increased exponentially.

There were people among us who had Kenyan citizenship. They had some unfortunate encounters

The Eastleigh neighborhood in Nairobi, Kenya

with the *askaris* too, but not as bad as the ones who were refugees. So they began to help the refugees who were experiencing problems by going out and buying them groceries and other basic needs since they themselves were not able to do it. Our neighbor Hawa became a helping hand whenever someone needed to buy diapers or groceries from the stores nearby—she never said no to anyone.

Tables appeared to have turned when, on a fortunate afternoon, my mother received a phone call from the UNHCR, an agency that helps refugees by resettling them to stable and safe countries. Mother tightly clutched the phone against her ear, her lower lip quivering as she uttered, "Thank you!" repeatedly. She stood still, staring at the reflection of her smile in the thin sheen of her cell phone screen. The UNHCR was considering my family for resettlement. We did not know how long the process would take, but hey, better half a piece of bread than none! For a brief moment, a blanket of relief smothered everything else that was going on.

For a month or so, we hardly ever saw any security forces in the streets. People were speculating that the *askaris* were eyeing the perfect time to pounce on their prey. I decided to take advantage of their "time-out" to roam the streets that I had not seen for quite a while. My mind was mainly focused on avoiding the *askaris*. The sun's embers poured into the clouds like molten lava. I passed by an elderly woman rocking in a chair that was probably older than she was, sewing her stress away. Her skin was wrinkled and thin like old parchments. She gave me a look that screamed, "What are you doing outside at a time like this?" I threw her a gentle wave, but she shook her head and looked down at her work, embellishments growing from her needles.

I took my usual spot on the wooden bench under the tall tree with finger-like branches that brushed our building. I closed my eyes and exhaled softly, the harassment and pain we had endured flashing through my eyes. I could feel my eyes getting watery, my throat getting dry. The only thing keeping me together was the solace that I sought in my family. "We will get through this as a family," the comforting voice of my mother rang in my head, a token of my poise and rationality. I stood up as soon as my face glowed with the last orange ray of the sun—a reminder to head home. I walked down the dusty streets that were once filled with people and music, and my tears came rolling down. A friend walked towards me and offered me a shoulder to cry on, and I gladly accepted it. "I am stronger than this," I murmured to her. But it seemed like I was trying to convince myself.

Mom's cafe's long run came to an end during the Usalama Watch. Although she insisted on keeping it open at first, she gave up when no one showed up. She sold it to the Swahili man who owned the shop next door, who then combined the two shops to make a bigger one. When it was time for her to pick out her belongings, I went to help her out. The colorful decorations on the walls, the lights, the feeling of being at home, and the savory aroma were all gone when my mother and I went there to pick up whatever was left. They were replaced by darkness, emptiness, and the smell of cement and iron. I tried to collect whatever I could find—baskets, thermoses, and containers—

avoiding the mud puddles and the construction tools that were scattered everywhere. "Let's get out of here," Mom finally said, breaking the silence that was closing in on us. She locked the door that was hanging on its last few hinges and glanced down at the wilting succulent that was placed behind it. She took a bottle of water from her purse and started watering it. "It's already dead," I told her. "It'll make it through," she said as she picked it up. My lips curved upwards.

The security forces started the usual routine up again. They moved from street to street as though they were washing dishes. Tired of being cooped up in the house, our neighbor Hibo paid us a visit. With her tear-jerking stories, her company was greatly appreciated. She and my mother were enjoying some cups of tea when a phone rang. Hibo answered her cell phone and her eyes flew wide. She put down the phone on our circular wooden table and raced to the metal-framed single pane window in our living room. I ran after her. The officers were walking on our pavements, randomly knocking on people's doors. Their murmurs lingered in my ears like the smoke of a blown out candle.

Hibo's brows creased. "I need to get back to my boys," she said.

Mother quickly shot down her thought. "If they catch you, you might never see your boys again," she said.

With a firm grip on our brass door knob, Hibo battled with her inner thoughts. Would she risk being captured? She knew there was no coming back from that. So she stayed back, hoping to see her boys one more time.

Hafsa as an infant

"They are with their grandmother. She will keep them safe," Mother reassuringly told Hibo, who was gulping down cups of tea as though it would dampen her unease. Her arms—as thin as the shoots of an olive branch—shook so much that splatters of tea gathered on the table top as she drank. Slowly, everything went dead silent. It was the kind of silence that pressed down on your ears. Images of what could be done to us flashed through my mind. What I had seen on the television made me question humanity. My siblings were silently huddled around each other, which was dismal but also amusing, since it was the first time that they had ever been still and hushed. Grandma snickered and wagged her cane at them. "If it takes a bunch of *askaris* to keep y'all orderly, then man, I need them around all the time."

We heard a loud *bang!* that must have been on the big gate right outside our apartments. I winced at the screech of the gate as it swung open, scraping along the pavers. I peeked through the window. My breathing hitched as soon as I heard voices that sounded like sandpaper over rough wood. Beside me, Hibo stood mute. There stood two *askaris* dressed in green uniforms with red berets. They were talking brazenly to what seemed to be a middle aged man.

"We can't accept the same amount as last time, *kijana*. Who do you think we are?" one of the officers spat.

The man's back tensed as he spoke. "This is all I have collected. These people are basically out of money."

The same officer spoke again while he rubbed his brow with his thumb and forefinger. "And why am I supposed to care?"

The man spoke again, "Then get back to wherever the hell you came from and stop terrorizing these people."

Had I not been worried about getting caught, I might have snorted.

The officer yanked the man by the collar of his blue button-up shirt. I can still see the way the man put his hands up in defense, the way his face quickly drained of color, the way his eyes were about to pop out of their sockets, and I can still hear the way he quietly said, "All I am saying is give us some time. We will have your demand ready by tomorrow night."

The officer's eyes held the man's eyes for a minute, searching for a speck of a lie, and when he couldn't find any, he released him. "We better not

be disappointed!" they roared and walked out of the gate, slamming it hard.

One night not long after that, I woke to the jangling of phones, voices rising and doors being opened. I could feel someone walking past me in a rush, but my vision was blurry. I went back to sleep, hoping that the commotions were fragments of nightmares.

I was dead wrong. Hibo had been repatriated.

"Why didn't you wake me up?" I asked Mom.

"What could you have done? Huh? Hell, what could *anyone* have done? Nothing. We are all useless!"

I watched as she broke down, scared to utter a word. She took me into her arms and rested her head on top of mine. "I watched them drag her out of the shop. She was just buying bread for her children."

I patted her shoulder, trying to comfort her. "Where are they taking her?"

"I have no idea," Mother said.

"What will happen to her resettlement process? What about her kids? Can we call her?"

Mother did not reply. She shook her head and tightened her arms around my back.

I kept quiet, scared to ask about the elephant in the room: would that happen to us?

"I hope we all go through this safe and sound," she said.

The resettlement process took months and required many appointments. There were police outside looking for refugees to capture at that time, but my mother was more worried about missing her appointments, because if anyone ever missed their appointments their resettlement process would be post-poned. The agency's office was far from our home. We usually took a bus. There would be a long queue of refugees all waiting to get inside the office, and sometimes we had to wait for hours. After our wait was over, we were checked for security purposes then were able to get inside the refugee agency's office.

Then one day Mom got a phone call from the agency. "We are finally moving to the United States!" she squealed. I let the spark of hope rekindle in my heart, the same heart that once beat with despair. We had a chance that most people would not get. My family and I were being moved to a safe and stable land.

We just had to complete the remaining steps of the resettlement process, which would take a few months. Mom continued going to every appointment the agency asked her to.

Despite everyone's eagerness to land their feet in the Land of the Free, I felt unsure. I wasn't certain about what was waiting for me across the oceans. I felt like I was walking on a cliff blindfolded. As I saw my siblings smiling with ease, I thought about how clueless they were about everything. Weren't they going to miss the familiar faces they'd known and grown comfortable with?

We eventually got a letter officially granting us passage to America. We were getting close. But the letter only listed my mom's name and the names of all of us children. No mention of Dad or Grandma. Mom called the agency and they explained that since Dad and Grandma had not moved to Kenya at the same time the rest of us had, they could not travel to the U.S. at the same time as us.

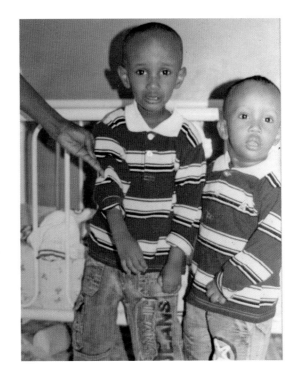

Hafsa's grandmother, Aisha Harun

A moment like this was supposed to be the beginning of my happily ever after. Wasn't that what everyone around me used to say? Maybe that wasn't the way my world worked or perhaps the way the world worked at all. I could not stop the clouds that rained sorrow down on me. Was I afraid to leave what I was accustomed to, or was it the fact that my father and grandmother couldn't go with us that disturbed me? Maybe I was lucky to have something that made saying goodbye so hard. I was overwhelmed with the feeling of losing something valuable, the feeling that what I once cherished was starting to feel like a memory, a shadow lingering in my mind.

My parents disguised everything that was flawed from my siblings and me. They told us, "Everything is alright. We are happy and so should you be." But I could see beneath their masks. How my father's brown eyes shifted to the sides and glazed whenever my siblings talked about leaving. How he would smile—not the kind that exposed his silver canine but the kind that made the corner of his lips tug downward as if tinged with a bit of gloom. Part of me wanted my siblings to know the truth, to pop their little bubble of glee and show them what was happening behind the curtains. But I didn't. Because I wished I hadn't popped mine, I wished that leaving wouldn't put a sour flavor in my mouth.

"I can't do that," Mom whimpered. She crumpled the paper that she was reading into a ball and tossed it aside.

Dad stood and started to uncrumple the paper. He strained his eyes at the black ink, glanced up at her, pursed his mouth and furrowed his brows—giving away all of his thoughts concurrently.

"What?" she asked, then immediately scowled as if she already knew what he was going to voice. "No!" she said.

"That's absurd, Ayan! Starting over the whole process isn't a choice here. Take the kids somewhere safe," said Grandma, her under-chin wobbling gently as she spoke. She hunched over in her chair, her back curved from age and wisdom. The map of wrinkles rooted under her eyes narrated tales of past laughter.

I stood still, chipping away the paint on our cobalt blue door, and hoped for a distraction to mask what was happening. Their voices rose and their expressions hardened. Mom was still clinging to the fear of everything falling apart. The fear that she would lose the family that she adored. And honestly, so did I, but I didn't voice that, partly because I was scared that they would notice me there and probably kick me out since they expected me to believe that everything was cherries.

Dad finally spoke. "She is right. You and the kids can't stay here. I am sure we won't either. It will take a couple of weeks and we will join you."

"Just because we weren't registered at the same time, doesn't mean that we can't leave together—as a family. There has to be another way!" Mom uttered. "I can't take care of them all alone. And besides, my mother needs me. Who knows what America is going to be. This is a bad idea."

Was it? It didn't matter how much Mom objected, though; they were at an impasse.

Grandma shook her head, stomped her cane—the breaking point of her tolerance—and said, "No, I am going to be alright. Go!"

That was when I slipped out of the room before I could make things worse. I slept that night with the anticipation of something beautiful and tragic in the fallout.

The standoff lasted for weeks. Mom argued with Dad and Grandma every day. She kept going to her appointments with the resettlement agency, though, which left the door open for us. In the end, Mom caved. We were moving to the U.S.

We had gone through pre-screening by the resettlement support center. Once we were eligible for resettlement, we had done a handful of interviews by the Refugee Corps. After we passed, we had moved on to security clearance and fingerprinting. We had waited three months for the placement allocations, then taken cultural orientation classes for a week. The last step was medical screening, which usually took about two months. Just two months to endure the *askaris*. They could still come any second and drag us out. Just two more months and we would no longer be in their iron grip. We had to make endless visits to the Nairobi medical facilities to establish our medical records and take some shots to ensure that we were ready to embark on our journey.

I curled my fingers around the thin hem of my scarf and waved it, creating a little air flow. We sat in elegant but uncomfortable leather chairs. A television hung in one corner displaying some tedious commercials about giving kids shots and other healthcare topics, and the clip-clopping of shoes down the tiled hallways drove me crazy. I kept checking the time but it seemed to flow like cement. My foot tapped rhythmically up and down to the crying of the little boy who was receiving shots.

We were called in to pick up our medical records. *Tick tock, tick tock.* Beside me my parents and siblings all waited patiently, except my little sister who kept running around as though an invisible storm were chasing her. *How long do we have to wait?*

As soon as I got on my feet, I met two captivating blue eyes framed with thick long lashes. Her red suit had a tailored look that was bold against her pale skin. She wore her long black hair in a bun. I took a step back and sank gracefully into my seat. The wait was over. Her eyes scanned the room in search of someone. The stranger in the black stilettos smiled when she saw my mom, who stood up and went with her. If I were to wear such shoes, I would hobble around like a newborn trying to stand for the first time. To my left, small children played with colorful toys as their parents kept a watchful eye on them. I glanced at the window but unfortunately a big old red truck was blocking the view. Yeah, my day wasn't going great.

Ms. Red Suit appeared. The words came out of her perfectly outlined lips: "You're up next for the shots."

Trembling hands decided to play my heart like a drum. "What shots? I thought we were only picking up our medical papers," I asked my mother, who was as confused as I was. I turned around to ask Ms. Red Suit but she had walked away, her heels clicking in time with the ticking of the gigantic clock mounted above our heads. I stared blankly at her perfect sculpted back, scared to take a step. But I knew I had to do it because I didn't want to look like a gazelle caught in the den of a lion. So I walked lead-footed towards the slightly-opened door to my right.

The rest of the suitcases were rolled in and lined up against a wall that I sat across from. *This is it*. I got up from the chair my body was dissolving into and as soon as I entered our living room, my lips curved upwards.

"Who's going to tell me what they want when we go to America?" Dad asked.

"Video game!" Keyse chipped excitedly.

"I want a phone!" Mohamed yelled.

"Chocolate! Chocolate! Chocolate!" Hinda, our youngest, cried out.

What did I want? "What about you, Mom?" I asked her. She looked past me, miles away, thinking. "What I want is a home that will make us feel safe and loved," she replied. And so did I. "That's why," she continued, "you kids, will be leaving with me. Your father and grandmother will be joining us a couple of weeks later."

Weeks? My siblings groaned, but they were eventually laughing, climbing on Dad's shoulders and reminiscing. *Just a couple of weeks.* A couple of weeks wasn't that bad, as long as we were going to end up together. For the beauty of the roses we have to water the thorns too, right? I moved to a mirror set on the wall. I was leaving behind my loved ones, friends, and even the stray cat that I had been taking care of. I stared at the dark brown eyes that looked back at me from the mirror. I thought about the wilting succulent that was now radiant and what Mother had said. There was hint of calmness in me—high hopes.

The still morning chill, the empty rooms and the suitcases were making me realize that the moment buzzing in my head would come and when it did, I would not know how to act or feel. It was as if all my emotions settled into a socket and someone flipped it on.

"Stand still," Dad said as he tied Anas's shoelaces.

"I don't like this color. I want Ahmed's," Anas cried out.

"No, no, this looks perfect," Dad convinced him. "Ready. Gather around," he called for us once we got ready.

We huddled around the sofa that he was sitting on. Hinda climbed onto his lap while Zakariya cannonballed himself to the corner of the sofa—*bam!*—and then grunted, "Yeah!"

"Okay, listen, everybody. When you leave today, I want y'all to promise me something. Take care of your mother and of each other. Promise." We nodded. "We can't wait to join you." Grandma nodded. Hinda had already fallen asleep in Dad's arms while holding the hard candy that she had been licking. He chuckled and tried to take it from her, but she tightened her grip on the stick. He let her have it. He said, "And if anyone causes trouble, I will board the fastest plane." He faced Zakariya. "Okay? I love you all."

Just a few weeks, I would constantly remind myself.

"Come here." He opened up his arms to us. We rushed for hugs and ended up falling over each other.

"I nearly passed out my first time on a plane," Grandma chimed in.

"Did airplanes exist back then?" Mohamed asked innocently, with a straight face. Everyone busted out laughing. Long gone was the emptiness that had been drowning us.

"How old do you think I am?" Grandma said, clearly irritated. Ahh! Good times are the remedy of sorrow. We gave her hugs and kisses before we left.

We were set to leave home at exactly 2:00 p.m. The weather outside was sunny and calm. Cars flew by the roads. Some of the neighbors were cooking food outside on their balconies. We were supposed to arrive at a gathering hall before going directly to the airport. We were traveling with an agency called IOM, the International Organization for Migration. When we arrived at the hall, our luggage was weighed. There were a lot of other people who were traveling to other countries. A middle aged woman who was traveling with her daughter started yelling at one of the IOM officers. They yelled back, "Ma'am! You have to remove some of your items from this bag. It is beyond the permitted size." She squinted her eyes while glaring at him and crossed her arms. "No, this is all my items. I paid for them." They kept talking to each other, their tones getting louder and angrier. Another man came out to talk with her. Eventually, she agreed to remove two huge jackets from her bag. She put on both of the coats and said "I will not go to America and freeze. That place is very cold."

Fortunately, nobody else was told to remove anything. Moments later, two gigantic travel buses arrived at a distance. As soon as the engine of the bus roared to life, my heart sunk. This was the last time that I would ever see this place again—the place where I had grown up.

We arrived at Jomo Kenyatta airport half an hour later. We sat down once we got through the sliding door and waited as a petite woman assigned to us by the IOM filled out some paperwork. Mom was handed a white tote that had the IOM logo on it to differentiate us from all the other people who were boarding the plane; anyone who had that bag would be assisted immediately if they had problems. After what felt like forever, the IOM lady came back. "Our plane does not take off for like two hours, *sawasawa*," she informed us. I looked at the vertical screen that displayed the times and destinations. Our first stop was at Zurich, Switzerland. My phone was buzzing with messages from my friends who were all wishing us a safe flight.

Eventually it was our turn to board the airplane. I was nervous because it was my first time ever on an airplane. To add salt to the wound, I was terrified of heights. But I did not want to whine about it and give my siblings something they could use against me.

"Everyone make sure to buckle up. It is going to be a seven hour flight. We will first stop at Tanzania and then our flight is going to end in Zurich, at around 9:30 a.m.," the IOM lady informed us over the voice of the flight attendant who was saying the same thing.

On July 7, 2015, my eight siblings, my mother, and I arrived in Louisville, Kentucky. We were completely worn out. The scorching summer sun was striking, its rays bolting through the colossal airport windows and casting shadows across the tiled floors. We had been told that our caseworkers would be around, and sure enough, they were there. A woman in a long black dress with a dark green hijab and two casually dressed men were holding a whiteboard with my mother's name written on it. We followed them to two black SUVs parked right outside the airport. We divided into two groups. The engine roared to life and so did the bickering.

Zakariya mumbled against the window, "Oh, look, a doggy!"

They all rushed to the dark tinted windows. Aisha and Farhan asked, "Where? Where?" The golden retriever wagged its tail from side to side. Farhan said, "He's adorable. Can I pick him up? Can I? He can live with me and I won't even tell Mom. I promise."

I listened to their conversion heavy eyed. *What is wrong with them? Weren't we just enclosed in a plane for sixteen hours?*

Aisha said, "It's a girl, dummy!"

Zakariya, whose face is still against the window, said, "First of all, it is a he, and second of all I am the one who found him first, so I am keeping him."

Seriously. The owner, a young brunette, was standing beside it with a red leash wrapped around her hand while we were stuck at a red light.

Aisha said, "Look at that dog. She's too pretty to be a boy."

A couple of "aha" and "how dare you" expressions displayed on my brothers' faces.

Farhan said, "Two against one. We win, dummy."

Aisha looked around. She's never one to admit defeat. "Hafsa, tell them it's a girl." She pulled on my shirt. "TELL THEM!"

At this point, they were ruffling my feathers. The car started moving again.

Zakariya said, "No, tell him to stop the car."

Farhan pleaded, "Come on. Tell him, please."

Their constant nagging was aggravating my head, which was pounding like those tom tom drums of West Africa. *That's it. I've had enough.* "I will kick y'all out and you'll have to walk home," I warned.

Farhan said, "You can't do that."

I faced him. "Oh yes I can! Mom is in the other car and she won't know anything."

The rest of the ride was soundless. I woke up to the faint shadows of the tall trees that stood like guards as we raced down strange paths. Before I could register the darkness, we pulled up to a narrow street with houses lined on either side.

"I think we have…," I began.

They were all asleep. Aisha dozed on Farhan's shoulder while Zakariya was laying his head against the car seat. *Why can't they be like this all the time?* The green shrubbery all around looked almost black. The stars winked as though we shared a funny joke. The house in front of us had pastel pink walls that looked as though they were dipped in cotton candy. Beside it was a tall tree that hung down, its long branches brushing the ground. The lawn looked freshly mown. Night had finally fallen and so had the realization that we had finally arrived at our new home, but it felt as though a dash of something was missing. Familiarity? As soon as I stepped inside, I felt a train of sleep hitting me. I fought hard but eventually gave in.

I walked along the pavements of my neighborhood, which was starting to feel like home after a few months of living there. The amber and tangerine orb of the sun sunk lower until it dipped down into the horizon, painting the sky. The air was damp and cool, smelling faintly of a car's exhaust fumes and the cloudless sky promised an unfettered view of heaven.

6/6   'The woman ahead'   hafsa

The Woman Ahead, a self-portrait linocut print by Hafsa Jama

There was a crunch of gravel that took me out of my world. I was walking with Sophie, a friend of mine. Although we did not go to school together, we lived near each other. She is an outgoing and charming person with a personality that would light up an entire house. Her hair fluttered in the air, her brown hazel eyes sparkling against the settling sun. With legs as long and thin as string cheese, she strolled down the familiar streets, matching my steps. Soon enough we reached home and took seats on an old bench. The wooden bench creaked as our bodies conformed to its shape and we sunk as if pulled by invisible strings gently downward. I ran my fingers over the rough paint on its handles that seemed to vanish as time went by. I closed my eyes and exhaled softly as bygone moments flooded my mind.

I could picture myself back at home, to the familiar streets and to the people I grew up with. I could see the sidewalks that looked as though an elephant with stilettos had staggered down them, causing great cobwebs of cracks. I could see the trees with branches that protruded like vines up towards the sky and brushed the nearby buildings like a paintbrush. Then I was back in Kenya, engulfed by the sweet scent of my grandma's home baked bread. My siblings were there, some glued to the television, while the others were turning the house upside down, something they are still good at doing.

Suddenly, I felt a tap on my knee and as I look up to see Sophie getting up. "It is getting darker. I think we should head home," she says. I nodded as I tried to quell the tears in my eyes and the lump in my throat. No matter what, the past beats inside me like a second heart.

I had goose bumps on my arms from the evening chill. There was no hint of warmth left. We had clearly underestimated this night. Sophie sighed heavily and exclaimed how a hot cup of chocolate would save our day. What is about a hot mug of chocolate that brings smiles? "And do not forget the marshmallows," I added, and we laughed.

Soon enough we were on Sophie's doorstep. Inside was warm. I greeted her mother with a smile on my face. She was a spitting image of Sophie with an avalanche of dark brown hair fanning over her shoulders like a settling dust cloud. In her floral skirt and baby blue blouse, she looked stunning. She wrapped her arms around us, giving us a quick hug. We bathed in her warmth and the smell of freshly laundered clothes.

"You girls are freezing. How long have you been out?" she asked.

"Mom, we just went for a walk and came back just in time. We are fine, right Hafsa?" said Sophie.

I glanced up to meet four similar eyes looking at me. "Yeah, yeah. We are perfectly fine," I concurred.

Sophie looked up at her mother to reassure her that we were fine and she finally seemed convinced. We followed her to the kitchen where she served us hot mugs of chocolate and a long lecture about dressing appropriately next time we left our houses.

"And I will let your mother know that you are here safe," Sophie's mother informed me.

"Thank you!" I replied. I sat next to Sophie on the sofa and I wrapped my fingers around the mug, enjoying the heat that spread through my hands into my body.

Sophie exhaled loudly and took a sip from her mug. "Now that is a wish come true," she announced, as though everything has been lifted off her shoulders.

The night was wonderful and I was without a doubt feeling at home. I kept thinking about my life back in Kenya. How I was separated from the people who I grew up with. How I arrived at a new place with nothing but my family beside me. I never thought that I would be at a friend's house, sipping hot chocolate and binge-watching *The Office*. Yes, I had left valuable memories behind, but as life moved on, I would make a some new ones.

"Hey guys, come talk to Dad!" Mom usually yells for us whenever Dad calls. Due to the different time zones between Kenya and Kentucky, we hardly get time to talk with him. Nairobi is eight hours ahead of Louisville. When he calls, we are usually asleep, and vice versa, but he still manages to check up on us. My siblings jostle each other as they try to fit their heads around the laptop screen. They call out to him. Our youngest, Hinda, tries to touch his face through the screen.

"Hey! Hey! I am right here," he says.

Then all of my siblings speak at once. "Dad, I got an A!" "So did I!" "Dad, look at what I got for my birthday!" "He is pushing me!" "No, I am not!" "Yes, you are!" "Dad, did you cut your hair?"

Dad tries to calm them down. "Ahmed, stop pushing your brother." It is complete chaos. I listen as he talks with them and it does not feel like he is miles away. It seems that he is right there with them just like two years ago, engulfed in their happiness.

My siblings explain to him every single thing that happens in their lives and he does the same. Mom chimes in here and there.

"How's your process going?" I ask him.

"It is still going. They are working on it," he says. His process gets more complicated with everything going on, such as the travel bans.

"Soon he will be with us," Mom says, her eyes lingering on hope. "It just takes time, just like it did with us. One day we'll be united."

My favorite part of when Dad calls us is when he asks about my siblings' behavior. They look at each other, waiting for someone to let the cat out of the bag. They all get quiet and put on their "angel faces." Mom usually covers for them because "they are just kids." "I won't say anything if you will all help me out with my chores," I tell them. They agree and no one receives one of dad's speeches.

"They have been behaving wonderful today," Mom says as I snicker.

We initially thought that Dad would be able to follow us here two weeks after we resettled, but it has been two years now and we have no idea how long it will be until we are reunited. Since we are here without Dad, I have tried to step in and give a helping hand to my family. Since Mom works a job to pay for all the expenses at home, I help take care of my siblings and do most of the cooking at home. And I have to balance my family responsibilities and my school responsibilities. As the first born, I try to be a role model to my younger siblings, to be someone they look up to and respect. Although life without Dad is sometimes overwhelming, we have pushed our way through it.

Oriental sofas with back and arm rest pillows are spread in a semicircle throughout our living room. Across from the sofas is a television, and two yellow artificial roses are placed on each side of the television stand. A colossal red carpet covers the whole tiled floor. Two long curtains, red with black floral embellishments, hang from the window. On the wall across from the window is a framed painting of a river that always seems like it is flowing when you get close to it. A lot of activities take place here, from hosting guests, to informal hanging out, to the whole family just sitting together enjoying quality time. This is the place where my mom has her gatherings. She and a couple of friends get together weekly.

Before her friends arrive, Mom usually lights up a Somali incense called *unsi* in a *dabqaad,* a ceramic incense burner that has some decorative details on its sides. She puts two pieces of coal on the top plate of the *dabqaad* and plugs it in. After a couple of minutes, the coal heats up, she places the *unsi* on the burning coal, and it melts away. After a few seconds the whole house is fragrant, and I start swimming in waves of nostalgia. I always find it fascinating how that smell takes me back to when I was young, to when we used to play pretend and to when my father used to spin us around on his shoulder, his hoarse laughter hovering over our giggles. Then she brings a set of demitasse cups, a jug of creamer, and a thermos filled with her signature freshly boiled tea and sets them on the coffee table. For the tea, she heats up two quarts of water, then crushes equal amounts of cardamom pods and cloves. She adds a stick of cinnamon, four bags of black tea, a teaspoon of ginger, sugar, and the crushed ingredients to the boiling water. She lets it boil for a few more minutes. To go along with the tea are biscuits and *halwa,* a sweet snack made up of sugar, cornstarch, oil, and spices.

"A lot of Somali households are like that. We host these gatherings to get closer and support each other," Mom says. After my mother's work hours at the daycare are done, she rests for a couple of hours as she prepares lunch for us. Cooking is something she considers relaxing. Not me. I love cooking, but for me it is not relaxing at all. I am constantly worried: *What if the food burns? Did I add too much salt?* Sometimes, I think Mom was born to cook. After the cooking is done, she doesn't just sit down and relax; she constantly checks for something to do. Cleaning here and there. Dusting the walls. Name any chore, she would want to do it.

Soon the awaited friends and neighbors join her and they all sit together. They engage in conversations about how their days have been. She passes the food around and her friends say "mmmh" and "this is great" as they take bites. Since everyone is mostly busy, they do not get together often and when they do, everyone receives calls numerous times. "Mom, where did you put the keys?" or "Where are the diapers for the baby?" They get all kinds of questions. I am guilty of interrupting too. Whenever I am looking for something, the first person I ask is Mom, and she always seems to find it or know where it is. One of my favorite things that they do is henna night. Henna is a temporary dye obtained from a plant that is made into a paste and used as a temporary tattoo. They put the paste into a plastic cone and paint the patterns that they want on their hands.

Items for sale at the International Mall

After that, they drink, eat, and just talk until the henna dries up. Later on, they pick off the crust of dried henna and it turns out beautifully.

"This is how we stayed connected," Mom has said to me. "I did not have a phone to constantly text and talk with and honestly it is much better to just sit together and enjoy each other's company," she continues. "Nowadays we don't get time to get together. Work, family, and other responsibilities hinder our time to socialize." I have always admired a lot of things about her—how she sacrifices everything for us, how she values togetherness, the way she listens without judgment, her cooking skills, but most importantly her ambition for happy endings through the hardships. During the worst parts of the Usalama Watch, Mom would say, "Don't worry. One day we won't be afraid of stepping outside anymore." When I hear about the Somali travel ban on the news, she tells me that she will make sure that she brings Dad home with us.

Hafsa's sister Hinda

When I was younger, I always believed that every book had a happy ending until I came upon one that didn't—a book called *City of Bones*. How could a writer obliterate such a beautiful story with a stroke of a pen? Younger me was devastated until months later, when I learned that there was a sequel to that book. And guess what, it had a happy ending. Indeed, a story's conclusion depends on where it stops.

A Lot of Explaining

AYAN IBRAHIM

I sat down with my mother to talk about her life in Kenya and Somalia, immigration, her transition to America, and what her life's like now. I thought that I knew almost everything about her, but as we sat down and her words fell through the air like confetti, I heard things that I had never known about. I learned a lot of things about her childhood and interesting facts about some of my relatives and the Somali culture.

—HAFSA

I was born in Mogadishu, Somalia. The place where I grew up was called Howl-wadag. I lived in a house with four rooms and a big backyard with my parents and eight siblings Intisar, Hinda, Abdikadir, Mohamed, Ahmed, Said, Kaltun, and Faiza. My brothers played outside while my sisters and I stayed inside and did work. My life was normal and good. My father had a store that sold food, and my brothers worked there. It helped us with paying the rent, school fees, and our meals. My mother was a chef, and she taught me how to cook. The first thing I cooked was *anjera*—after a couple trials I managed to cook one. I also cooked rice, pasta, sauce, and other things. We didn't have a car so we basically used cabs, taxis, and buses to travel around, although it wasn't cheap.

I usually helped my parents with housework and anything they needed me to do: cleaning, doing laundry, and other things. Just like how you help me around the house. When my mother would give me money for something I did, I would run and buy *samosas* or *mandazi*. Sometimes I would steal candies from our shop and hide them from my siblings.

The market was near us and so was our school. I had two best friends that I used to go to school with. At first, school seemed hard. I was learning religious lessons and the standard education. After a while I started getting used to school, finding friends, and learning, and I enjoyed it. My favorite subject was geography because it was interesting and because its questions had direct answers and they were small, unlike science, which required a lot of explaining.

Things changed when the war broke in Somalia. All the streets were destroyed and even our houses, and we moved. A war has been going on for about 28 years now. Nothing is the same anymore.

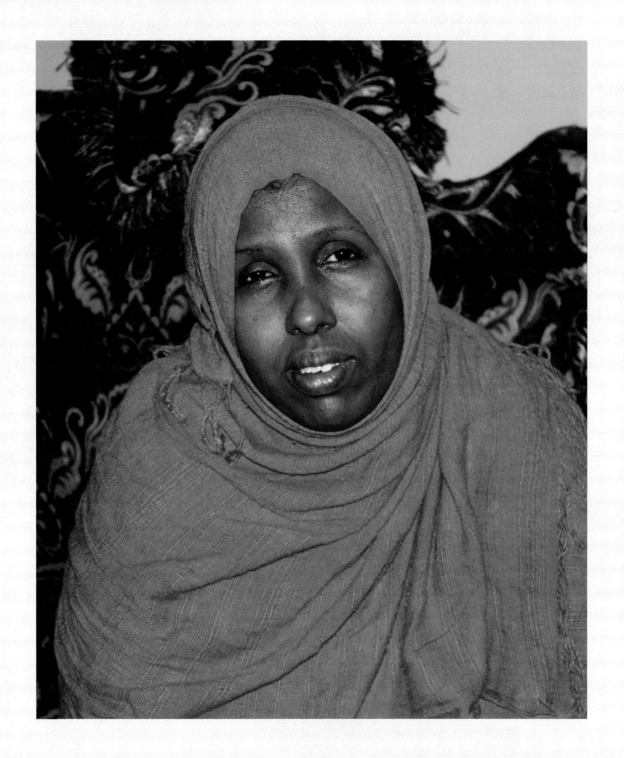

I moved to Kenya in March 2007 with my husband, kids and mother. Kenya was close, it had a good government, and it was safe. My first night in Kenya was very rainy. We spent the night at a lodge then we moved when we found an apartment. I was helped by Somalis who gave us food, clothes, and transportation to the place to get my refugee ID.

Finances were a major problem in Kenya, and I was missing people I was close to who were back in Somalia. But I was surrounded by my family members and a loving community. We found most of our cultural foods in Kenya because a lot of Somalis were living there. We also found out that there were Somali schools and mosques too. The Somali community in Kenya was really helpful. They helped us when we needed help. They also acted as middlemen between the Somalis and Kenyans. The Kenyan police always asked for a Kenyan ID and if you didn't have one they would arrest us. To be released, the UN had to issue a certificate to the refugees so that they couldn't be arrested.

Somalia and Kenya spoke different languages, had different cultures, and the environment was different too. It was hard to interact with people when you couldn't understand what they were actually saying. Learning the language was my first goal when I arrived in Kenya and was also a problem for me. If I wanted to live in Kenya, I had to speak Swahili. It took me quite some time to learn it. I went to a language school that helped me to learn the basics first, like what to say when you need to buy something or need help. It was a really nice school. After quite some time I quit going to the school because I had to take care of my kids.

It took my kids quite a while to know the country. Eventually they were all doing great. They would often hang out with the neighborhood kids, who showed them around. I loved the Kenyan culture. It was so interesting and colorful. The people were nice and hard workers.

When I came to America, it was my first time on a plane. My kids and I were a little bit terrified. The kids were like, "Are we going to fall?" But they got used to it. The flight was amazing, and although I didn't like the food they had, it was an unforgettable event.

We arrived at 7:00 p.m. on July 7, 2015. The language was going to be a problem for me, and your father was not allowed to come with us, but when I arrived through Catholic Charities that night, I felt like everything was going to be okay. Two American men and my caseworker, who was Somali, accompanied me to our house. They gave us food and water. They helped me settle down. I am grateful for that. I thought that I had finally made it. I was now able to live a life that I'd always dreamed of.

My first night in America was unusual. I had a problem with turning on the stove. It was a gas one and I heard a sad story about an accident with a gas stove, so I didn't use it until I called my caseworker. My kids were all sleeping but I had barely slept.

One of the funniest and most terrifying moments for me was when I first tried to use an elevator. I wanted to go to the second floor, but instead I went to the tenth floor. I didn't know where to go or which button to push, so it just kept going. I kept thinking, "Where am I going?" I was trapped in a small box. At last, on the tenth floor I found someone to help me. When I look back on, it I laugh.

Ayan Ibrahim with some of her children

At first I lived in a house on the east side of Louisville. Then I recently moved to a place near the daycare where I work. I go to work at 7:00 a.m., then leave at 1:00 p.m. My kids go to that daycare, too. I take care of the little babies: I change their diapers and clothes, give them food, and make them happy.

Living in poverty, insecurity, and fear made me forget what life looked like. Being here reminds me that I can live my life. I get medical and food support, I have a government that supports me, I have a home with everything that I need, and I live without fear. I have learned a lot and am hoping to get my license so that I can drive myself around. My kids are doing great. Even my youngest kid has started speaking English. They are passing their classes and their health has improved. I make sure they get enough sleep and good nutrition, and I make sure that they keep up with their work.

I want my kids to finish school, go to college, and be the best. I also want to be able to help other people who want to start a new life in America, just like I was helped.

From Dadaab to Kentucky

MARYAN MOHAMED OMAR

In the summer of 2017, I sat down with Maryan, who is from Dadaab, Kenya, which is home to the largest refugee complex in the world—three of the world's largest refugee camps are in Dadaab. Accompanied by her family, she recently resettled to the United States in 2014. She graduated from Iroquois High School in 2017 and she now goes to Jefferson Community and Technical College, where she studies nursing. We talked about her substandard yet often enjoyable life in Dadaab and Kakuma, which is the only refugee camp larger than Dadaab's biggest camps. We also talked about her family, the horrifying experiences that she went through, and her favorite childhood memories.

—HAFSA

I was born in Kenya, but my parents are from Mogadishu, Somalia. I am nineteen years old. I was seventeen when I came to the U.S. In Kenya I lived with my parents, siblings, and some close relatives. In 2008, my mother died, and my father stepped in and took care of us. I had seven sisters and one brother. Two of my sisters died when they were young, and three of them are married. The oldest one lives in Minnesota with her husband and four kids, and the others are here.

We lived in Dadaab but then moved to Garissa. My aunt welcomed us in Garissa. She prepared food and everything for us. *Mashallah,* Garissa was wonderful but very hot. The fruits and vegetables there were extraordinary! Fruits such as bananas and papayas were fresh and cheap. I used to go to school on Saturday and Sunday with my friends. Sometimes, we took the bus, but most of the time we walked to school since the bus was so expensive. My father used to pay the school fees monthly.

We didn't have the diversity that we have in schools here. The school was mostly a Muslim school. The students were mostly Somali and so was the principal. Our school uniform was red. If you didn't wear red clothing, you would be sent home or even punished. There were Kenyan teachers that taught us Swahili and English, but Swahili was the main language. There were other schools that only focused on English classes but they were expensive. Some classes focused on academics while others

were religious classes. The academic classes were math, English, conversation, writing, science, social studies, and others. On the religious side, we used to learn *Fiqi, Towheed, Hadith,* and Arabic. We went to school at 6:00 in the morning and came back at 3:00. We had breaks for breakfast and lunch. You could eat there and pay for it or you could go home and eat.

On Saturdays, extra classes were offered from 8:00 to 12:00. The main class was conversation, where teachers helped us with our speaking skills. I liked school because that was where I could hang out with my friends and see them a lot every day. On my last day, I got a certificate that showed what I had accomplished. Sadly, I left it in Kenya and don't know where it is. But I don't think it would be useful here.

My parents always wanted me to continue with my education. They would always advise me, "Go to school. Don't give up." My father used to work in Nairobi so that he could pay the school fees, but he transferred his work to Daadab when mom died. He opened two stores there. My older sister and brother managed these.

I was the quiet one, while my younger sister Raho was a troublemaker. There was this small garden of flowers outside of our house and kids liked to play with them. They would pluck the flowers on their way from school. Raho used to chase them around with a stick whenever she saw the kids approaching. We would hear their screams as she chased them around. But when she grew up, she calmed down. They used to call her *Shudo.* The kids would be like, "Oh, *Shudo* is coming, *Shudo* is coming!" People who knew her back then did not know her as Raho.

Then we were registered at Kakuma for our resettlement process. We moved there at the end of 2012 and stayed there for seven or eight months. There were a lot of open markets there. People came from places like Hagardere and Dagahley. We stayed at a *tendo,* or tent, but then they moved us to more a permanent residence.

Kakuma was mostly populated with the Turkanas, a local ethnic group. They mostly sold firewood and bags of these chopped black briquettes, like charcoal. We would exchange a pack of flour or a bag of grain for a small bag of charcoal, although some of the Turkanas preferred to be paid.

Sometimes Turkanas would break into our homes. There were a lot of fights. The police were often called, and they would investigate the incidents. Sometimes they would even call to you and check you when they saw you on the streets. It was peaceful most of the time, but the police would sometimes beat up people with the backs of their guns whenever they got angry or when fights started. One day, when I was walking home, a fight broke out. I didn't know what to do. Everyone was running and I ran to a nearby house. I was so scared because the police could arrive anytime and beat whoever they found there, innocent or not. Even women. I used to hear these stories but never thought I would experience it. They went around knocking on people's doors, looking for suspects. Thank God, they never knocked on ours. I thought I was going to die that day, but I guess it is God's will that I was supposed to get here.

All the people there have high hopes to move to the U.S. or other stable places. But it all depends on luck. Some are relocated while others are still waiting for the call. The rejected ones either stayed back and kept on trying or left when they couldn't find help. Those who were accepted were transferred to Kakuma. In Kakuma, the ladies were advised not to give birth because that would lengthen their cases and make it more difficult. There is a girl that I know, Nasteha, whose mother had seven boys and two girls. They were the first people there, but due to the births, her case got held back a lot.

I didn't like Kakuma that much. We only stayed there because of our resettlement process. The refugee agency told us that the rest of our process would take place there. I didn't like it because it was dusty and hot. We did the medical screening and everything else there. After that, our flight was posted. On August 2014, we arrived here in Kentucky. We haven't moved since.

I was very happy because it was like a wish come true. The U.S. sounded like a huge name to us. I was going to get a chance to continue with my education and looked forward to a better future.

The flight was difficult for me. We boarded the plane in Nairobi. I was kind of feeling sick and I got locked inside one of the bathrooms. I didn't know how to open the door. So I banged the door and a guy came to help me. He asked what the problem was. I spoke in English. I told him that I was locked inside. He told me how to open it. So, after that, I didn't go back because I was afraid. We used three planes from Nairobi to here. We stopped at London, New York, and some other place that I don't remember. Our last stop was here, Kentucky. A guy called Hassan helped us to our house here in Crums Lane. We are still living there.

Learning the language was really hard. I got into the ESL program. My English was somehow good since I started learning English back in Kenya, but I am learning to perfect my English. I went to Newcomer Academy, and after six months I was transferred to Iroquois High School, which I graduated from. Iroquois was amazing. The teachers helped me a lot.

I am going to JCTC to learn nursing. When I went to visit JCTC, it was so different from high school. The classes are bigger. The books are expensive. I am going to be managing myself there. I am planning to have everything ready before start college, *inshallah*. Maybe someday I can go back and work as a nurse in Kenya or back home, because there are not many nurses there and I could help out a lot of people who can't afford medical care.

Acknowledgments

This book would not exist without important contributions from a diverse array of individuals and institutions in the Louisville community. While we don't have space to sufficiently express our gratitude, we would like to briefly acknowledge some of those folks.

First and foremost, thank you to the families of the authors, for actively participating in this project and/or providing loving support to the authors during the course of developing this book: Mohamed Alsaadi, LaTanya Anderson, Nancy Báez, Robert Brown, Arnaldo Coca, Ayan Ibrahim, Norma Izquierdo, Pablo Izquierdo, Abdi Jama, Maroo Jan, Al Lawler, Joyce Lawler, Ghaidaa Obaid, Amy Riedling, Yordan Socias, Kimberly Watts, Robert Wilson, and Arfin & Tauskhan Zaminkhan.

To the passionate, dedicated folks at Iroquois High School, especially Kim Courtney, whose close, daily partnership was absolutely essential in more ways than we have space to enumerate. Her unwavering support of and fierce advocacy for her students in the face of overwhelming challenges is nothing short of inspiring. To Kyle Gordon, for contributing beautiful photographs and important research to the project, and for resolutely having the authors' backs. To Areti Masero-Baldwin, for laying the groundwork and working out the logistics to make this crazy project possible in the first place. To Principal Clay Holbrook for agreeing to this unusual partnership. To all of the other teachers and staff, too numerous to name, who have embraced the project and cheered the authors along the way.

To book designer extraordinaire Shellee Marie Jones and cover artist Kathleen Lolley for creating a stunning visual package that honors and elevates the authors' work so beautifully. Extra special thanks to Shellee for her patience, flexibility, positivity, and resourcefulness as we translated the manuscript into book form.

To everyone who allowed the authors to inverview them and thus enriched this project in so many ways.

To Spalding University, for all of the support they provide to keep our overhead low, and for being such wonderful, welcoming neighbors.

To SummerWorks, for their flexibility and creativity in establishing an unconventional partnership that fueled so much of the authors' fantastic work.

To the other major supporters of this project: Louisville Metro Government, the C. E. and S. Foundation, the Gheens Foundation, the Norton Foundation, the Cralle Foundation, the Snowy Owl Foundation, Mrs. Christina Lee Brown, Matthew Barzun & Brooke Brown Barzun, the Republic Bank Foundation, the Fund for the Arts, Brown-Forman, Charles Merinoff, Mimi Zinniel, Emily Bingham & Stephen Reily, the John Evarts Speed Memorial Fund, and the Kentucky Oral History Commission.

To Tim Morton for his tireless, skillful work in producing the pitch-perfect project video, to Ben Freedman for shooting b-roll and stills while visiting from the UK, and to Kertis Creative for lending a camera to Ben.

To Cat Sar, Laura Kirwan, Chloe Teets, Sarah Dyson, Siddeq Samadi, Ed Wong, Elizabeth Kuhn, Nicole Gaines, Derek Burke, Chastedy Johnson, Jim Miller, and Judy Hoge for assisting with transcription and/or translation of oral history interviews.

To Sophie Maier, arguably the purest-hearted human on the planet, for helping some of the authors secure interviewees, and for her general support and cheerleading.

To the Festival of Faiths, for giving the authors of this book their first public platform, and for making that experience so unforgettable.

To everyone who provided financial support, especially Roy & Julie Elis, Haydee Canovas, Ellen Sears, Cassie R. Blausey, Phil & Landis Thompson, Erin & Stephen George, Elizabeth L. Matera, Susan M. Bentley, Jason & Kate Lacy Crosby, Jennie Jean Davidson, Yvette Gentry, J. Andrew Goodman, Martin & Trudy Ray, Elizabeth & Jason Behnke, Barbara Woodson Dillon (in memoriam), Lori Hudson Flanery, Stephen Kertis, Melissa & Nate Kratzer, Hongwoo Lee, Judy & Fred Look, Keith Look & Carlotta Kustes, David López, Bob & Bo Manning, Anne McKune, Beth & Doug Peabody, Scott Schaftlein, and Wendy Carson Yoder.

To Louisville's bookstores and to the other local businesses who sell and promote our books and/or support us with donations.

To everyone else who has played a role keeping LSP going and making this book happen: our write-a-thoners, the folks who vociferously urge other people to read our authors' books, the educators who use our books in their courses, everyone who has given our authors recognition or amplified their voices. It takes every single one of you.

And to you, reader, for taking the authors of this book seriously, and for listening intently.

DARCY THOMPSON & JOE MANNING
Louisville Story Program